YOUR FUTURE SELF

YOUR FUTURE SELF

HOW TO MAKE TOMORROW
BETTER TODAY

HAL HERSHFIELD

Little, Brown Spark
New York   Boston   London

Little, Brown Spark
Hachette Book Group
1290 Avenue of the Americas, New York, NY 10104
littlebrownspark.com

First Edition: June 2023

Little, Brown Spark is an imprint of Little, Brown and Company, a division of Hachette Book Group, Inc. The Little, Brown Spark name and logo are trademarks of Hachette Book Group, Inc.

The publisher is not responsible for websites (or their content) that are not owned by the publisher.

The Hachette Speakers Bureau provides a wide range of authors for speaking events. To find out more, go to hachettespeakersbureau.com or email hachettespeakers@hbgusa.com.

Little, Brown and Company books may be purchased in bulk for business, educational, or promotional use. For information, please contact your local bookseller or the Hachette Book Group Special Markets Department at special.markets@hbgusa.com.

Cartoon on page 153 reprinted by permission of Zachary Kanin / The New Yorker Collection/The Cartoon Bank.

ISBN 9780316421256
LCCN 2023934895

Printing 1, 2023

LSC-C

Printed in the United States of America

To Jennifer, Hayes, and Smith,
who help me celebrate both the present and the future

CONTENTS

INTRODUCTION

Walking through a dense forest, you suddenly find yourself in front of a wrought iron gate. A rustic-looking sign on the entrance reads, "Pathway to the Future." On the other side, there's a gravel road that bends into the trees. Feeling curious, you decide to go for it.

You open the gate and walk down the path, immediately noticing that the air is cooler than it was just seconds earlier. Before long, you're back in your neighborhood, but twenty years in the future. Arriving at your house, you see someone coming out the front door and find yourself staring at...you. Or a version of you, twenty years older, with all the markings of time to prove it. There are a few extra pounds around your waist, more wrinkles on your face, and a softer demeanor to your gait.

Approaching your future self, you're overwhelmed with all the possible conversation topics. It's like catching up with an old friend you haven't seen in years: you can't decide what to ask about first.

Sure, you're interested in your spouse and your children and in what ways the world around you has changed, not to mention twenty years' worth of gossip. High on the list of questions are likely ones about your health and money, career satisfaction, and personal happiness. What did you learn about your life and how you lived it that made you proud? Where have you found meaning and joy? What regrets do you have? What disappointments? What do you imagine your legacy will be when all is said and done?

But wait: before you start grilling your future self, it's worth taking a moment to consider how much you really want to know about the next twenty years of your life. Are there any aspects of your future that you'd rather remain a secret? Most important, how will your conversation with your future self change the way you think and live your life today, once you return through the gate?

The scenario I've just described is based on a novella by Ted Chiang called *The Merchant and the Alchemist's Gate,* in which the narrator — a merchant — visits an alchemist who has, as the title might suggest, a magic gate that allows for meetings between past, present, and future selves. Although the story is science fiction, I assign it to my students in marketing and behavioral decision-making at UCLA. I have also told my friends and family members in an all-too-eager manner that they simply have to read it.

I do so because the tale brilliantly shines a light on the notion of time travel, something that people are surprisingly good at. Not in the way that the characters in countless science fiction novels have done, of course, but in our minds.

Because here's the amazing part: you've already been through the magic gate.

———

When neuroimaging research was in its early days, researchers often spent their time studying basic — but critical — questions.

One of them was: what happens in our brains when we are simply resting, not thinking about anything in particular? People were asked to lie still in a scanner and put their minds to rest. The scientists who conducted this early work had been expecting the brain activity to look like a blank slate, kind of like what you'd see if you'd just switched off your TV. What they discovered, however, was what's now known as the "default network."

The default network fires up when we think about a presentation we're working on...which makes us consider what that presentation will mean for our career prospects...which reminds us—ugh—that we forgot to send some research for that presentation to a colleague as we had promised...which makes us remember the other things we need to follow up on (today!). And suddenly, we remember that card we need to buy for our father's birthday next week, which makes us reflect on what kind of father he was when we were growing up. A moment later, we're thinking ahead ten years to what we can teach our children as they enter adolescence.

In the span of a few seconds, our thoughts can careen back and forth from the present into the near or far future, back to the present, then to the past, and back to the distant future, in what's known as *mental time travel*. It comes so easily to us that we often don't appreciate its significance; when we're just resting, after all, our default networks are actively supporting our mental trips. But our skill at such time travel may be, as Steven Johnson wrote in the *New York Times,* "the defining property of human intelligence." Psychologist Martin Seligman and his coauthor John Tierney go further. What sets our species apart, they claim, is the "ability to contemplate the future...we thrive by considering our prospects."

Sometimes we engage in this sort of time travel deliberately. Take, for instance, Shawdi Rahbar. On May 6, 2020, she sat down at her desk to write a letter about the relationships in her life and her quest for happiness. It wasn't a regular diary entry, nor was it a letter to a close friend. It was a letter she would send to herself that wouldn't be delivered for another year. Rahbar was one of more than eighteen thousand people that particular day, and ten million overall, who have written letters to themselves on the hugely popular platform FutureMe. It's modeled after the time capsule that so many of us created in elementary school—a cache of letters, pictures, and other objects and mementos stored in a box of some kind and then buried, only to be dug up in five or ten years.

The letters on FutureMe are filled with a range of emotions and topics. Some are riddled with anxieties about which big-picture direction to go in ("I'm so scared. So, so scared. So many paths in life to take and I don't know which one is for me"). Some offer encouragement ("But I want you to know...I'm always here cheering you on"). And some are just funny ("Dear Future me, wanna know the difference between you and me? You're older").

What was once a high school rite of passage—writing letters to ourselves in our freshman year to be given to ourselves at graduation—gained new currency when the COVID-19 pandemic hit. I suspect that many people were more curious than ever about what the future held. And, maybe more than ever, people wanted to take advantage of the brief pause in their lives to change the paths of their future selves.

Matt Sly, the founder of FutureMe, recently told me that he started the site because he had written a letter to his twenty-year-old self when he was in elementary school but was disappointed when he realized that, upon turning twenty, he never received the letter. Couldn't his former teacher have sent it to him? What would it be like, he wondered, to be able to communicate between present and future selves? His site appeals to that curiosity we all have. Even though it was a side project for Sly with no marketing budget, traffic on FutureMe exploded from about four thousand letters a day in 2019 to as many as twenty-five thousand a day a year later, as people tried to gain perspective on their lives and connect with the persons they would be in the future. More than five million letters were sent in 2020 alone; clearly, knowing what the future holds is appealing to many of us (but writing letters, which I'll dig into more in Chapter 7, is just one way of expressing such a desire).

My research focuses on understanding how this ability to time travel—albeit in our own minds—can help us manage our emotions and improve our decisions about the things that matter. Things, for example, like our finances or our health. Those are just two of the areas where our present-day wants run up against our long-term wishes. We want the slightly over-budget, nicer car; we want the extra cocktail or delicious-looking dessert. And yet at the same time, we wish to be financially stable and physically healthy.

However, by strengthening the connections between our

past, present, and future selves, we can gain a new perspective on what's important—and help create the future we want. That, in essence, is one of the main points of this book.

Just because time travel takes place inside our heads doesn't mean it can't change reality. How you think about your future can have a huge impact on your present *and* future selves.

Okay, but what do I mean by your "future self"? Conventional wisdom holds that we are just one self throughout our lives. After all, we keep our first names, our memories, and most of our likes and dislikes. Sure, our cells replace themselves, our fashions are constantly updated, our friendships change, and our faces age, but "we are who we are." My research tells a different story: instead of there being a central self at our core, we are instead an aggregation of separate, distinct selves. You are actually a *we*.

Think about the different ways we live our lives: We have a nighttime self, who stays up late and watches television. But we also have a morning self, when we walk the dog or go to the gym or anxiously anticipate the events that will unfold in the day ahead. More broadly, we clearly see our present self, in our current job, with our current associates and friends. And we remember a different self from ten years ago, when we were in school or just starting out in the job market. And we can easily imagine we will be yet a different self again ten or twenty-five years in the future, with more experience, skills, and emotional maturity.

When it comes to thinking about our future selves, the details of *how* we time travel can have a big impact. If I want to be healthy and fit in five years so that I can continue playing actively with my kids, I may be thinking about a future self who's about five years older than I am now. Yet, there are lots of future selves along the way between now and then. What's important, as some psychologists have suggested, is whether there are aspects of future me that are relevant to what I'm doing today. Maybe, for instance, I've decided that part of the process of getting healthier is to go for a run first thing tomorrow morning. My morning self isn't totally foreign to me in the way that my self five years from now is, but I may still have a hard time getting in touch with tomorrow morning's self's feelings (and he might not be all that in touch with mine when I've set the alarm for 5:30 a.m.!). In order to wake up and go for a run, I need to tap into what tomorrow-morning me will be feeling—will he be tired and groggy and not want to get out of bed? Put another way, how can I help my tomorrow self stay motivated? Would it help, for instance, if I program the coffee maker to turn on at 5:25 a.m.?

The larger lesson is that learning how to effectively time travel can improve the way we think about and treat these different future selves, and thus help us create a better future.

Marketers for charities have taught us that the more vivid they make people appear, the more likely we are to give money. Could we get people to think about *themselves* in the future in a similarly vivid way?

One solution: in my research, I've *shown* people images of their future selves. We took photos of the participants with a blank expression and ran them through a software package to create digitally aged avatars. Mimicking all the fun things that happen with age, we made their hair grayer, their ears droopier, and their under-eyes . . . baggier.

And we made the experience immersive. Using virtual reality projections, participants would *encounter themselves* in a virtual mirror. Half were shown their present self, and half were shown their aged, future self. Afterward, we had them fill out surveys. Those who confronted their future selves ended up putting more money into a hypothetical savings account than those who did not. I've since tested this same sort of intervention on thousands of people, recording the decisions they made with their hard-earned dollars and cents.

This is just one possible fix, but there's a larger lesson to be drawn from it: to make better decisions today that create happier tomorrows, we need to find ways to close the gap between our current and future selves. We need to make time travel easier, to help ourselves cross through that magic gate. That is the goal of this book.

In lieu of inventing a time-travel machine, my plan is to offer a better understanding of how we think about ourselves over our lives. The first section of the book lays out the philosophy and science behind this journey. In traveling to distant futures — at least in our minds — I'm hoping to convince you that our future selves may represent different versions of the people we are today. We strive for permanence, and so the idea that we may have multiple versions of ourselves, spread out over time, may be off-putting. I maintain, though, that the idea of our future selves as being different people altogether should be a comforting one. If we can treat those distant selves as if they are close others—people we care about, love, and want to support—then we can start making choices for them that appreciably improve our lives now and later.

But we can also use this same idea—the notion that our future selves are "others"—to better understand why we so often fall short of our goals. This is the focus of the book's second section. In it, I highlight three common time-travel "mistakes" we make. We "miss our flights," or get overly anchored on present-day concerns, failing to consider the future at all. We engage in "poor trip planning," thinking ahead in some surface-level way, without deeply considering what the future will look like. And finally, we "pack the wrong clothes," relying too much on our present self's feelings and circumstances and projecting them onto a future self who might not feel the same way.

Of course, it's one thing to understand our mistakes, but another to do something about them. And so the last section is all about solutions—solutions that are meant to smooth the trip from now to later. There, I focus on ways we can draw our future selves closer to our present selves, as well as methods that help us "stay the course." But creating a better tomorrow shouldn't be all about pain, so I also highlight techniques that make present-day sacrifices feel easier to tackle. At the same time, it may be just as important to occasionally celebrate the present in service of better todays and tomorrows.

In Chiang's science fiction story, the merchant is disappointed to learn that traveling through the gate won't allow him to alter the future. Yet the alchemist notes that by traveling ahead in time, he can at least get to *know* the future.

We can go beyond knowing, though. Because in reflecting on our possible future selves, we can plan for them. Shape them. Change them.

Your fate is not fixed. Not even close.

PART I

THE JOURNEY AHEAD

Who Are We as We Travel Through Time?

CHAPTER 1

ARE WE THE "SAME" OVER TIME?

Pedro Rodrigues Filho was born with a dented skull. The injury was inflicted by a particularly violent father, who had tragically beaten Filho's mother while she was pregnant with him. In the spectrum of nature versus nurture, Pedro seemed to get violent tendencies from both sides of the equation. And it was these acts of violence that ended up playing a starring role in Pedro's life, as he eventually became one of the twentieth century's most prolific serial killers.

Why am I starting a book that's supposedly about increasing long-term well-being with the story of a man who turned into a real-life Dexter? Here's the answer: The person Pedro is now, as you'll see, is very different from the one he once was. And the arc of his life raises a key question: what determines who we become? Put another way, how do we ensure that our future self is the person our present self wants them to be? It's a question that applies not just to extreme cases like Pedro's, but to the rest of our lives as well.

A PAST YOU WOULDN'T WANT

In 1966, when he was thirteen, Pedro was beaten up by an older cousin. He was small for his age, and losing a fight to his relative caused the rest of his family and neighborhood kids to laugh at him. Bent on revenge, he waited until both he and his cousin were working at their grandfather's factory before he pushed his older relative into a sugarcane press. The press severely mangled his cousin's arm and shoulder but spared his life.

A year later, Pedro Sr. was fired from his job as a school security guard for allegedly stealing from the school store. Although he swore the daytime guard had committed the thefts, he was fired just the same. According to his autobiography, Pedro couldn't bear the thought of his father being falsely accused, gathered guns and knives from his family's house, and left for a thirty-day trip in the woods, where he hunted for food and thought about retribution. Returning to town, he sought out the man who had fired his father—the town's deputy mayor—and shot and killed him. Still consumed with rage about his father's unjust treatment, he tracked down the daytime guard, shot him twice, covered the body with furniture and boxes, and set it on fire.

But these were just the first of what would come to be many episodes of brutal violence. And by the time he was eighteen, Pedro had earned himself the nickname "Pedro Matador" or "Killer Petey." He tattooed "I kill for pleasure" on his right forearm and his late fiancée's name alongside the phrase "I can kill for love" on his left arm.

Once he was finally caught by law enforcement, he was charged with eighteen murders and ordered to a notoriously brutal São Paulo prison. For the transfer from jail to prison, he was put in the back of a police car with a serial rapist. The serial rapist did not survive the trip.

By 1985, Pedro had killed seventy-one people — one of whom was his own father! — and his prison sentence was increased to four hundred years. But the killing still didn't stop. While he was locked up, he was responsible for murdering an additional forty-seven inmates, though he claims it was more than one hundred. This doesn't excuse his violence, of course, but it does speak to his murderous talents: these prison victims represented some of society's worst criminals.

When Pedro wasn't killing other prisoners, he took up a rigorous exercise program, learned to read and write, and started receiving and answering fan mail.

In the early 2000s, the Brazilian authorities realized that they had a problem, and it wasn't that Killer Petey was systematically thinning out the prison population. Instead, they noticed that the Brazilian penal code was created when life expectancy in Brazil was forty-three years. According to the code, inmates were not to be detained for a period longer than thirty years.

Fearing the release of one of the country's most notorious criminals, judges found a legal loophole: prisoners could receive extended sentences for crimes committed after the original ones were prosecuted. Pedro, however, appealed his additional punishment and won.

Which is how in April 2007, after thirty-four years behind

bars—only four more than the current maximum—he was released.

There's not a robust resocialization program in Brazil. Yet, Pedro managed to adjust to a much quieter life, moving to a pink cottage in a remote part of Brazil. Authorities, however, were desperate to put him back in prison, and in 2011, they arrested him for riots that occurred during his prior jailing. On December 2017, he was rereleased. At the age of sixty-four, he had a youthful physique, maintained his calisthenics routine, and started a YouTube channel with the help of a neighbor, where he began sharing inspirational messages and stories.

By his account—which should admittedly be scrutinized—he hasn't killed in years and no longer feels the need to do so. Can a man who was once diagnosed as a psychopath, who has killed dozens of people but now lives an ascetic (seemingly upstanding) life, be considered a *new* man?

I decided to ask him.

Setting up the meeting wasn't easy. My translator, a Portuguese-speaking graduate student, was wary of giving his contact details to a convicted serial killer. So he first created an alias email address for himself and then arranged a time for all of us to speak. It was the middle of the pandemic, and given that both my wife and I were working from home, I asked her if I could use the office to take the call so I wouldn't be distracted. But our appointment kept getting pushed back, until my wife ultimately needed the office for her own work (she's a child psychologist and was about to go into a teletherapy session with a kid in need... which, I have to admit, was hard to prioritize below my interview with Pedro).

As a result, I found myself sitting in a rocking chair across from my infant son's crib while talking to Brazil's best-known serial killer. I started by asking Pedro if he thought that he was in some way the same as his younger self, or if, instead, he was fundamentally different.

His answer contained no uncertain terms: "I'm disgusted by who I once was, and I consider myself to be a new person now."

I wanted to know, though, if there was a specific moment when he became this new version of himself. He said that it was somewhat gradual but that, yes, one specific event set off his transformation.

When he was being transferred between cells, three other prisoners ganged up and stabbed him many times—in the face, mouth, nose, stomach, all over his body. Fighting back, he killed one of them. As a result, he was placed in solitary confinement, and when he was there, he had a "negotiation" of sorts between himself and his God.

He promised God that he would become a new and different person if he could just get released from prison. In many ways, it seems like he may have lived up to his promise. For one, he no longer has the urge to kill. And while he used to be "explosive," reacting violently to anyone who upset him, he now deals with frustrations in more socially acceptable ways (for example, he's become a big fan of exercise).

These days, Pedro wakes up at 4 a.m. to work out and earns a small income at a recycling plant. He describes himself as essentially a hermit, avoiding alcohol, parties, and large gatherings. In his spare time, he advises younger people who have committed crimes on how to change their lives. Even though I don't understand Portuguese, Pedro's tone sounded genuine when he told me that he takes great pleasure in "transforming" others, counseling them away from crime.

But he also noted the challenges of transformation: although he's seen other people from prison change their lives (one even became a preacher), the vast majority of prisoners "are who they are," and it's hard to completely change when "all you know is what's inside the prison walls."

So, even though his day-to-day life has transformed, is Pedro the *same* person now as the one he once was? Or is Pedro — who now goes by "Pedro *ex*-Matador" — a completely different person?

More to the point: can our present and future selves differ from each other in substantial ways, and does it matter?

This question is one that philosophers have been debating for centuries. I'm aware that one extremely efficient way to get people to stop paying attention is to include the words "philosophers," "debating," and "centuries" in the same sentence. But understanding what makes us the same — or different — over time presents an ideal jumping-off point for learning why we sometimes treat our future selves poorly — why we sometimes make choices today that we'll later regret — and how we can do better.

THE BOAT THAT TRAVELED AROUND THE WORLD

Imagine that you have decided to take a few years off from life as you know it, buy a boat, and sail around the world. (I know, I know, the two happiest days of owning a boat are the day you buy it and the day you sell it, but for this little exercise, let's just pretend that this is a dream of yours.) Knowing that you'll hit some strong winds along the way, and being a big fan of puns, you've decided to name your new boat *The Whirled Traveler*. You plan to take your newly purchased yacht (if you're going to get a boat, you might as well go big) and start off the coast of Northern Europe, travel west across the Atlantic, and make your first stop at one of the Caribbean islands—let's say Aruba.

You experience a few storms, and by the time you arrive in Aruba, you notice that one of your sails has gotten a bit tattered during the long journey. No problem, though. You replace the sail with a new one and continue on through the Panama Canal toward French Polynesia. Once you're there, however, you see that some of your floorboards have started cracking, and now *those* need to be replaced.

As luck would have it, this sort of thing keeps happening on your trip. And by the time you make it back safely to Northern Europe almost three years later, you've replaced every part of your yacht, from the sail to the floorboards, and, yes, even the hull. If that sounds insane, please remember that I've just asked you to picture leaving your job to travel around the world, which itself is pretty crazy.

The big question is this: after sailing for three years, and replacing all the parts of your boat, is it still *The Whirled Traveler,* or is it now an entirely different boat?

I should note: I'm clearly not the first to ask these questions. Centuries ago, Plutarch discussed such issues through the story of the Greek hero Theseus, the founder of Athens. Theseus had reportedly killed several monsters on his journeys, the most famous of which was the Minotaur. Yet, he became better known for his sailing vessel than for these heroic exploits. When he returned to Athens from Crete, the Athenians—to honor him—decided to preserve his ship in the harbor. As one board rotted, it would be replaced with another so that the monument to Theseus would remain standing. Over centuries, the whole boat must have been replaced.

Among ancient philosophers, Theseus's ship became an anchor for an argument that never really ended. I imagine them sitting around late at night, drinking wine, using the boat to debate the idea of change. One side would hold that the ship, despite all its parts being swapped out, was still the same boat it once was, while the other would claim that, no, in fact, it could not be.

But if we want to attempt to answer this question, I think it's helpful to take a step back and ask: What makes a boat a boat? More to the point: how many parts of us need to change before we become someone else?

ARE YOU THE SAME NOW AS WHEN YOU WERE EIGHT?

I freely admit that this is a funny question to ask. "Of course I'm the same person over time!" you might exclaim if you were prone to shouting at books you were reading.

Most of us, I'd bet, believe that we are who we are; surface-level characteristics may get altered, but not our "core" selves.

After all, the kid who knocked out his front tooth in second grade, roughhousing with friends, isn't some other person—that's still fundamentally me!

Take Jerzy Bielecki and Cyla Cybulska, who met and fell in love in the Nazi concentration camp Auschwitz in 1943. Working with a friend in the uniform warehouse, Jerzy made a fake SS guard uniform. He then forged a document giving him authority to take a prisoner to a nearby farm. On a summer day in 1944, a sleep-deprived guard let Jerzy lead Cyla out of the camp. They walked for ten nights till they arrived at Jerzy's uncle's house. Jerzy, feeling a strong need to help others, joined the Polish underground army. After some time, and due to a series of miscommunications, Jerzy and Cyla believed the other had died.

Almost forty years later, Cyla, then living in Brooklyn, sadly told her housekeeper the story of the man who had saved her but then died. Coincidentally, the housekeeper had just seen a man tell the same story on Polish TV and asked whether it could be the same person—perhaps he wasn't dead?

A week after that conversation, Cyla stepped off a plane in Krakow and was greeted by Jerzy carrying thirty-nine roses, one for each year they had been separated. Both had been widowed, and they saw each other about fifteen more times before Cyla died in 2005. In one of his final interviews before his death in 2010, Jerzy stated that he was still very much in love with his former lover.

The idea that this couple, who had known each other only briefly when they were eighteen, could still be in love sixty-seven years later makes a powerful statement about the stability of a person's identity. With that amount of time and the trauma they had both experienced, it's not hard to imagine that they could have changed and grown in ways unrecognizable to the other: their reunion could have just as likely been an awkward meeting between strangers.

We cling to and celebrate stories like Jerzy and Cyla's because we seek permanence in our long-term partners. Part of the unspoken promise of marriage is that throughout your lives together, your partner will still be that same person whose smile you noticed when you first started dating. (Sure, part of the promise is that you'll also *grow* together, but you're most likely not marrying someone whose entire identity you'd like to change.)

This desire for permanence, however, may be a foolish one.

One of the most popular articles published in the *New York Times* was entitled "Why You Will Marry the Wrong Person." In it, philosopher Alain de Botton made the pessimistic but reassuring claim that there are no perfect unions and no perfect partners. We marry others not necessarily because we want to be happy (although that's why we think we marry!), but because we want to make permanent the feelings we had at a relationship's beginning. That urge, though, might not be entirely rational. "We marry," de Botton writes, "to bottle the joy we felt when the thought of proposing first came to us," failing to fully recognize that our feelings for our partners will morph and shift in ways we can't anticipate. In the same way, our partners—and we too—will also morph and shift.

So, what *does* stay the same over time? And what changes?

These are questions that Brent Roberts, a personality psychologist, has studied for much of his adult life. With Rodica Damian and other colleagues, he recently published a paper that looked at personality continuity—and change—over a period of five decades. In 1960, almost half a million American high school students (about 5 percent of students) spent two and a half days taking various surveys and tests. Called Project Talent, the idea was conceived by psychologist John C. Flanagan, who believed that many young adults were not landing careers in which they could thrive. His solution was to assess the abilities and aspirations of America's high school students so they could eventually be matched with more ideal job prospects.

Fifty years later, almost five thousand of these original students were surveyed again. This group was carefully selected to represent the original group—it was composed of roughly the same number of men and women from similar geographic regions as the original sample. Analyzing survey responses from 1960 and 2010, Damian and Roberts could see what happens when a sixteen-year-old teenager morphs into a sixty-six-year-old adult. How stable, they wondered, are core personality traits over fifty years?

The best answer is that it depends on how you ask the question.

Here's one way to think about it: if you were the shiest teenager in your class, there's a decent chance you'd be among the shier in your adult friend group. As Brent explained it to me, imagine you wanted to bet on how likely it would be that a teenager who was gregarious relative to her peers would turn into an adult who was also gregarious relative to her peers. You'd have about a 60 percent chance of making a correct guess. Better than a random roll of the dice but still far from a sure bet.

Our experiences powerfully shape who we become, so there's no guarantee that our adult selves will resemble our teenage selves. Part of the motivation for this paper came from Rodica's experiences growing up in war-torn Romania in the 1990s. As she explained it to me, she found it curious that some people she knew as a child continued to thrive and to alter their personalities in positive ways even in the face of adversity, while others suffered.

So, there is some stability in where you stand compared to others, but it's still possible to show growth in important traits. For instance, most people change in terms of how conscientious and how emotionally stable they are as they grow older. But there are significant differences across people: some change a great deal, while others, not so much. In the Project Talent data set, for example, 40 percent of adults showed reliable change for any given trait, whereas the other 60 percent did not.

That doesn't mean we all turn into different people from our teens to our sixties. We have five core personality traits—openness to new experiences, conscientiousness, agreeableness, extraversion, and neuroticism—and most people show significant change in one of them across ten years. That's something—one big trait changes over a decade! But four out of five remain pretty much the same. Continuity seems to be the pattern that wins out. As Brent said, "It's not as if people are reformulating their character in its entirety in a decade's time."

So, whether we are the same person over time isn't a simple question to answer. In some ways, we are the same, but in others, we're not. To return to the yacht metaphor—we might replace the sails or paint, but our floorboards stay the same. Or maybe we put in new floorboards but keep the original mast. We're not an entirely new boat, but we're definitely not the *same* boat.

These inevitable changes in your future self raise a rather practical set of questions. Given that we'll change, and change in unexpected ways, what determines how these changes impact our perceptions of self-continuity? Pedro Rodrigues Filho, for instance, was convinced that he was an entirely new person because he no longer had homicidal instincts. Likewise, a ship given a new paint job might feel new, even if the frame remains the same.

The reason these perceptions of continuity matter is because they have a big impact on our behavior. If *The Whirled Traveler* still feels like *our* boat, then we'll treat it better. We'll keep replacing parts as needed, and maybe even invest in some upgrades. However, if it starts to feel like a different boat—a machine to which we have little attachment or with which we have little shared history—then we'll start treating it like the last rental car we took on a family trip.

The same logic applies to your identity. If you feel a strong connection between your present and future selves—even though your present self is different from your past self, and your future self will be different from who you are today—you are much more likely to perform the hard work of self-improvement.

IT'S ALL ABOUT YOUR BODY

When you show up to your high school reunion, no one will call you by your best friend's name. Your friends—or the people who you now just sort of know on social media—would see you and recognize that you are the same person who once inhabited an eighteen-year-old high school senior's body. Sure, your face might have aged, and you might have a different hairstyle, but you are still in the body that your friends spent time with all those years ago. As some philosophers maintain, when it comes to your identity, what persists over time is the physical.

But your skin cells do turn over, your red blood cells get recycled, and you will most likely get shorter (or taller, if you're like my father-in-law, who is fond of telling me how his degenerative disc surgery gave him an extra inch of height). Of course, those are just a few bodily alterations you can expect to face over time. How much, though, needs to change in your body for you to stop being you?

Here's one slightly silly way to figure this out: You've decided to become friends with a mad scientist, and he has a proposition for you. He's going to take everything inside your head—all your thoughts, feelings, and memories—and transfer them into someone else's brain. After he has gone through this complicated and time-consuming surgery, there will be two bodies. One that looks like you but no longer has the contents of your mind, and one that doesn't look like you but does have your thoughts and feelings.

He ups the ante and has decided to give one of the bodies a

million dollars. The other body, however? Well, that one will get tortured. Before your surgery, you get to decide which one gets tortured and which one will finally have enough money for their kids to attend college. Which one do you pick?

My guess is that you doled out the money to the body with your mind and assigned the torture to the body your mind once was in. If you did pick that way, it would suggest that maybe our bodies aren't the key to our identities.

But wait: let me give you another thought experiment. Imagine you had a tumor that would kill you unless you underwent a brain transplant procedure. You'd remain living, but your memories, preferences, plans—essentially, your entire mental life—would be destroyed. Would you do it? You'll die if you don't go through with the surgery, but you might die if you *do* go through with it.

So, the "body" theory, as some have called it, says that what makes you continue to stay "you" is your body. Yet, these quick thought experiments show that it's hard to say if that's *really* what makes you the same person over time.

IT'S ALL ABOUT YOUR MEMORIES

To John Locke, the seventeenth-century British philosopher, the body couldn't be the answer. Instead, his insight was that what makes you the same over time is your "consciousness." Here's one way of interpreting that perspective: what matters is your memory. So, if you're thirty-five years old, you contain the "you" of today and the version of you when you were fifteen. Those two versions share an identity because the later person can remember the earlier person's thoughts and actions. Think about a sort of chain of memory — you at thirty-five remember thoughts and feelings from when you were fifteen, and that version of you remembers being twelve years old, and so on down the line.

Your identity stays the same, in other words, because you have memories from different points in time, and each memory is linked to earlier ones. Locke suggests that if you can remember your first day of, say, second grade, then you can remember that version of you. If the person you are now shares memories with the person you were then, a persistent identity is retained across all those years.

As with the body theory, there are, of course, issues with this account. For instance, if I forget what I had for breakfast yesterday, does that mean I am no longer the same person I was then? Perhaps a more significant problem: no one remembers the very early days of their lives. Does that mean that the baby version of us was a different person, since we retain no memories from that time? Do we not become ourselves until, say, we have our first memories?

MAYBE IT'S SOMETHING ELSE ENTIRELY

There's an old joke about a dean at a university who is frustrated that the physics department requires so much money for research. He asks, "Why can't you be like the math department — all they need are pencils, paper, and trash cans. Or even better, like the philosophy department. All they need are pencils and paper." I know that jokes are never funny once they're explained, but here's the point: philosophers come up with ideas without ever needing to test them. In the context of identity over time, it's all well and good for philosophers to create theories about what makes people the same—or different—throughout their lives. But how well do these theories map onto the way we actually think about the issue in real life?

Put differently, what do everyday people think matters when it comes to continuity of the self over time?

That's precisely the question that Sergey Blok, at the time a psychology graduate student at Northwestern University, set out to answer in the early 2000s. He asked his research participants to imagine that an accountant named Jim was involved in a terrible car accident. The only way he could survive? You guessed it—a brain transplant! This time it's a crazy medical experiment where his brain will be carefully removed and placed in a robot.

Thankfully, the transplant is successful. When the scientists turn the robot on, they scan Jim's brain inside it and find that all his memories are intact. Or at least, that's what half of the participants read. The other half learned that even though the brain survived, when the scientists scanned it, they found that none of its memories were the same as those from before the operation.

If the robot is "still" Jim, even without his old memories, that would be a point in favor of the body theory. But, if memories are necessary for Jim to continue being Jim, we would need to score one for the memory theory. In this study, which admittedly had a small number of people in it, there was a clear winner: people were roughly three times more likely to say that the robot could still be considered Jim when the memories survived the transplant procedure compared to when they did not.

When figuring out the ingredients of continuity, there's value in learning what everyday people and philosophers believe. But in both cases, we're dealing with imaginary scenarios, the likes of which probably won't happen in our lifetimes. And that makes it hard to determine what matters when it comes to our identities over time.

So, how do you test such ideas without relying on thought experiments?

Nina Strohminger, a professor at the Wharton School, decided to take a nontraditional approach to understand what ties our past, current, and future selves together.

Sitting in her Philadelphia loft, with faint parrot squawks in the background, she told me that although she had done her fair share of thought experiments, she didn't think they should be the only source of evidence. So, she turned to nursing homes.

Specifically, she reached out to caregivers of patients with neurodegenerative disorders. These are disorders where the brain has changed fundamentally — much like those of the characters in those philosophical vignettes.

She focused on three groups of patients. One group had Alzheimer's disease, where patients' bodies were healthy, but their memories were vanishing. Another group had amyotrophic lateral sclerosis (ALS), where patients' minds remained healthy, but their bodily functions were deteriorating. And the final group had frontotemporal dementia (FTD), where motor abilities and most memories are intact, but moral impairments occur.

For example, many patients with FTD show reduced empathy, become dishonest, and no longer pay much attention to social norms.

The caretakers responded to a battery of survey questions, including "Do you feel like you still know who the patient is?" and "Does the patient seem like a stranger to you?" Patients with ALS, the disease primarily affecting the body but not the mind, were perceived to have the least identity disruption. Alzheimer's came next. But frontotemporal dementia was seen as having by far the most identity disruption.

The debate about what makes us who we are as we progress through life has often boiled down to the "body" versus the "mind." The fact that FTD patients seem least like their former selves suggests that there may be something more to consider. What, though, might that be?

As Nina and her coauthor, Shaun Nichols, explain, what makes us stay who we are — or become different people altogether — is our sense of a "moral self." Whether a person is kind or biting, empathetic or callous, polite or brusque: these are the aspects that most significantly tie a younger person to their older self.

When these moral traits are fundamentally altered, Nina and her colleagues have found that our relationships seem to be altered, too. Nina related a telling example to me: She asked one of her friends, a woman who was an artist, what would have to change about her personality for her partner to no longer see her as the same person over time. After considering the question, her friend replied, "I think if I became really bad at art. If I became a bad artist, my partner would leave me—she'd say, 'That's not the person I married, and I don't love her anymore.'"

Nina then flipped the question around. "What," she asked, "are some ways your wife could change, and you would say, she's no longer the person I married? What change would need to take place for you to say, she's no longer the same person, and I don't love her anymore?" And to that, her friend quickly replied, "Hmm . . . I guess if she became a bitch."

There's an interesting blind spot here—when it came to her own traits, Nina's friend assumed that art was such a core part of her identity that were it to be altered, she'd no longer be the same person in the eyes of her spouse. Yet when the question was switched around, things changed. Now what mattered most was her wife's sense of kindness. That makes sense: kindness, after all, is what Nina and her colleagues call an "essential moral trait."

This anecdote is a perfect illustration of how these sorts of moral traits, when changed, can impact not only our sense of identity stability but our relationships as well. Yes, we change friends and lovers, but if all of them were to change, it would present a serious challenge to our sense of a continuous self over time.

———

So, is Pedro ex-Matador a fundamentally different person now, or is he the same person he once was?

I believe that the research on the "essential moral self" is the closest we can get to an answer. When core moral traits remain intact, even if many other things change, we can see a thread of continuity in people. It's why we see some people as maintaining a sense of sameness over time, but recognize complete change in others.

What happens, though, when we turn the lens on ourselves? Sure, we can see continuity — and the lack of continuity — in others; we recognize the transformation of Pedro ex-Matador from a cold-blooded killer into an evangelist for nonviolence. But how likely are we to see our own future selves as the same or as completely different from who we are now? And how might those beliefs impact the decisions we make today? That's the set of questions I'll tackle in the next chapter.

The answers could have serious implications for your diet and your bank account, among other things.

Highlights

- Do we change over time? Some aspects of our personality change, while others remain the same.
- It's difficult to make long-term decisions (such as whom to marry) if our future selves are different from our present selves.
- If people retain their moral traits over time, we're likely to see their present and future selves as similar.

CHAPTER 2

IS FUTURE ME REALLY...ME?

Just outside Keflavik, Iceland, there's a tourist attraction known as the Blue Lagoon. It's known for its deep azure color, shockingly hot temperatures, and therapeutic qualities. (The mineral-rich water and white pasty dirt are good for the soul and also your skin—studies have shown that the lagoon can help treat psoriasis and reduce wrinkles.) Although the Blue Lagoon might seem like another Icelandic natural wonder, it was actually formed in the late 1970s by runoff from a nearby geothermal power plant.

I'd always wanted to visit Iceland and its lagoon, which is why I leapt at the chance to attend an academic conference there (a definite upgrade from the usual airport Hilton). The meeting was sponsored by the University of Sydney, and it featured talks focused on how people think about time.

Sitting in the back of the conference room, I stared out the large glass window at the towel-wrapped tourists heading to the steaming thermal springs. My wife, who had joined me on the trip, was either somewhere in those springs or out taking pictures at a nearby glacier. This meant that I was a bit distracted when Laurie Paul, a Yale philosophy professor, took the podium. I wanted to be lounging in the Blue Lagoon, not stuck inside a drab hotel.

"Imagine that you have a onetime opportunity to become a vampire," started Paul. "Things are a little different now, and vampires don't drink the blood of other humans, but rather, of humanely farmed animals."

It was a gripping way to start an academic talk—I suddenly stopped thinking about those tourists and the Blue Lagoon and started contemplating my possible life as a vampire. As Paul noted, many people are intrigued by the idea, since becoming a vampire comes with immortality, power, and speed. But let's say that you're not 100 percent convinced: Do you really want to become "undead"? Do you really want to drink blood? To help make the decision, you decide to ask your vampire friends for advice.

They're having the time of their lives—they truly love being vampires! And they assure you that you'd love the experience, too. You already wear black clothes all the time (probably not true, but just pretend), you like exotic foods and are willing to try new ones, and you love to stay up late at night. Becoming a vampire, in other words, would suit you quite well. You want to know more, but when you ask, you're told that you need to just take the plunge.

But there's a catch.

Once you become a vampire, you can't undo your decision. You can't dabble in this new way of life and then decide, nah, that's not for me, and go back to your mortal existence.

Vampires are forever.

WHAT DO VAMPIRES HAVE TO DO WITH FUTURE SELVES?

A few days before I started thinking about vampires, my wife and I were in our bathroom getting ready for our last pre-vacation workday. I was engaged in a profound internal debate regarding which shaving cream to take on the trip (was there enough left in the travel-size can? would the regular-size one get confiscated at security?), when she tapped me on the shoulder. With a knowing smile, she handed me a pregnancy test stick that showed two distinct dark pink bars on it.

Wait, I wondered, was I really seeing two lines there? Were we *really* going to become parents? Of course, I was thrilled. I had wanted to be a parent for some time and started to fantasize about the fun things I'd eventually do with my future kid (which admittedly boiled down to introducing them to good music and movies).

But then, while listening to the lecture in Iceland, my expectant joy was replaced by a creeping sense of anxiety.

Was becoming a parent all that different from becoming a vampire?

I'd told myself that I knew what life would be like once we had a kid — I knew other people with kids! I even knew some kids! But did I really understand parenthood? Would I still be able to maintain my interests and passions? Would I be patient / have fun / be a good partner / still be able to sleep?

I had asked friends to tell me more about becoming a first-time parent, and they told me that it was great, and meaningful, and that they couldn't imagine life any other way (except for the sleepless part)—all the things you'd expect new parents to say.

Yes, they said, you should do it if you can. And when I asked for more information? Well, I would just have to have a kid to find out what being a parent was *actually* like.

In the midst of my own spiraling anxiety, Paul stopped her thought experiment. The vampire problem, she noted, was nothing more than a thinly veiled analogy to... becoming a new parent! Becoming a vampire is an irrevocable decision, and so too is becoming a parent.

In drawing this parallel, she was raising a compelling idea: we can never really know our future selves. Even with the very best time-travel efforts, it may be impossible to know what these distant versions of us will feel and think. Because just like a vampire, or a parent, when we turn into new versions of ourselves—when we become our future selves—our thoughts and feelings may change in ways we can't anticipate. To reiterate, it's not just that we can't know what our day-to-day lives will be like. Rather, we can't know what we will think and feel, since those thoughts and feelings may change drastically once we turn into our future selves.

This means that our futures are defined by a sense of existential uncertainty. Our future selves, on some level, will always be strangers to us.

On hearing this, though, I didn't fully despair, and neither should you.

Consider the lessons of the last chapter: when we think about other people, we are able to see a connection—a thread of continuity—between their past, present, and future selves as long as their moral traits remain intact.

If we can be confident that our future selves will maintain some of our core moral values, then perhaps it's all right to still care for them and plan for those distant versions of us, even if they are enshrouded in a cloak of unknowability. My future self as a dad might be a stranger to me, but as long as he maintains my commitments to the Red Sox, empathy for others, and Reese's peanut butter cups (you may say that's not a core moral trait, but I disagree), then perhaps I can justify spending my time thinking about him and planning for his life.

But how should we think about our own selves over time? What allows us to see connections between today's self and tomorrow's self? More to the point: do we think about our future selves as if they are continuous extensions of who we are today, or do we think about them *as if* they are other people altogether?

As you'll see, gaining a better understanding of how we view our future selves—as either extensions of us or as *other* people—can provide insight into the choices we make today.

THE SUITCASE AND THE PHILOSOPHERS

We're surprisingly young when we start thinking about our identities in terms of who we are to others: between the ages of six and nine, children start to define themselves through their relationships with family and friends. We are sons, daughters, brothers, sisters, parents, husbands, and wives. It's a hopeful habit: because we assume these relationships will remain stable, we tether our identity to them, trusting that this will make our personal identity stable as well.

In the last chapter, we talked about Theseus's ship, and how difficult it is to tell whether objects—and other people—remain the "same" or become different over time. Similar questions can apply to ourselves over time, but because we know our own self that much better than we know others, there are some twists. If you want a useful analogy for addressing questions of sameness and ourselves, think about a good piece of luggage that you bought early in your life. You take it with you on trip after trip, filling it with different items and souvenirs. Over time, the suitcase gets tattered from use, battered by luggage carousels, overhead bins, and spilled toiletries. Nevertheless, you'd probably say that it's still the same suitcase, not a different one altogether. So too with our selves: like that old suitcase, they may change and grow and get stained, but they still remain a single entity over time, largely because of those abiding relationships.

This might seem obvious—of course I'm the same person over time! Who else would I be? Nevertheless, this idea of a single, continuous self has certainly had its detractors. David Hume, an eighteenth-century Scottish philosopher, rejected the idea outright. In his boldly titled *A Treatise of Human Nature*, Hume argued that there is no such thing as a self. You are not a suitcase.

Why? To Hume, for something to maintain an identity means that that thing has to possess the same set of properties from any given point in time to the next. This clearly isn't the case for human beings, who are constantly changing their opinions and preferences. According to Hume, we'd be wise to retire the idea of one stable identity over time.

Derek Parfit, another British philosopher, also weighed in on this debate. Parfit, who died in 2017, was a quirky and brilliant thinker. Not wanting to waste time on matters unrelated to his writing and scholarship, he wore the same thing—white button-down, black pants—every day. For much of his adult life, he even had the same meal each morning: sausage, yogurt, green peppers, and a banana, all mixed up in the same bowl. (He adopted this diet for health reasons, thinking that it was the epitome of a healthy breakfast, but when he found out from a nutritionist friend that this was not the case, he changed up the recipe the next day and never looked back.)

Like Hume, Parfit was obsessed with the problem of identity. To explore the paradoxes of the self, he came up with clever thought experiments to try to gain some insight into what makes us continuous—or not—over time. Watching his old lectures is a little like watching the intersection of a *Star Trek* episode and a cult leader discussing his most recent revelations. Tall and skinny, with a gaunt face, imposing glasses, and a shock of white hair, he looks like an absurd caricature of a modern-day philosopher.

He starts by asking that you imagine a tele-transporter machine. It copies all of you—your body, mind, skin, memories—and transports you to Mars. Now let's think about a new, updated version of this body transporter. While you're being scanned, you're accidentally left behind on Earth, but the copy of you still gets sent to Mars and lives there. Now there are two of you. But which one is the "real" you?

Just as the body transporter made a copy of you that landed on Mars, Parfit suggests that we might apply this notion of copies to ourselves over time. Rather than a single constant self—a stable identity—maybe we are really more of a collection of *separate* selves.

Here's another analogy that might be useful in understanding the idea Parfit raises: think about the "single self" versus "separate selves" comparison like the difference between a solo entrepreneur and a small start-up. The solo entrepreneur, like the single self, does all the jobs of many people but is still just one worker. In this view, we are an individual person throughout our lives, even though our interests, likes, beliefs, and relationships may change.

The small start-up, by contrast, is akin to the "separate selves" model: it has many people working for it, each of whom performs a different job. In this view, we may have many *different* selves over time, each of whom has his or her own interests, likes, beliefs, talents, and so on. Although these people are all working for the same company, it's important to acknowledge their differences.

The idea of separate selves can be a little jarring. When I talk about it in my teaching, I'm sometimes met with small existential crises from my students. If I'm a collection of separate selves, who am I really? How can we hold people accountable for things they've done earlier, if a previous version of them is separate from who they are now? And is the person I married a different person from the one I'm married to now? (If so, OMG, what good are wedding vows?!)

To Parfit, what matters is the sense of connection that each separate self has with the others. Think again about the start-up with several different employees. Over the lifetime of the company, as it evolves from start-up to more established firm, there may be new employees who start and old ones who leave.

By overlapping with one another for a few weeks or months, older employees will be able to pass on crucial information and company culture to the newer ones. And they, in turn, will pass that on to future employees in the years to come. In this way, interlocking bonds connect the very first employees to the later ones. But breaks in the chain may occur — some employees might only stay a short while and barely overlap with newer ones; or some information may just simply not get passed along. With enough of these sorts of breaks, some later employees may feel no sense of connection at all to the earlier ones. They may seem like strangers to one another.

In a similar way, our identities can be thought of as a series of interlocking selves over time.

Each successive self has a lot in common with the one before it and the one after it. But with enough distance between selves — that is, with enough distance over time — we start to lose some of those connections.

And at some point, with a lot of distance — a large expanse of time — long-ago past selves or faraway future selves may seem like *strangers* to us. They may seem like different people altogether.

WHO CARES IF MY FUTURE SELF IS
A STRANGER TO ME?

Okay, but so what? Why does it matter if future versions of ourselves are like strangers?

This matters for a very simple reason: *we treat strangers differently.* Consider a coworker of yours whom you don't interact with all that often. Other than their name and the department in which they work, you probably don't know much about their life. And if they asked you to help them out on the weekend—say, assist them in moving furniture from their old apartment to a new one—you'd probably say no. After all, you've got a lot of other things to take care of, and there's no real obligation to help out a stranger like this. Even nice people tend to act in self-interested ways, prioritizing themselves and their friends and family. It's not how we *always* act, but it can be a strong tendency.

To take a sad example: Roughly a year after the COVID-19 vaccine was available, the people who were most vulnerable to the illness—older adults—were also the ones most likely to get vaccinated (89 percent of adults over sixty-five were fully vaccinated by the end of 2021). It was in their best self-interest, after all, to get vaccinated, since they were most at risk. By contrast, only about two-thirds of adults between twenty-five and forty-nine were fully vaccinated by the end of 2021. For this younger cohort, who were far less vulnerable to the virus, one of the main benefits of vaccination—in addition to preventing severe illness—was to protect others and stop the spread of COVID. When an action benefits ourselves, we may be more likely to follow through. Yet when complete strangers are the beneficiaries, we may be more likely to act on behalf of ourselves; there are caveats, but for younger adults, this meant not going to the trouble of getting a shot.

Connect the dots here: if we view our future selves as if they are strangers, and if we tend to act in self-interested ways, then what rational reason could there be to do things for our future selves' benefit? It would almost be irrational to do so!

Eat that extra slice of chocolate cake that's bad for your waistline? Why not! That waistline isn't "mine" but my future self's — a future self I don't even know! Spend a little more on the higher-end 4K TV or put that money in my 401(k)? Buy the TV! Who cares about the future, retired version of me? That's just some stranger. Go to the gym or binge the next Netflix series? Netflix, of course — why sweat for some other self?

Derek Parfit talks about this concept in terms of an adolescent boy who takes up cigarettes. The boy knows but hardly cares that smoking might cause his later-aged self to suffer significantly. "This boy," writes Parfit, "does not identify with his future self. His attitude toward this future self is in some ways like his attitude toward other people."

Or consider the philosophical comedy of Jerry Seinfeld. As part of his stand-up gigs in the 1990s, Seinfeld noticed the strangeness of appliance ads that aired around Christmastime, many of which promised no payments until March of the following year. No payments until March? he wondered. It's as if March will never arrive! Sure, I don't have money now, but that guy in March — maybe *he'll* have money. Cleverly, Seinfeld observed that he is guilty of the same sort of error with his own body, staying up late at night and not worrying how his morning self will feel after only five hours of sleep:

> So, you get up in the morning, with your alarm, and you're exhausted and groggy...Oh, I hate that "night guy"! Ya see, "night guy" always screws "morning guy." There's nothing "morning guy" can do. The only thing "morning guy" can do is try to oversleep often enough so that "day guy" loses his job and "night guy" has no money to go out anymore.

When Seinfeld recounted this problem on the *Tonight Show,* host Jay Leno listened and then offered a solution: "If morning guy got up extra early, then night guy would be tired!" "Yes," responded Seinfeld, and after a pause, he added, "Unless day guy takes a nap."

Seinfeld, with his characteristic wit, identifies a relatable truth first noticed by philosophers: we may indeed view our future selves as if they are strangers.

By studying the mind and the brain, we can better understand why we sometimes treat our future selves as strangers, and how we can eventually learn to be kinder to them.

ON BIRTHDAYS AND GROSS DRINKS

Picture your next birthday. What do you see in the scene?

Now picture your birthday in the distant future — say, twenty years from now. What do you see then?

In both cases, you probably thought of the typical things that are associated with birthdays: cake, drinks, and friends.

But did the two scenarios differ in any way?

Emily Pronin, a psychology professor at Princeton, asked different groups of people a version of these questions. The first group was asked to describe a meal that they were currently eating (she surveyed them in college dining halls). When they wrote about their meals, they did so largely from a first-person perspective. They described the scene as it unfolded in front of them, through their own eyes.

A second group was asked instead to picture a meal in the very distant future (which, for college students, was "sometime after they were 40"). This group showed one key difference: rather than adopting a first-person perspective, they were more likely to use a third-person point of view. They saw themselves *in* the image itself, as if they were observers witnessing the scene; they used, for example, "he" or "she" to describe their future selves, rather than "I."

In the mind's eye, the future self looks as if it is another person!

Pronin next wanted to know if this view has consequences: do we also *treat* our future selves like someone else? To answer this question, she asked people about their preferences for drinking a disgusting drink. She fibbed and told her subjects that she was studying disgust, which would be induced when they consumed an "unpleasant-tasting liquid." (The scary-looking concoction was actually a mixture of ketchup, soy sauce, and water.) To persuade the students to give the drink a try, Pronin reminded them that they were contributing to science.

Here's where things got interesting. One group was asked how much they would be willing to drink—that is, actually drink—at the end of the research survey. The second group was asked how much they'd drink but were told that, due to administrative issues, they wouldn't be able to consume the drink until the start of the next semester (if they didn't return, they'd lose the class credit they were getting for participating). And a third group was asked how much of the drink they'd like to assign to the next research participant.

On average, people chose to consume about three tablespoons for themselves right now. (I'm frankly surprised it was this high; perhaps Princeton students are just really excited about doing things for "the sake of science.") When it came to assigning the disgusting liquid to another person, the amount was closer to half a cup (about eight tablespoons). And for the future self? Also about half a cup.

This suggests that, in many ways, we don't just see our future selves as if they are other people—we *treat* them as others, too.

MATT DAMON, NATALIE PORTMAN, AND A GRAD STUDENT WALK INTO A ROOM...

MRI scanners are extremely expensive to use. (Maybe you've had the pleasure of being inside one. The experience is akin to being locked in a noisy coffin for forty-five minutes or so.) There are the costs associated with the machine's maintenance, the staff who operate it, and the physicists and computer scientists who make sure the background programs are working up to speed. For a researcher, using a scanner can cost upwards of $1,000 an hour.

Unless . . . you use the scanner from midnight to 4 a.m. Then, it's only half as much. Since I was at a point in my graduate school career when I could easily stay up late and didn't have a lot in the way of research funding, I showed up at Stanford's neuroimaging center at 12:30 a.m., trying to understand if there was any basis, in our brains, for the idea that our future self might be another person.

The room was cold, sterile, and furnished with a few computers and a glass window. On the other side of the window was a giant hospital-grade MRI scanner. But unlike the typical MRI machines that are used to take images of lungs and knees, this one contained a bed and a small mirror inside that reflected images from a computer screen. The next day, after processing the scans, I could watch the activity in the brains of participants as they experienced a range of thoughts and feelings.

One of the early questions that psychologists asked when using this sort of functional MRI (fMRI) was: can the brain easily tell what's "me" and what's "not me"? Can the brain figure out, in other words, the difference between self and other? This may seem like an academic question, but "locating" the self in the brain might represent a key step toward understanding consciousness.

One group of researchers had people come to their scanner, lie down, and look at a list of trait words (like "daring," "talkative," and "dependent") flash across the screen above their heads. Just above those words, they'd see either "SELF" or "BUSH." (At the time, George W. was president, so he seemed like a good choice for another person.) Holding a button clicker in their hand, the research participant's task was simple: if the trait word applied to the person they were thinking about (themselves or George Bush), they'd have to click one button; if it didn't, they'd have to click the other.

There's a part of the brain known as the medial prefrontal cortex that sits just behind your forehead. No bigger than a credit card, this region was more active when people thought about themselves compared to when they thought about another person. In other words, it wasn't particularly interested in George Bush—it cared about *you*.

To neuroscientists and social psychologists, this was a big deal: it showed that there was something special about the "self."

Having read the paper describing this study, I couldn't help but wonder: if the brain can tell what's me and what's not me, *and* if the future self is seen as if it's a stranger, well then . . . could it be the case that the future self looks like *another person* in our brains?

I thought I'd bring the idea to one of my mentors, a psychology and neuroscience professor named Brian Knutson, to see if he would advise the project and, well, pay for me to sit at the scanner and run it. Brian has more IQ points than many people I know and had an easy time saying no to projects that didn't interest him. So I was delighted when he was excited about the project and wanted to jump in.

The setup was straightforward. Research participants would

lie down in the scanner and make judgments about trait words that applied to their current self, to their future self, and to another person now and in ten years.

Although previous researchers had used George Bush as the "other person" in these neuroscience tasks, we didn't think that was such a good idea. For one, he was a more controversial president at the time I was carrying out my research compared to when the earlier work was done.

Who, then, should we use to represent the "other"? We decided to have undergraduates help us figure it out. We asked them to select the most well-known yet least controversial people they were familiar with. Two answers received a majority of the votes: Matt Damon and Natalie Portman.

This was in 2007, and although the names would surely be different today, the goal was to find people who were known by everyone and not particularly provocative. We wanted to make sure that any differences we saw in the brain were legitimate and not due to something else, like strong emotions.

The picture that follows shows what happened in the part of the brain that can tell the difference between the self and another person. The lines represent blood flow to that region, which is another way to measure just how active a part of the brain is when you think or feel something. (More blood equals more activity.)

Think of the horizontal axis as time during the scanning task: on the left is when a trait word was shown to a participant, and toward the center is about four seconds after that trait word was shown. That's the point in time when you expect to most

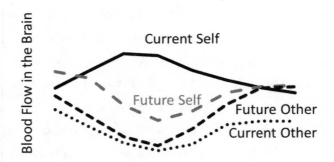

strongly see the effect of a given thought on blood flow in a given part of the brain.

You can probably tell right away what's happening. Check out the dashed gray line — that's the activity in the brain that arises when thinking about the future self. And it's most similar to the activity that is produced from thoughts about another person — whether that other person is in the present or the future.

It's probably worth repeating: in the brain, the future self looks more like another person than like the current self!

Brian, my adviser, asked me to rerun the study just to make sure these findings were reliable. After I spent another two months of sleepless nights at the scanner, the same results showed up.

Other studies have since come to similar conclusions. Let me share my favorite one, which used a neuroimaging tool called transcranial magnetic stimulation (or TMS for short). TMS sends a little magnetic pulse across the brain and effectively shuts off whatever region is targeted. For people with chronic depression, TMS is currently being used to turn on and off the parts of the brain involved in mood regulation, leading to significant improvements in symptoms.

There's a small section of the brain called the temporal parietal junction, which helps us step into the minds of others so that we can empathize with them and take their perspective. When researchers "turned off" the temporal parietal junction, participants didn't suddenly turn into cold-blooded sociopaths. But they did show drops in scores on scales that measure empathy. As a result, they couldn't step as easily into other people's minds.

Here's the wild part. Not only did people have a hard time stepping into the minds of others—they also had a hard time stepping into the minds of their future selves. When the mind-traveling region of the brain was shut off, people opted to spend more of their money right now rather than save that money.

When the ability to empathize with others was dialed down, people also had a difficult time empathizing with their future selves, treating them as if *they* were other people, too. Why save for your retirement? That older self is a stranger.

WHY DO WE SEE OUR FUTURE
SELVES AS OTHERS?

Our tendency to engage in this type of thinking—that is, to see our future selves as if they are other people—may be due to a basic quirk of perception.

If you were to peer out your kitchen window at two bees buzzing around, you'd be able to see both in clear view. But if you were to notice two bees in the distance, it would be harder to tell the two apart—their images would most likely blur together, making it more difficult to tell where one ends and the other begins.

Something similar may be happening when we make comparisons between our present and future selves. As demonstrated by psychologists Sasha Brietzke and Meghan Meyer, people see a clear separation between present selves and future selves that are nearby. Just like the two bees at the window, we're able to easily see differences, for instance, between today's self and a future self in three months' time. Yet, when asked to compare future selves that were three, six, nine, and twelve months out *to one another,* those selves were seen as relatively similar to one another. This tendency to smoosh future selves together even showed up in the brain: future selves that were farther away from the present shared a neural activity pattern.

We have a hard time seeing the details of objects that are far away. Our future selves, far away from us in time, may be similarly blurry. In contrast, our present self is extremely vivid, just like an object within reach. This suggests that part of the reason our distant selves are not seen as "us" might be caused by the fact that we can't see them all that clearly.

As we'll discuss in Chapter 7, though, there are tricks that we can employ to improve our perceptions of our future selves.

OKAY, SO FUTURE ME IS ANOTHER PERSON... IS THAT BAD?

Thinking about future selves as if they are other people is, of course, just an analogy. I was once asked a tough question during a presentation to financial advisers: if the future self is really another person, can we marry them? I'm going to go with a "no" on that one.

Just the same, it's a *useful* analogy. If we think about our future selves as if they are other people, then it makes sense why we sometimes treat them so poorly. It's understandable to not diet, save, or exercise for those temporally distant strangers, especially when we have this very vivid present self who is hungry and lazy and really wants that new iPhone.

Remember: there are times when we may be fundamentally self-interested, often acting in ways that increase our own well-being but not the well-being of others. If my future self is another person—a stranger—then maybe there's no compelling case to act on his behalf.

But . . . we aren't *always* self-interested in our actions.

We make sacrifices all the time—whether it's for our kids, our best friends, our aging parents, our spouses, and yes, sometimes our coworkers (at least, the ones we like).

To put it clearly: We may see our future selves as if they are other people. But what truly matters is what *sort* of other people they are.

If our future selves are strangers—like that coworker you barely know—then sure, there aren't many good reasons to sacrifice for them. Just like in the scenario where we turn into a vampire or a parent or any other new version of ourselves, we can never truly know the future selves we'll become. But if our distant selves are seen as more emotionally close to us—more like best friends or loved ones—then we may be considerably more likely to do things today that benefit us tomorrow.

In the next chapter, we'll learn more about those relationships with our future selves and how they make a difference in important arenas of our lives.

Highlights

- We can't truly know our future selves because when we become them, our thoughts and feelings may change in ways we can't anticipate. But we can still care about and plan for those selves.
- Multiple versions of us spread out over time. We can think of those selves as being linked together like a series of interlocking chains. But over time, the links in the chain may be weakened so that faraway versions of us may seem like strangers.
- We treat strangers differently than we treat ourselves, often failing to consider their interests. If our future selves seem like strangers, it's no wonder we so often do things today that we then regret tomorrow.
- In a variety of ways, we see our distant selves as if they are other people. What matters is the relationships we have with those other people.

CHAPTER 3

RELATIONSHIPS WITH OUR FUTURE SELVES

I n 1773, Ben Franklin wrote a letter to his friend Jacques Barbeu-Duborg in which he expressed his desire to come back to life in a hundred or so years. Franklin desperately wanted to see what would become of the country he helped found.

But as an inventor, Franklin wasn't satisfied with abstract wishes. Rather, he delved into the logistics of resurrection: "I should prefer an ordinary death, [and then be] immersed with a few friends in a cask of Madeira." After a century's time, he wanted to "be recalled to life by the solar warmth of my dear country!"

It's hard to imagine a more extreme—and improbable—version of connecting with a future self. And yet, there is a growing group of people today who engage in something just like what Franklin was imagining more than two hundred years ago. Not with a group of friends in a vat of sweet wine (though that does sound like a fun way to be preserved), but in a nitrogen-filled steel bin where temperatures plunge into the subfreezing range.

ARIZONA: A PERFECT SPOT TO FREEZE

In the late 1960s, Linda McClintock and Fred Chamberlain independently read an obscure book titled *The Prospect of Immortality*, a treatise on the concept of life preservation. At the time, the idea was truly science fiction. However, after meeting at a cryonics community convention in Southern California, and subsequently falling in love, the two decided to explore the possibility of cryopreservation in earnest. They were motivated in part by Fred's father, who had recently suffered a debilitating stroke and was quite frail.

And so, in 1972, Fred and Linda Chamberlain founded their cryopreservation company, Alcor, in Scottsdale, Arizona. The climate there is arid and the city's location makes it relatively impervious to the sorts of natural disasters, like hurricanes, tornadoes, blizzards, and earthquakes, that plague many other regions of the United States. Nobody wants their peaceful afterlife interrupted by a flood or collapsed building.

Four years later, Fred's father became Alcor's first cryopreserved patient. With gleaming halls and shiny preservation bins housing rows of frozen bodies, the state-of-the-art facility in which he now resides is a far cry from the way things looked in the early days of the company's existence. Back then, Alcor had only one patient (Fred's father) and five members who had committed to being preserved. The organization now boasts close to two hundred patients and almost fourteen hundred members.

But the general approach has remained roughly the same over time: As soon as a person is declared legally dead, a cryonics

team travels to the death site, artificially restores blood circula-
tion and breathing, and then places the patient's body in an ice
bath. As the patient cools, they are protected with about ten
medications, their blood is replaced with an organ preservation
solution if they need to be flown to Alcor on a commercial air-
line, and they are transported (carefully!) to Scottsdale, where
"cryoprotectants" are injected into their bodies (to prevent later
damage to their body and organs). Over the course of the next
five to seven days, the patient's body is cooled to –320°F, which
allows it to be preserved and stored in a solid state for—in theory—thousands of years (however, with the current pace of
medical and technological advances, Alcor estimates that their
patients will only have to wait approximately fifty to one hundred years).

The hopeful promise of this procedure is that some future
generation will develop the technology to allow for an eventual
"revival." Some cryocustomers freeze just their heads and brains,
assuming that if the technology exists for resurrection then we'd
also have technology to regenerate the body. Approximately half
of Alcor's members, though, decide to freeze their whole body—
it costs significantly more, but they don't want to come back to
life with a stranger's limbs.

MAKING COMMITMENTS TO UNKNOWN SELVES

Perhaps I'm too constrained by existing scientific paradigms, but
the idea of forking over upwards of $200,000 for this procedure
just seems like . . . a lot, especially for what essentially amounts to

hope rather than evidence. However, listening to members of the cryonics community talk about their plans is, to some extent, inspiring.

For many of them, their faith in eventual revival is motivated by a desire to connect to loved ones past and present. (In fact, the youngest cryopatient is two years old; her parents decided to preserve her when she was diagnosed with, and then succumbed to, brain cancer.)

The same seems to be true for Linda. I asked what she'd most want to know or see when she was eventually revived, and after a short pause, she poignantly exclaimed, "Well...Fred!" (He was cryopreserved in 2012.)

Even though I had a number of additional questions about cryopreservation itself (what if the power goes out? apparently not a major concern, as the deep freeze just requires a dedicated worker who can top off the liquid nitrogen from time to time), I was most curious about Linda's relationship to her future self.

In many respects, Linda — and the cryonics community generally speaking— represents an extreme test of the idea that our relationships to our future selves shape our decisions, behavior, and well-being. By definition, it seems that anyone willing to spend a small fortune on cryopreservation has to feel very connected to that distant future self they may one day become.

Sure enough, Linda's present-day life fully reflects her intense connections to future Linda. Having maintained a vegetarian diet for twenty years, she's now become fully vegan. She made that switch after reading research that links a plant-based diet to the prevention of cognitive decline. In terms of exercise and eating, she claims that everything she does is based on optimizing her long-term brain health; revival, which is already a long shot, will be that much more difficult if there is any underlying neurodegeneration.

Linda Chamberlain may be an outlier. Her beliefs about life extension are certainly on the fringes of society, though they are starting to be more accepted by mainstream science. Her strong link to her future self—and the healthy behaviors that have resulted from it—may seem extreme. But there are others like her in the cryonics community. In fact, attendees at an "Undoing Aging" conference—for life extension supporters—were asked how much of a connection they felt to their *very* distant selves (at 180 years old). They reported significantly higher feelings of connection to their future selves than did a group of healthy adults who were not part of the conference.

This makes sense: if they weren't so connected, they'd probably find other ways to spend that $200,000.

FUTURE SELVES AMONG THE NONFROZEN

It's clear that feeling close to your future self is important for cryonics customers. But this finding raises a larger set of questions: Does the way we relate to our future selves matter in other contexts? What are the practical implications of our relationship to these hypothetical beings?

These are the questions I've been trying to answer for some time now.

The first challenge is to figure out how to ask someone about their future self. After all, if you're not used to actively thinking about your future self or your relationship with them, then this line of questioning can be confusing.

Here's what you shouldn't do: you shouldn't ask people how much they *like* their future selves. Or at least, don't ask an American sample of undergrads that question.

When I did—in one of my first attempts at measuring relationships with future selves—just about everybody said, "Oh, I love my future self," or something along those lines.

I just didn't think it could be the case, though, that everyone would feel such a strong bond toward their distant selves. If they did, then we wouldn't see so many cases in which future selves were left high and dry. Your local gym would be much more crowded. And Dunkin' Donuts wouldn't be a national chain.

I figured there had to be a different way to get at our true connections to future selves.

The answer came in the form of a gentle-mannered psychologist named Art Aron. Aron, a psychology professor at SUNY Stony Brook, wears, on most days, a light sweater (beige, brown, or sometimes patterned) over a button-down shirt as well as a backpack draped over his shoulders.

When he was starting graduate school at the University of California, Berkeley, in the 1970s, Aron was desperate to find a research topic that suited him. The normal thing to do back then was to study something that no one else had studied before. Around this time, he had fallen in love with Elaine, to whom he's now been married for more than forty years. So, he decided to study what he was feeling: love. Or more specifically, romantic relationships. How they start, what keeps them going over the course of a long marriage, and what the biological basis of love is.

Even though Aron is best known for generating thirty-six questions to ask someone if you want to fall in love — questions that he derived and published with Elaine — another line of research that he also conducted with his wife is equally powerful.

Together, they developed a theory about close relationships, noting that one of the key ingredients was a feeling that your romantic partner (or loved one) was included in your sense of self. If you've ever forgotten whether a story happened to you or your partner, for instance, that's a form of including your partner in your self. Or, if you'd be equally excited at the prospect of your partner receiving a job promotion as if you were receiving the promotion, that's another good example. When Jerry Maguire tells Dorothy Boyd that she completes him, that shows, too, how love creates overlapping selves, so that we feel incomplete without our partner.

Aron and Aron came up with a simple drawing to measure this concept of "inclusion in the self." The drawing shows seven sets of circles that progress from being totally separate to almost totally overlapping.

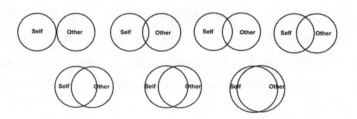

Even though the instructions were simple — "pick the group of circles that best represents the way you think about your partner" — the responses were important. The more overlap people reported, the more likely they were to still be with their partner up to three months later, the more satisfied they were with their relationship, and the more of a commitment they were willing to make to their partner.

A RELATIONSHIP WITH FUTURE YOU

When I first started trying to measure the relationship quality we have with our future selves, I was working with a master's student named Tess Garton. She had come across the Arons' "circles measure" and asked if it might be useful in our research.

The idea instantly made sense. There are already tests out there that have been shown to successfully measure the connections we have to *other people*. So, let's use them to assess the quality of our links to our future selves, who are sort of like other people, at least from the perspective of the brain.

We started small and asked a group of undergrads to pick the set of circles that depicted how "similar" they felt to their future selves. Specifically, we asked about a future self who was ten years out, reasoning that this would allow us to see a lot of differences among people. After all, if we had picked one month out, we suspected that *most* people would say they felt quite similar to that self; and if we'd picked a really distant time like forty years out, we suspected that most would say they felt no sense of similarity.

We tried to keep this question straightforward and ask only about similarity. This seemed like a good place to start: the more similarity you feel that you share with a stranger, the more you like them and feel bonded to them. And we figured the same should be true of our future selves.

We also gave our research participants a set of financial choices, where they had to choose between small amounts of money that they could receive immediately (say, sixteen dollars tonight) and larger amounts of money that they could get at a later time (say, thirty dollars in thirty-five days).

If our relationships with our future selves matter — that is, if feeling closer to our future selves helps us do right by them, whether that means investing in cryonics or saving for retirement — then the answer on the circles scale should match up with answers on the financial task. Indeed, social closeness matters in other decisions: we're more likely to forgo money for ourselves and give it to other people, *if* those others feel emotionally close to us. And so, people who feel more similar to their distant selves should, in theory, be more patient with their money choices, and more willing to wait for larger amounts of money rather than take smaller amounts now.

I wasn't sure what we'd find, though. After all, the idea of expressing a connection to your future self is still quite abstract. Sure, giving people a picture of circles made it a bit more concrete, but would answers on that little scale really correspond to financial choices?

In fact, a significant correlation existed between which set of circles people chose and how willing they were to delay a payout. In short, the more similar people reported being to their future selves, the more likely they were to wait for a bigger prize.

Okay, a skeptic might say, that's a neat finding, but this study used only undergrads... and how meaningful is an imaginary choice between sixteen dollars tonight and thirty dollars in roughly a month, anyway?

It's a valid criticism, so we decided to take it further. We recruited another 150 people, but rather than college students, we invited community members to take part in our study. And instead of asking about hypothetical monetary choices, we took a detailed accounting of their financial lives.

Once again, future-self relationships mattered. The people who felt more similar to their later selves had also accumulated more assets over time.

Of course, there might be other factors that could explain *both* a sense of connection with your future self and your assets. You could imagine, for instance, that people who were older would also feel more bonded with their future selves, and that, due to their age, they'd also be more likely to amass wealth. And yet, when we controlled for factors like age, education, income, and gender, the link between future-self connection and assets was still there.

The Consumer Financial Protection Bureau recently gave a version of our future-self question to a group of more than six thousand Americans—people from all fifty states across the spectrum in terms of income, age, race, education, and personality traits like conscientiousness and extraversion. This time, rather than circles, respondents were simply asked how "connected" they felt to their future selves on a scale that ranged from 1 to 100. And again: the more of a connection people felt with their future selves, the more they had saved, and the better their overall financial well-being was. This correlation held up even when we took into account demographic and personality characteristics.

We see similar results when we study the brain. Remember how, on a neural level, the future self *looks* more like another person than like the current self? Well, that finding is based on an average: on average, the brain responds to your future self in a way that's similar to how it responds to a stranger.

The problem with averages, however, is that they may obscure meaningful differences among people.

Sure enough, when we looked more closely at our data, we noticed that for some people, the difference in brain activity between thinking about future selves and thinking about current selves was quite large. For those folks, the future self *really* looked a lot like another person. But for others, the difference was much smaller, with the future self looking more like the current self.

We suspected these differences between people might be meaningful. Previous research had found that if you were to think about someone very similar to you — your best friend, your parent, a close loved one — you'd see relatively small differences in your brain when you thought about them compared to when you thought about yourself. Your feelings of closeness, in other words, are reflected in your brain activity.

We decided to see, then, if the brain differences we identified could predict the sorts of financial decisions people made. Two weeks after we scanned their brains, our research participants came back to the laboratory to participate in a quick decision-making task.

They had to make choices between smaller amounts of money that they could get immediately versus larger amounts for which they'd have to wait. (The choices were real: they received the money at the time they had specified.)

Sure enough, the more the future self looked like another person according to brain activity, the more impatient people tended to be with their financial choices. Put another way, the "otherness" of the future self was linked to a preference for small amounts of money today, rather than larger amounts later.

MOVING PAST DOLLARS AND CENTS

These links to our future selves, and the power they hold over our decisions, apply beyond just dollars and cents. The more people feel a sense of connection with their future selves, for instance, the more likely they are to take an ethical path when given the choice. That's because choosing a rewarding but ethically dubious route is, in a practical sense, a way to prioritize today over tomorrow. (You're offloading the risk of being caught onto your future self.) And the more connected people are to their future selves, the better the grades they get in high school and college, and the more likely they are to exercise.

To me, the most impressive outcome of our relationships with our future selves comes in the form of psychological well-being—specifically, life satisfaction. Back in 1995, almost five thousand adults, aged twenty to seventy-five, took part in what's known as the Midlife Development in the United States survey, answering a variety of questions about their current-day traits (like how calm, caring, and wise they were), and how they thought they'd fare on those traits in ten years. Those who felt close to their future selves imagined a greater overlap in traits between their current self and future self. Conversely, those who felt less close were more likely to imagine their future self as a different person with different traits.

A decade later, in 2005, these adults were surveyed again. One of my students, Joey Reiff, got ahold of this data set and realized that it allowed us to "check in" with the future selves people eventually became. Who ended up being more satisfied with their lives — those who envisioned more change and difference over time or those who envisioned more similarity?

Similarity won out: the degree of overlap between selves was more strongly linked to well-being than any amount of predicted change. And that was true regardless of whether the change that people anticipated was positive or negative. Sure, it could be the case that people who see more similarity are also living more stable lives at the moment and expect to continue to do so. But in our research, we were careful to adjust for things that might otherwise lead to greater well-being — things like demographic characteristics and socioeconomic status.

It's worth taking a moment to really reflect on this result, because I think it reveals so much about the nature of our relationship to our future selves. Imagine that in 1995, you took two middle-aged women who had relatively similar life circumstances and asked them to predict how similar they would be to their current selves in ten years' time. If one predicted more similarity and the other predicted more change, it would be the one who envisioned similarity — at least in this data set — who would end up more satisfied with her life ten years later.

Why might this be the case? Well, we already know that people who see more similarity between their current and future selves tend to do things like save more, exercise more frequently, and choose the more ethical path. It's possible — though we can't know for sure — that years of such behavior lead to a life that's more satisfying.

But doesn't this finding — that more similarity is linked to more life satisfaction — fly in the face of the very American notion that we should all be striving for self-improvement? Probably not.

Researchers Sarah Molouki and Dan Bartels have found that when people consider what makes them feel a sense of connection with future versions of themselves, they naturally incorporate the idea of self-improvement. I can feel a bond with my future self — sensing that he and I are similar and share a connection — but still anticipate that I'll get better at the things that make me "me" over time. I won't become a different person, just a better one.

THE ARROW POINTS THIS WAY

It's a cliché of social science: "Correlation does not equal causation." It's also true. The outcomes I've been discussing so far —

that strong relationships with our future selves are linked to improved long-term behaviors — all represent correlations. They leave open questions about which things *cause* which outcomes.

Is it the case that connections to our future selves lead to more patient financial decision-making, or could it be equally plausible that people who are wealthier and more patient simply end up being more bonded with their future selves?

To properly answer this question, you'd ideally want to don your mad scientist hat, find thousands of people to take part in a giant experiment, and split them into two groups.

With one group, you'd give them a whole bunch of money and see if that changed how connected and how similar they felt to their future selves. And with the other, you'd somehow make them feel more of a sense of connection with their future selves, and then see if they engaged in more positive future-oriented behaviors.

Doing so would conclusively tell you whether strong relationships with our future selves *cause* better behavior, or if the causal arrow spins the other way. No one has truly done that particular experiment, however. It does seem possible, though, that these processes are related. If you feel more of a sense of connection to your future self, it would make sense that you'd want to invest more in them. At the same time, if your life is stable and comfortable, then it might be easier to think ahead to the future and feel connected to the person you will become. (In fact, as people grow older and they experience more stability in their lives, they report feeling higher levels of connection with their future selves.)

But there is compelling evidence suggesting that the arrow points more strongly in one direction.

First, from surveys of thousands of adults, we've observed that those who have received a large sum of money in the past year (through, say, winning the lottery or an inheritance) don't actually report higher degrees of connection with their future selves compared to adults who haven't been so lucky. It's not necessarily the case, in other words, that an immediately better financial scenario *leads* to a stronger bond between current and future selves.

A second piece of evidence comes from Dan Bartels, whom I mentioned earlier, and his colleague Oleg Urminsky. They asked graduating college seniors to read a short passage indicating either that they could expect to see a lot of change in their core personality traits after college or, alternatively, that they'd see very little change in those traits. The ones who read about similarity between their current and future selves were more likely to be patient when it came to choosing between small gift certificates that they could get immediately or larger ones for which they'd have to wait. It was just a simple intervention, but it suggests that changing your sense of connection to your future self can boost your willingness to take more actions on their behalf.

And perhaps, I might speculate, on behalf of others as well.

CONNECTING TO OTHERS, BEYOND NOW

When he was thirty-two years old, Arne Johansen was diagnosed with Lou Gehrig's disease. It's a tragically young age to be given a prognosis of only a few years to live. Arne was a father of four, extremely active in his community, and a coach on his kids' sports teams. His oldest child, Ryan, was just eleven when the diagnosis was made.

As Ryan told me, he and Arne were extremely close. So much so that they talked in depth and at length about the reality of what his father was facing.

Although they continued to spend significant amounts of time together, Ryan noticed that his dad started spending hours each day writing letters—almost immediately upon receiving the diagnosis. When Arne's motor skills deteriorated (which happened fairly quickly), typing became difficult. This was in the early 1990s, and sophisticated dictation technology wasn't yet in existence. "I remember seeing him typing all the time, and then, when he couldn't type anymore, we had these mechanical arms installed on his wheelchair—and they'd hold his hands out with little eraser tips on his fingers, which would allow him to press the typewriter keys," Ryan recalled.

When that rudimentary technology failed, and as Arne's health continued to deteriorate, the family hired a nurse. Even then, Arne continued to write letters by dictating what he wanted to say to his nurse.

Ryan, wanting to be a caretaker of sorts, would check in on his father every morning before heading off to school or football practice. On one of those mornings, about three years after the initial diagnosis, Ryan found that his father had "left."

Now the chief of police of San Bruno, a small city just south of San Francisco, Ryan has grown used to dealing with extraordinarily difficult situations but acknowledged that that moment was particularly awful. For many people, that's the moment "that you remember forever—what it's like to see your dad, lifeless like that."

That's not his dominant or most vivid memory of the morning, though.

Rather, after discovering that his father had died, he went to get his mother and tell her what had happened. Ten minutes later, she handed him a manila envelope.

In it was a short letter from Arne.

More than the trauma of the death and the negativity associated with that loss, what Ryan remembers is the letter. It was written to him—not to the other kids, not to his mom—but to him. And even though it was only a paragraph, it was an effort to be there through what "would probably be the most difficult time of my young life, and a time when I would want my dad to be there, but he couldn't be," Ryan related to me.

What he didn't know was that there would be many more such letters to come. In one of them, Arne wrote that he wasn't necessarily afraid to die—he had come to terms with that fact around the time of his diagnosis. No, what he was most afraid of was not being able to be there for his wife and kids in the years ahead. He recognized that all the normal rite-of-passage moments—moments that should provoke pure joy—would forever be marked by the grief associated with his absence.

And so, in an effort to reduce some of that sadness, he wrote letters to mark almost every significant life experience that his children would encounter in the future.

Now in his mid-forties, Ryan has received notes from his dad on the day of the funeral, the first anniversary of his father's death, his high school and college graduations, his wedding day, and the birth of his first child. There's even a letter waiting for the birth of his first grandchild.

Arne wrote dozens of these letters—letters for his other children, for his wife, and for others as well.

These letters are a powerful reminder that we can maintain a sense of connection to people even after they're gone. In thinking of his own future self, and of life beyond the existence of that self, Arne ended up shaping the future selves of others, too.

Thanks to the letters, Ryan continues to feel close to his father—he remains an important influence in his life. More unexpectedly, the letters have allowed his own kids to get to know their grandfather better—to get to know his voice, his personality, and his "self," all of which seem to have peeked through in the writing.

His father's letters even prompted Ryan to form his own company. When he became a cop two decades ago, he was with the San Diego Police Department and was assigned a beat in a particularly violent neighborhood.

In his first year, he was involved in an incident where he was shot multiple times. Although his father had the "luxury" of several years to plan out his remaining time, Ryan realized that in his line of work, he could die at any moment.

So, he sat down to start to write the same kinds of letters that his father wrote. The task, however, was exceedingly difficult— it took him forever to get through just half of one letter.

Maybe, he thought, he could use his webcam to record a

video "letter." Yet, that also proved harder than he anticipated. Recording a video that was meant to be a source of support on his daughter's wedding day turned instead into more of a pile of sobs attached to a barely intelligible message.

His struggles led Ryan to found EverPresent. With the company, Ryan has tried to create a forum for just about anybody, whether healthy or sick, to create these sorts of "legacy" videos so that they can be shared with loved ones after their death.

As Ryan noted, and as weird as it sounds coming from a chief of police, the video prompts actually follow standard interrogation techniques: a user is asked a series of questions aimed at getting them to tell a narrative. That, as it turns out, is much easier to do than sitting down in front a camera with no real script or sense of order.

For Ryan, the process has had an impact. Because it has forced him to think more deeply about loved ones, creating the videos has drawn Ryan closer to them. Other users of EverPresent have had similar experiences. In one testimonial, for instance, a user notes that although he purchased a membership for his mother as a Christmas present, it's been a gift for the whole family since she created her videos.

But there's another benefit: in leading Ryan to think beyond his lifetime, the videos have allowed him to feel more comfortable about the prospect of his own mortality—in part because he knows he won't have left any loose ends dangling with his family.

Being less afraid of dying, in turn, has made it easier to show compassion in key decision-making moments that he faces as a cop. "You might be a little more willing to talk before you pull out your gun," he told me, because, if you were to die, you know you'd have more closure with your family—even if just in the form of video "letters."

And it's not just Ryan: doctors at Stanford Health Care have taken on a similar letter-writing project with their patients. In an effort to get patients to think more deeply about their end-of-life wishes, palliative care physicians have introduced an advance directive that takes the form of a letter. Though not quite the same as what Ryan has achieved with EverPresent, there's a similar strategy. Patients are asked to write about both what matters most to them now and what they think will matter at the end of their lives, as well as how they want to be remembered by their families. Doing so has allowed patients to more completely express their preferences to their doctors. To the extent that clear and well-documented end-of-life plans lead to "better" deaths (for both patients and caretakers), it stands to reason that such letter-writing exercises could make life's most difficult stage just a little easier.

There's a larger lesson here. To philosophers like Derek Parfit, considering connections with future selves is something that can make death a little less scary. If we think there is but one "self," then life ends when death arrives. "After death," writes Parfit, "there will be no one living who will be me."

But if our lives are better defined as a collection of separate selves—who experience some degree of connection to one another—then perhaps death shouldn't inspire quite so much terror. Yes, as Parfit notes, death will create a strong divide "between my present experiences and future experiences, but it will not break various other relations." We can live on in the hearts and minds of loved ones. Glimmers of the self survive.

The meaning of this insight is that we need not be defined by our faces, our interests, our memories, or the meat clinging to our bones. Those aspects of our selves will surely cease to exist upon death. Other aspects, though, can persist, and they do so largely through our closest relationships. Whether it is through core values of ours that we impart to others, the impressions we make on them, or the stories they tell about us, we can continue to impact the world even after we're gone.

Just ask Ryan, or perhaps even the folks at Alcor.

Recognizing connections among selves over time can strongly influence our behavior and life satisfaction. Whether through financial decisions or health choices, ethical paths or posthumous relationships with loved ones, maintaining strong bonds with our distant selves is linked to positive outcomes. In short, the closer you feel to your future self, the better you'll prepare for your future, whatever it may bring.

But before we discuss ways to bridge the gap between current and future selves (which we'll do in the final section of the book), it's important to understand the dark side of relationships with our distant selves. What happens when our future-self connections are frayed, and what, if anything, can impoverished connections with our future selves tell us about the mistakes that we so often make in our daily lives?

Highlights

- The relationships we have with our future selves play a crucial role in the decisions we make.
- Stronger connections to our distant selves are linked to positive outcomes.
- These improved outcomes can be found in a variety of areas, like enhanced financial well-being, a greater likelihood to exercise, better grades, and better psychological well-being.
- Strengthening your connection to your future self can boost your willingness to take more actions on your future self's behalf.

PART II

TURBULENCE

*Understanding the Mistakes We Make as
We Move from Now to Later*

CHAPTER 4

MISSING YOUR FLIGHT

When Groupon started in 2008, its focus was on deeply discounted deals that were "group activated": a certain number of consumers would have to buy the sale before it become active. As a grad student on a budget, I thought the company offered an excellent service, and I often gladly bought coupons for things that I "needed" or felt that I needed.

About two years into Groupon's existence, I was living in Chicago teaching MBA students for the first time. This meant that my go-to outfit of shorts and a T-shirt wasn't cutting it—I needed some dress clothes for the classroom.

I was delighted when I saw a Groupon offer for two dress shirts for ninety dollars. This wasn't my first Groupon experience, though, and I was well aware of the temptation I'd feel when I went to use the coupon. I knew I'd likely buy more than the coupon allotment, pouring more than ninety dollars into shirts I didn't need. In other words, I'd go broke saving money.

But I had a solution. In what I thought was a move of

sophisticated foresight, I asked my wife if she'd accompany me to the store, imploring her to help me buy only two shirts.

Before our dedicated shopping day, I was already feeling a little anxious that I'd blow through my budget—the store was just off of Chicago's upscale Michigan Avenue shopping district and had the fancy-sounding "Clothiers" in its name.

After we'd walked up the stairs, a handsome and impeccably dressed salesman named Jake greeted us. His hair was perfectly done, and his button-down seemed to fit just right. Before I could say, "I'm here for the Groupon deal," he immediately reached out to shake my hand and asked if either of us would like something to drink—tea, coffee, or perhaps wine or beer? Okay, I thought, a beer would be pretty nice.

When he returned with our drinks, I again tried to tell him that I was there for the Groupon deal, but he quickly started asking us how our day was going and complimented me on my outfit. Finally, I let him know that I had the coupon for two shirts and that that would be all I'd need that day.

"Sure," he said, "but let me first show you our suits."

"No, no," I protested, "I'm truly just here for the two shirts and no more." I'd like to think that I might have even tried to tell him that he'd already complimented my outfit, so why did I need more than two shirts? But I'm pretty sure I didn't have the courage. Besides, he was a professional—he knew exactly what he was doing.

"Okay," he relented, "just the two shirts. But we have to walk by the suit area anyway, so I might as well show you those."

There were three categories of suits, he told me. The "lower-end" ones were about $500. The middle grouping, where apparently "most of the customers shopped," was about $900. And the final category? Well, that was roughly $18,000 a suit.

Eighteen thousand dollars?

What on earth, I asked him, would make a suit cost so much? Sure, the material looked nice, or as nice as I could tell, but it also kind of looked like a regular pin-striped suit.

Jake noted that it was all hand-sewn—made exactly as a customer would like, to fit perfectly. But the pinstripes? "Take a closer look," he said. As I stepped up to the suit, I could immediately tell that the pinstripes were...monogrammed.

"Just think about it," Jake said in a dreamy tone, "your suit could say 'HAL, HAL, HAL, HAL' all over it!" And what's more—as if you could imagine something being "more" about such a suit—the thread was dipped in nothing other than liquid gold.

Obviously, I didn't buy the suit. I would have just as soon purchased a new car! And to be fair, I don't think Jake was really trying to sell me on it.

However, what he was doing—and quite effectively at that—was drawing my attention to a much higher price than the ninety dollars I was prepared to spend.

An hour later, as I clutched my receipt for four shirts—twice as many as I'd wanted to buy—I proudly told my wife (and myself) that at least I hadn't gotten suckered into spending tons of money on a suit I couldn't afford!

ANCHORS AND TIME TRAVEL

What Jake had done was "anchor" me on a very high price. As a talented salesman, he knew that I'd probably get stuck on that number and then be willing to purchase more than the two shirts I was planning to buy.

You might have heard of this phenomenon—it's a concept that's moved from the academic world of behavioral economics into popular conversation. The basic idea is that when making decisions that involve numerical information, we sometimes pay far too much attention to an initial number, failing to adjust for the hook it sets in our minds.

When a boat drops its anchor in the sea, it stays close to where the anchor is. Sure, it can still float a bit in one direction or another, but at day's end, it will still be roughly where the anchor was initially dropped.

So, too, is the case with numbers. We get anchored on an initial value, and even though we know we can and should move away from it, we don't do so sufficiently. I knew I would never pay in the neighborhood of twenty grand for a suit with HAL pinstripes, but in thinking so much about that big number, I failed to see that even an extra hundred dollars was still much more than I had planned to spend.

This concept of anchoring is at the core of the first time-traveling error we make. Just as we hew too closely to initial numbers, even when they're not relevant, we often focus too much on our current selves. The present becomes our anchor, distorting our decisions about the future.

As an example, imagine you've planned an elaborate trip to a faraway spot. You arrive at the airport well in advance of your flight. After making it through security, however, you decide to have a few drinks at the airport bar. It's vacation, after all! Unfortunately, you lose track of time and regrettably miss your flight.

A similar issue can happen with time travel: rather than making the trip to the future in our minds — and acting in a way that benefits ourselves in the future — we get sucked in by the present and miss our "flight." In the decisions we make, in other words, we anchor on and pay too much attention to the thoughts and whims of our present selves, who are perfectly happy drinking beer in an airport bar.

IMAGINE YOU'RE A SCRATCH-OFF LOTTERY TICKET FANATIC...

Let me try to illustrate what's going on here with the help of some magic lottery tickets. Imagine, with me, for a minute, that you're a fan of scratch-off lottery tickets.

A few times a week, your morning ritual is to buy a ticket and scratch it off at your desk before you start work. On this particular crisp fall day, you've got your scratch-off ticket and a hot cup of coffee sitting right next to it.

You scratch off your lottery ticket, and bam, you see that you've won $1,000! When you look more closely at the ticket, you see it says, "You've won $1,000! Redeemable in six months."

You're a little disappointed because you were expecting to be able to cash in on the money right away; but still, this will be an extra thousand bucks for your bank account. You're only a block away from the convenience store where you bought the ticket, and you're excited enough that you decide to take a stroll over there to share the good news with the shop owner, Izzy.

When you go in to tell Izzy about your winnings, he explains to you that, actually, since you two have recently become friends, he'd happily pay you the money right now. Or you can choose to wait to receive your money in six months (as the ticket says).

Why wait? If you were given the opportunity to receive $1,000 right now or that same amount of money in a month, you'd most likely take the money right now.

That choice is a version of missing our flight and staying too close to the present—we are opting for the money now rather than the money later. And yet, we'd be hard-pressed to find the mistake in prioritizing the $1,000 right now over that same amount in six months.

But now, let's say that a few weeks have gone by since you've won your $1,000. It's a rainy day in November, and you've got your lottery ticket and your coffee at your desk (if you won once, you figure, why not try again?). You scratch off the ticket. Either you're the luckiest lottery player ever, or your local convenience store is blessed, but you've won another time! Again, though, the prize is $1,000, redeemable in six months.

Just the same, you decide that you'll go tell your friend at the store about your most recent streak of good luck. Who knows— maybe he'll pay out your earnings again. But when you get to the store, the owner suggests something else.

"Listen," Izzy says, "I can pay you your $1,000 in six months.

Or, if you want, I could pay you now, but this time, I need to take a cut — so I could give you $990."

Should you opt for the lower amount that you can get immediately? Or wait for the larger one? For a variety of reasons, it might make sense to take the money right now. Could you, for instance, do more with the smaller amount? Could you invest it or put it to some other use that would leave your future self in a better position?

If so, it probably wouldn't be a mistake, so to speak, to take the $990 right now. The point being, there are circumstances in which it makes sense to choose slightly smaller amounts of money now over more significant amounts of money later. When you choose that smaller amount, that's called "discounting the value of a future reward." You are, in other words, valuing some future reward a little bit less than something that you could get right now.

If you kept winning lottery tickets, and Izzy kept lowering the amount that he was offering you to take immediately — $980, $970 ... $500 ... and so on — at some point, you'd probably say, "Okay, okay, I'll wait for the $1,000!" It just wouldn't be worth it to give up, say, $100 or $200 or whatever your specific "indifference point" is.

Who am I to say which of your choices in these scenarios are mistakes? Maybe you need the money right now, so taking $900 — or $600, or whatever it is — instead of waiting a whole six months makes sense. It's okay to be impatient, provided you've got a good reason.

But the real time-traveling mistake — the mistake of missing our flight because of those airport drinks—arises when we engage in this tendency to discount future rewards in a way that's contrary to how we'd ideally wish to behave. You wanted to go on that trip. You booked the flight, found the hotel, read the guidebooks.

It was only your present self who, momentarily, made a bad choice.

I'LL HAVE SOME ICE CREAM WITH THAT DANCE MUSIC, PLEASE

What would you imagine generates the most profit in Las Vegas: the slot machines, the blackjack tables, the hotel suites, the elaborate shows, or the extravagant meals? It turns out it's none of the above. The real profit machine in Vegas is actually the clubs.

At enormous ones like Hakkasan, Tao, or Jewel, some of the world's most famous DJs start their elaborate sets around one or two in the morning and don't finish until dawn. The multilevel clubs are packed with people who waited hours in line or spent huge sums of money to avoid the lines. Patrons burn through so much money on entry fees and drinks (table service can run into the thousands of dollars) that some DJs earn upwards of hundreds of thousands of dollars *a night.*

But many of these young DJs have a hard time holding on to that windfall. One of the most famous of them, Afrojack, has spent a large portion of his vast income—he makes millions of dollars a year—on splurges. Several years ago, when he was already in possession of a Ferrari, a Mercedes, and three Audis, he decided to buy yet another Ferrari and crashed it after only forty-five minutes, driving over an oil slick. His lavish lifestyle extends beyond cars; he rented an eighty-foot yacht to celebrate his daughter's birthday and hired a private Jetstream plane (for $38,000) to take him to one of his shows.

In a *New Yorker* profile of the six-foot-nine megastar, he seemed to be aware that he was living his life in a way that could be considered, at minimum, "outlandish." Yet, when asked about it, he offered an answer that, if nothing else, represents a unique description of extreme discounting: "If someone gives you a whole bunch of ice cream, what are you going to do, put it in the refrigerator? No. You're going to fucking eat the ice cream."

I suspect that this desire is relatable, even if none of us can truly identify with Afrojack's specific circumstances. In thinking this way—that the ice cream will melt if we don't eat it right away—we overestimate the importance of what's happening in our lives *right now*. We prioritize the airport beer over tomorrow's vacation, or anchor to the comfy couch instead of getting on the treadmill.

This sort of desire is also what I'm talking about when I say that we might be acting contrary to how we'd behave in an ideal world.

WHEN THE FUTURE TURNS INTO THE PRESENT

Let's return to the lottery example for just a minute. After several amusing encounters with your friend at the convenience store, he decides to pose a question to you. "Imagine," he says, "that a year from now, you again scratch off a winning lottery ticket. And again, you could either take your full $1,000 in six months or come to me and cash your ticket in for $900 immediately."

What he's asking you to imagine, in other words, is that you could either have $900 in a year or wait a year and a half for the full $1,000.

What do you think? Would you tell him you'd prefer to have $900 in a year rather than $1,000 in a year and a half? My guess is that you'd opt to wait it out for the larger amount of money. In an ideal world, in other words, your preferred course of action would be the one where you need more patience.

Isn't it wildly inconsistent, then, to choose the larger amount of money when both choices occur well into the future (in a year versus a year and a half) but settle for the smaller amount today when the option is between getting it now versus six months from now? Logically, yes. But the reality is that as the future draws closer to the present, it becomes harder for us to exhibit patience. We have a harder and harder time, it seems, acting in ways that benefit our future selves. Instead, we start to shift our focus to our current selves.

In fact, in studies where people are given choices just like the ones I've been presenting, we often see evidence of these sorts of preference reversals. The basic idea is that in the absence of an immediately available reward, people *do* value the future and choose to act patiently. But when a temptation is available now (or close to now), the future and all that it holds are devalued more intensely.

Here's one example from a typical research study: When choosing between thirty dollars in eight days and thirty-four dollars in seventeen days, people opt to wait for the larger reward. But when one of the rewards is available now—say, thirty dollars right away versus thirty-four dollars in nine days—then the preferences reverse, and people opt for the smaller, immediate reward.

You can find these patterns in other areas as well. For instance, a week from now, would you rather have a banana, an apple, a chocolate bar, or some nuts (not boring, unroasted, unsalted nuts, but the good kind)?

If you're like many of the research participants who got this same question, you'd probably go for the healthy option in one week's time. But a week later, the same people were given the same choice, except this time, the rewards were available immediately. Most of them, and I'm betting you might do the same thing, switched course and went for the junk food over the healthy food. When choosing for our future selves, we choose the banana. But when the present self gets involved, we end up gorging on chocolate.

This sort of behavior—which is known as extreme discounting of future rewards—is associated with and even in some cases predictive of behaviors that many of us wish to avoid, like, for example, smoking, alcohol abuse and dependence, heroin and stimulant use, and even obesity and problematic gambling.

You can observe such preference reversals in nonhumans as well. When pigeons, for instance, were given access to grain for either two seconds or six seconds, they preferred the larger reward, so long as both rewards were going to be delivered at a future time. Or rather, a "future time" in pigeon terms: twenty-eight seconds later for the smaller reward and thirty-two seconds later for the larger one. Every single pigeon, in fact, chose the larger reward in this context.

Yet, when the amount of time between rewards was increased—with a two-second wait for the small reward and a six-second wait for the larger one—now the pigeons acted like the junk food–eating humans I mentioned earlier: they opted for the smaller bit of food that was available sooner. Rats have been shown to behave the same way, too.

In reality, it may be difficult to detect such "clean" reversals of preferences in our daily lives. We're rarely confronted with circumstances where we first express an explicit preference and then change course when facing temptation.

What's more common is that we hold general preferences about how we'd like to behave at some future point. You might generally want to be someone who eats healthy foods, for example. But when tonight rolls around, if it's been a long day, you may find yourself eating a bag of peanut M&M'S instead of the apple that would certainly be better for your body.

A TIGHTLY HELD SPARROW IS BETTER THAN A THOUSAND FLYING BIRDS

Why are we such impulsive creatures? Why can't we stick to our long-term preferences in the face of instant gratification?

One explanation revolves around the certainty—or rather,

uncertainty—of the future. Animals and humans alike can't know what the future will hold, and there's risk involved with waiting for the promise of some reward rather than snatching up a sure bet right now.

This is, of course, the sentiment underlying the old "bird in the hand" idiom, which made its first appearance back in the seventh century as "Better is a sparrow held tight in the hand than a thousand birds flying about in the air." (The author of this ancient text has a few other animal-related pieces of advice in the same vein, such as "A sheep's foot in thine own hand is better than a sheep's shoulder in the hands of a stranger.")

We've been aware for quite some time, it seems, that the future contains no guarantees, and it may be wise to go for what's available in the present, even if it's just a sheep's foot.

So, then, one of the reasons why we end up getting anchored on the present is because the present is more knowable than whatever exists beyond its limits.

This explanation is no doubt intuitively appealing. And yet, it's worth noting that there are still many instances in our lives when the future *is* decently certain and yet we still let down our future selves. (Think about the apple versus chocolate bar study. There's little risk of America running out of apples, and yet we still can't say no to the immediate pleasure of dessert.)

Why, then, do we prioritize the now? Why do we let ourselves get anchored to the present, even if it comes with a future cost? The answer, of course, isn't simple, in part because the tendency to overemphasize the present isn't due to just a single cause. There are, however, a few compelling explanations.

THE PRESENT IS A MAGNIFYING GLASS

Liz Dunn, a professor of psychology at the University of British Columbia, is both a leading international expert in the study of happiness and an avid surfer. When I had lunch with her a few years ago, I casually asked her if she had any good surfing stories to tell me while we waited for our food to arrive.

"Wait, have we never talked about surfing?" she asked. Based on her puzzled look, I figured that there was something I was missing. She went on. "Have I not told you about the time...a shark bit me?"

To be fair, I don't remember everything people tell me, but this surely would have been something I would have committed to memory. Her tale sounded just as you'd imagine a shark-attack story to sound.

She was in Hawaii and had hired a guide to take her around to local breaks—as she later told me, you don't want to end up in the wrong spot. After catching a wave that took her away from her guide and his friend, she quietly lay down on her surfboard so that she could paddle back to her party. Her tranquility, though, was disrupted by a giant bump underneath her. Assuming a clumsy sea turtle had swum into her board, she was obviously surprised when something suddenly bit her leg, leaving three big holes in her wetsuit and a wound that went all the way down to the bone.

All she saw of the shark was its giant tail fin, thankfully swimming away after having circled her menacingly for a while.

"What's funny about the experience," if there can be anything funny about this, she later told me, "was that afterward, all of these reporters were trying to ask me details about the context. Questions like 'How far out were you?'... 'What did the shark look like?' et cetera.... I'm like, 'I have no idea!'" Like a scene out of *Law and Order,* she was shown a lineup of possible sharks but wasn't able to identify the likely culprit. (She now uses this anecdote to discuss the unreliability of eyewitness testimony when teaching social psychology.)

All her attention, unsurprisingly, was focused on what was happening in the moment and whether the shark was about to attack again. Emotionally speaking, how could she not be focused on that moment? Or in her words, "It's not like I was thinking about what to have for dinner...or how I should plan for retirement!"

This is an extreme example of a very common habit: we pay a great deal of attention to the present. The here and now tends to consume our mental bandwidth, blocking out thoughts of the future, even if what's currently happening is far less salient than a shark attack. That observation reflects a line from a research paper Liz published a few years after the infamous Hawaii trip. "The present," she and her coauthors wrote, "seems to be viewed under an emotional magnifying glass."

Put another way, the emotions we feel at any given moment may simply seem more important than the ones we've felt in the past or those we can imagine feeling in the future.

If you're someone who has ever kept a journal, think back to some of the topics you wrote about and the feelings you had when doing so. How important, intense, and all-consuming were those past events in your life? I bet that for any given one of them, *while* you were in the midst of it, you probably experienced more intense emotions than you're experiencing now, as you look back on the past.

But even if you're not a journaler, you can still probably come up with examples of situations where that present-day magnifying glass rears its head. Of course, there's the classic "shopping while hungry" experience of buying lots of food while at the grocery store, only to realize once you've had dinner or can't find room in the fridge that you've bought too much.

Economists have pointed to "visceral factors" in explaining the tendency for our attention to be overly drawn to in-the-moment emotions. If we are hungry, thirsty, or feeling otherwise deprived in some visceral or deep-seated way, we will do our best to satisfy that need, even with something we'll later regret.

When we give in to those visceral impulses, it's as if there's an impetuous, toddler-like version of ourselves who wins out over the more patient adult inside us. Put in more biological terms, in our brains, we have a dopamine system (the toddler) as well as a system associated with our prefrontal cortex (the wise adult).

The dopamine system triggers an emotional reaction to whatever is right in front of us. It helps us code the value of everything—good and bad—in our environment. The prefrontal system, by contrast, allows us to keep the big picture in mind, helping us to exhibit patience in the face of temptations. We know about these systems, in part, from watching what happens to patients with lesions in their prefrontal regions. They suffer from something known as environmental dependency syndrome.

Without your prefrontal cortex to guide you, you'd end up entirely dependent on your dopamine system, acting according to whatever feelings your immediate environment prompts. In the 1980s, French neurologist François Lhermitte movingly described the case of a patient with this syndrome.

One of the most poignant scenes occurred when Dr. Lhermitte took one of his patients to his apartment. Upon seeing the bed in the doctor's bedroom, the patient casually undressed, got into bed, and settled in as if he were ready to go to sleep for the night. (Apparently, privacy concerns in the 1980s were different from what they are now, as the journal article contains pictures of the entire incident.)

Without the benefit of a fully functioning prefrontal cortex, the patient did whatever came to mind, as it came to mind. He was tired, so he simply climbed into the nearest bed, regardless of whom it belonged to.

In a less extreme case, researchers Baba Shiv and Alexander Fedorikhin asked people to choose between a piece of chocolate cake and a fruit salad (I don't think I need to spell out which one is more emotionally engaging here). You won't be surprised to find out that the chocolate cake was more likely to be chosen, but only when the prefrontal cortex was taxed. That is, one group of research participants was asked to memorize a series of numbers (a mentally taxing task!) while they were waiting to choose between cake and fruit, and they were the ones most likely to pick the cake.

There's a clear twenty-first-century takeaway from this finding. As conventional advice has put it, it may make sense to put your phone in another room when interacting with others. After all, even an incidental distraction in the form of a ding or buzz may tilt the scale in favor of the immediate present and away from a larger goal of being more engaged with our friends and families. Doing so will most likely provide more meaning in the long term than scrolling through the latest social media post.

Again, one of the reasons that we overvalue rewards that we can get immediately is that our present self's emotions may trump the ones we expect our future self to feel. With the help of our prefrontal cortices, we can sometimes tamp down those overly powerful emotions and keep our eyes on the long-term prize(s). We give in, however, when we're otherwise distracted — which is often! — or when the pull of the in-the-moment emotions is just too powerful.

As I hinted at earlier, this line of reasoning gives us one way to understand why we sometimes choose now over later even when we don't initially intend to. Another compelling explanation concerns the way that we think about time itself.

HOT STOVES AND PRETTY PEOPLE

Einstein famously said, "Sit with a pretty girl for an hour, and it feels like a minute; sit on a hot stove for a minute, and it feels like many hours. That's relativity." I always figured this was just a thought experiment until I read an article in *Scientific American* entitled "Einstein's Hot Time."

As the story goes, Einstein decided to test his idea one afternoon. To do so, he first fetches a small cooking stove from the garage that hasn't been used in a while. Then he awkwardly calls his friend Charlie Chaplin and his beautiful wife, Paulette Goddard, and asks if Paulette would mind visiting with him for an hour.

After spending what feels like a minute with Paulette, Einstein looks at his watch, and sure enough, just under an hour has passed. The first part of his hypothesis: confirmed!

The second part of his research project, however, ended prematurely when Einstein landed in the doctor's office with a slight burn on his left butt cheek.

Only years after reading this anecdote did it occur to me that it just might have been satire. Nonetheless, it makes a serious point: time's passage is relative. Or rather, the way we perceive the passing of time is relative — the same amount of objective time may *feel* longer or shorter depending on what's happening.

That's the conclusion the researchers at Yale came to in a series of experiments where people reported how long a given period felt using nothing more than a paper and pencil. Research participants were shown a line with the left end labeled "very short" and the right end labeled "very long." Different groups were asked to tick off how long three months, one year, and three years felt.

Now, objectively speaking, we all know that three years is longer than one year, and one year is longer than three months. Yet, subjective perceptions of time didn't map onto these differences. Subjectively, the one-year span only felt about 1.2 times longer than the three-month time frame (objectively, it should've been four times as long!). Even stranger, the three-year span was felt to be about equal to the one-year block of time.

Blocks of time feel compressed, in other words, the more they move away from "now."

The important implication of this work is that a day, spanning from right now until tomorrow, may feel as if it lasts longer than that same daylong period in three months. Similarly, consider your feelings about a long flight or drive: in advance, the whole trip might feel like one long block of time; midway through, however, the final hours may seem to stretch on and on as the destination gets closer and closer. Here's why this is significant: if a span of time feels like it lasts a long time, it'll be that much harder to exhibit patience and wait for some reward at the end.

Think about what this warping of time means for your likelihood to get overly swayed by what's happening in the present. If you have to choose between $100 in four weeks and $125 in six weeks, the gap between those two rewards might seem relatively short. You'd be willing to wait for the larger reward—it's just two weeks! But when you move both rewards up so that you're choosing between $100 now and $125 two weeks from now—well, that two-week gap may feel as if it lasts a subjectively longer amount of time. That lengthening of time might make it very hard to act patiently today. The end result is that we treat the present in a special way.

What, however, do we even mean by "the present"? Given the unique psychological power of the present, it seems like an important question to answer. Of course, the answer might seem blindingly obvious—the present is now! It's this very moment! But I hope to complicate that obvious answer.

At its core, the present moment is really about transitions. Let me explain with caterpillars.

OKAY, SO WHAT DO WE MEAN BY "THE PRESENT"?

When my daughter was little, she, like many other two-year-olds, grew obsessed with *The Very Hungry Caterpillar*. Upon reading it, I couldn't help but notice that the caterpillar's progression from tiny caterpillar to beautiful butterfly wasn't unlike time's march from the present to the future.

The analogy stuck with me (probably because we read Eric Carle's book night after night after night). So, I reached out to Naoki Yamanaka, an associate professor of entomology at the University of California, Riverside, to ask him some questions. (He's one of the world's experts in the study of metamorphosis.)

It was my first time talking to an actual entomologist, and not just a toddler who was really into bugs. And it lived up to all my expectations. Yamanaka even showed me vials of dozens and dozens of fruit flies at the beginning of our meeting. But when he turned his attention to describing the caterpillar-to-butterfly process, that's when he became really animated.

Yamanaka noted that scientists have crystal-clear markers for when you call a caterpillar a caterpillar and when you call it something else. When the creatures are moving nonstop and eating everything in sight? That's a caterpillar. But the moment they stop moving—when they're neither a caterpillar nor a butterfly—that's when they are known as a pupa. And when they break out of the shell that they were in, that's when they become a butterfly.

Time's delineations may follow a similar pattern.

Most of us, if pressed, would agree that there's a present and a future. But where does one end and the other begin?

Entomologists have a clear sense of when a bug is this or that, but psychologists don't have a clear sense of when the present gives way to the future. Instead, it's up to each of us as individuals to decide when we think the present ends and the future begins. In research I conducted with Sam Maglio, a professor at the University of Toronto, we asked thousands of people this very question. Just like the caterpillar-pupa-butterfly life cycle, our research participants identified three clear blocks when asked to give their general impressions about time: the present, some "in-between" period (sort of like the pupa), and the future. With no clear definition of where the present ends and the future begins to go on, people gave responses that ranged from "the next future starts whenever I move from one task to another" to "each present lasts about three days" to "the present ends when I finish this strange research study." To see where your answer stacks up relative to our research participants, see the figure that follows.

But one major finding stood out: nobody had a hard time giving us an answer, even if their definitions were different.

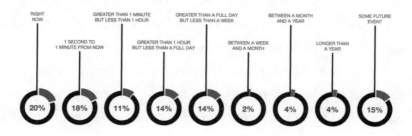

Perhaps that was the case because the present is the block of time in which we spend most of our lives. And, as a result, it's the one that we weight the most heavily.

Yamanaka shared a fact that's relevant here—something that seems to have escaped the pages of children's books. Caterpillars, he told me, have what's known as "imaginal discs" in their "spine" regions. If you were to dissect the caterpillar, the tiny groupings of cells would look like miniature DVDs. And although many of the cells die off over time, these particular groupings are tagged for what they will eventually become. Some turn into eyes, others into legs, and still others morph into the wings of the butterfly. In other words, the caterpillar already has the building blocks inside it to create its future, butterfly self. And remarkably, if you were to dissect the adult butterfly, you'd still be able to see remnants of its younger, caterpillar self.

A key point can be drawn from these cells: we easily separate the present from the future but often fail to recognize how each "present" adds up to an overall future.

What's happening to our current selves—the selves who live in the present—feels more significant than everything else.

We want to get one more beer in the airport bar; we *don't* want to get on our exercise bike; that chocolate doughnut is calling our name. Given the visceral pull of the present, it makes sense that we overweight it. Looping back to my research with Sam Maglio, the participants who said the present seemed especially big—meaning it occupied more space in their mind's eye—allocated fewer dollars to an imaginary long-term savings account. The bigger the present, the farther away the future; the farther away the future, the less weight their present selves give to it.

By overweighting "now" in this way, we treat the present as if it's an expanse of time that's divorced from the rest of our timelines, which it simply is not. Each period that we label "the present" subsequently turns into the next "present." We're like the hungry caterpillar happily devouring his fruit and candy, completely unaware that he'll soon be a pupa and then a butterfly. In short, we ignore our future variations, which can leave us terribly disappointed when our future selves aren't prepared for their own present. And so, we end up as disappointed butterflies, full of regrets about our caterpillar choices.

———

Placing too much of a priority on the present—missing our flight, so to speak—isn't the only time-traveling error we make, though. Even when we recognize the interconnections between present and future, we may still fail to do so in a way that treats the future, and the future self, realistically. We're like a caterpillar convinced he's going to turn into a grasshopper. I discuss this tendency—what I call "poor trip planning"—in the next chapter.

Highlights

- Our first time-traveling mistake is that we get overly focused on the present, failing to consider the future. There are at least three reasons for this tendency.
- First, the present is simply more certain than the future, and we'd rather take a sure bet now than a risky one later.
- Second, our present-day emotions seem more powerful than the ones we expect our future selves to feel.
- Third, time feels as if it lasts longer in the present, making it more difficult to exhibit patience.
- We may fail to see the ways in which our present selves add up to and become our future selves.

CHAPTER 5

POOR TRIP PLANNING

Mozart, the great and enduring musical genius, doesn't conform to our stereotypical notion of a musical prodigy.

Did he practice for hours per day? Nope.

Was he well-intentioned with his plans? Also no.

More of a partier than a conscientious adult, Mozart, as biographers have described him, was someone who was "much addicted to trifling amusement."

Perhaps it's not surprising, then, that he also wasn't known for finishing compositions promptly. In fact, in late October of 1787, after having all but wrapped up the score for *Don Giovanni*, he decided to go out for a night of drinking with buddies. Toward the end of the evening, one friend nervously turned to Mozart and remarked that with the opera due to be performed for the first time the next day, he couldn't believe that the overture hadn't been written yet!

Mozart hurriedly returned home to start—and hopefully finish—this missing piece. But, because he kept nodding off due to the alcohol and the late hour, he asked his wife, Constanze, to help him stay awake by telling him stories.

Amazingly, just three hours later, the overture was complete.

Without the benefit of photocopiers, copyists had to then transcribe the orchestra's parts by hand, and, as legend has it, the final pages made it to the theater only minutes before the curtain went up. The ink, in fact, was still wet when the orchestra members performed it for the first time. The opera was a success, and almost 250 years after that stressful debut, it's still performed regularly at opera houses worldwide.

Leaving things to the last minute is a bad habit that resonates with many of us. Take the story of Tim Urban, the creator of the popular blog *Wait But Why*. A self-proclaimed "master procrastinator," he has relayed the story of how, during his final year of college, he kept putting off writing his honors thesis.

Given that the thesis was meant to be a yearlong endeavor, the plan was to start in the fall months and slowly ramp up in January, maintaining a challenging pace of work until May, when it was due. Except that's not what happened. Finding excuse after excuse to not get started, he finally sat down to write it two nights before the due date. Pulling not one but two all-nighters in a row, he was able to dash all ninety pages off and get it in just in time.

As he relates on his blog and in a TED talk, he received a call from one of the college administrators about a week later.

"Mr. Urban, we need to talk about your thesis," the administrator said.

"Okay . . . ," Tim responded nervously.

The administrator continued. "Well . . . it's the best one we've ever seen."

In Urban's telling of the story, you can quickly see how stunned he was to get this news.

But then, after a pause, he says, "Actually, that didn't happen at all." It was, in fact, "a very, very bad thesis."

If only putting things off resulted in the sort of positive critical reception that *Don Giovanni* received. Most of us, however, have had experiences more like Urban's than Mozart's: procrastination doesn't typically garner awards.

WAIT, I THOUGHT THIS FLIGHT WAS GOING TO BOSTON!

Even though you may never have procrastinated like Mozart, I'm going to guess that you're intimately familiar with this behavior. Across the globe, about 20 percent of people are chronic procrastinators. And, while estimates of exactly how many people procrastinate to some extent are a little hard to nail down, one informal survey found that 85 percent do so in a way that bothers them.

Make no mistake: the tendency to put things off isn't just bad for college students trying to complete long papers. As psychologist Fuschia Sirois has documented, there may be far more severe consequences: chronic procrastination is associated with a litany of undesirable outcomes, including poor mental health, anxiety, hypertension, and cardiovascular disease. And this type of procrastination becomes a vicious cycle: procrastinators put off and fail to schedule the very doctor's appointments that could help lessen some of their healthcare woes.

Consider for a moment what procrastination actually is. The word is derived from the Latin *procrastinaire,* which means "put off until tomorrow." Okay, sure, you know that. Here's what's more interesting: procrastination is also conceptually related to the Greek word *akrasia,* which means doing something *despite* knowing that it's against your better judgment.

So, procrastination isn't just about putting something off until tomorrow that you could just as easily take care of today. It's also about knowing that even as you delay, you're harming yourself.

Think about this definition in light of our present and future selves.

When we're faced with an unpleasant task—say, folding the laundry or finally making that appointment with the cardiologist—and we decide *not* to do it, we prioritize our present self's desire to avoid negative emotions. To some extent, that's what we talked about in the previous chapter—we get anchored on our feelings in the present. But procrastination presents an additional wrinkle: in putting something off until a later point in time, we're also failing to consider how much our future self will want to avoid the same negative emotions that we're trying to avoid right now.

Note that it's not as if we're simply failing to consider our future selves. When we procrastinate, we do think about the future and our future selves...but not in a particularly deep or meaningful manner.

In this way, procrastination represents the second time-traveling mistake: poorly planning our trips. It's as if you're about to go on a weeklong Boston vacation and have in mind some ideas of what you want to do once you're there. You'd probably like to try some Boston-specific foods and maybe take in some of the rich cultural history. But only once you've boarded the plane do you realize that, outside of booking a hotel room, you've made very few plans. Maybe you'll still be able to get some clam chowder, but if you were hoping for a tour of Fenway Park or a visit to Paul Revere's house—attractions that could sell out quickly—your future self might end up disappointed.

You'll still be taking *a* trip to Boston, but one that differs significantly from the trip you intended to take.

So, too, is it the case with time travel: in thinking about the future in a merely surface-level way, we end up traveling to a different future than the one we meant to go to. It's as if we want to arrive at one particular version of the future—where we are happy, healthy, and financially secure—but allow ourselves to go down a path that could potentially land us in a very different place.

THE PROCRASTINATION PROFESSOR

Tim Pychyl, a psychology professor at Carleton University in Canada, has looked at just this sort of time-travel mistake.

In one study, he and his former student Eve-Marie Blouin-Hudon surveyed hundreds of college students. (While conducting research on undergraduates often comes with limitations, they present an excellent testing ground for all things having to do with not completing assignments on time.) The scientists asked the students about their procrastination habits as well as the relationships they have with their future selves. Those who felt more of a sense of similarity and emotional connection with their future selves, it turned out, were also the least likely to needlessly delay the critical tasks they set out to do.

It wasn't just a sense of similarity and connection that mattered, though. The research participants were also asked how vividly they imagined the future. For instance, if you were in this study, you'd be asked to think of an image of the sun rising over the ocean on a hazy day. In your mind's eye, how vivid is that image? At one extreme, it might be super clear—almost as if it's something you could see right in front of you. At the other extreme, though, it might be as if there's no image at all, but rather, you just sort of "know" you are thinking about the sun rising.

In Blouin-Hudon and Pychyl's research, the students who reported conjuring the most vivid mental images also felt the strongest relationships with their future selves and were the least likely to procrastinate.

These are correlations, but they're suggestive of something compelling. Having an easier time fully and vividly imagining ourselves in the future may make it harder to justify putting something off to the version of ourselves who will suffer from today's failures to act. Because we can conjure up the disappointment of our future self in Boston, we're more likely to exert the effort required to plan the "right" trip.

I reached out to Professor Pychyl to ask him a bit more about this work. I was naturally curious whether he—an international expert in the study of procrastination—ever finds himself, well, procrastinating.

"Almost never!" he told me with a laugh. But not, he cautioned, due to some great virtue on his part. Instead, he reportedly recognizes procrastination for what it is: a desire to have our future selves do the things our present selves want to avoid.

As he put it, "I know my future self isn't going to want to do this thing any more than my present self does. And I have empathy for my future self: he's going to be under enormous amounts of stress, so let's just do this thing now."

FORGIVING PAST YOU

But when Tim does act like the rest of us and procrastinate, he engages in self-forgiveness. Essentially, after putting something off in a detrimental way, there needs to be an acknowledgment and acceptance that a past version of you has done something to harm your present self. And then your present self has to forgive your lazy past self.

Let's say that you've been accumulating a stack of papers on your dining room table — a few bills, maybe some pieces of mail that you've been meaning to file away, and some artwork your kid has brought home from school. (This is all hypothetical, I swear.)

Your pile is cluttering up a part of the house that's meant to be clean; it's making your partner or roommate more annoyed with you with each day that you fail to tidy up; and you're putting yourself in danger of owing some late fees.

Clearly, putting off the great pile cleanup harms you in a variety of ways.

Part of the reason this keeps happening, as I've noted previously, is that there are a lot of negative emotions associated with your growing pile of paper. You probably feel bad that you have yet again failed to take care of the mess, and maybe that makes you think of other times you've failed to follow through on a promise either to yourself or to someone else. You're possibly also feeling a growing sense of shame in front of your partner or roommate and, irrational as it may be, some resentment toward them. Sure, it's your pile, but... couldn't *they* just help clean it up? Or maybe instead of nagging you about the dining room table they should put away those clothes you folded yesterday? (Again, this is all entirely hypothetical.)

A great way to avoid those negative emotions is just to avoid the dining room—and your cleanup—altogether! That's what we end up doing, day after day, until the pile grows ever larger.

What if, however, you were to acknowledge that you messed up and then forgave yourself for the transgression against... yourself? Doing so should, in theory, reduce some of those negative emotions that you've come to strongly associate with your pile of paper.

With forgiveness comes less avoidance of the very thing you're trying to avoid. Think about what happens when you forgive someone else for a transgression: reducing some of the anger, sadness, and so forth that you've associated with them makes it easier to spend time with them again. Similarly, forgiving a past version of yourself for procrastinating may make it more likely that you'll approach—rather than avoid—your bills, the doctor's appointment you need to schedule, those unanswered emails, and yes, that pile of paper. All things that should ultimately make life for your future self a tad better.

Pychyl's idea of applying self-forgiveness to procrastination is something he's tested in the context of studying for college exams. Over a semester, Tim and his collaborators sent questionnaires to first-year students right after their first midterm and then again right before their second midterm.

Imagine receiving questions like these as a first-year student: "Did you begin studying much later than you intended to?" "Did you delay studying to do other, less important things instead?" I certainly would've answered a shameful yes to both of them.

As you might have expected, the students who engaged in more procrastination received worse grades on their first midterm of the year. But the researchers also asked about self-forgiveness strategies. To what extent did the students put themselves down and blame themselves for studying less than they knew they should have? And to what extent did they let themselves off the hook?

Self-forgiveness, it turns out, isn't a strategy that has helped Tim just in his own life; it also conferred benefits to the students he and his collaborators assessed. Those who were more likely to engage in this practice were less likely to approach studying for their next midterm with strong negative emotions. And that, in turn, translated into less procrastination and improved grades on their next midterm.

As a note of caution: Accepting responsibility, apologizing, and forgiving other people in our lives isn't a simple process. Neither is self-forgiveness. We know, for instance, that there are flavors of apologies that won't work with others. Similarly, there are flavors of acceptance and forgiveness that won't work with your past self.

Think about two possible apologies you could offer after causing a fender bender: "Sorry I bumped your car—I know I should have been paying better attention, and I take full responsibility" or "Sorry I bumped your car—it's a natural consequence of the moon cycle that we're currently in." You don't have to be an expert in human behavior to recognize that the former will result in greater forgiveness than the latter.

The point here is that if you forgive yourself for procrastinating but don't genuinely accept blame, then you're robbing yourself of an opportunity to address the causes of your procrastination head-on. This is what psychologists Michael Wohl and Kendra McLaughlin have called "pseudo self-forgiveness," and it most likely won't result in any change in future behavior. Instead, if you want your future self's life to improve, then Current You needs to genuinely accept responsibility for your past self's mistakes. The dining room table isn't cluttered because of those moon cycles, or because I've been too busy with other chores. It's cluttered because I chose to avoid it. It's my fault.

So, procrastination is a battle between our past, current, and future selves. And it arises, in part, due to our tendency to engage in "poor trip planning"—that is, to consider our future selves, but not in a deep or meaningful enough way.

WHY IS IT SO HARD TO STEP INTO FUTURE YOU'S SHOES?

We've all procrastinated before and felt the negative impact of doing so. After a few such experiences, shouldn't we be able to think ahead to our future self's life and realize how difficult we're making things for them?

You'd think so. But due to a few psychological peculiarities, it can be pretty tricky to do just that.

Here's one quirk: we tend to think that the feelings we have in the future will somehow be less intense than the ones we have now. Consider this experiment: researchers asked people how happy they'd be if they won twenty dollars right now, and then how happy they thought they'd be winning the same amount of money in three months.

Just to be clear, this is *not* a question of "would you rather have money now or money later." Rather, the question here is how happy you'd be if you received some amount of money now and how happy you'd be if you were to receive that same amount in the future.

There shouldn't be a difference between the two answers, right? If you said you'd be an 8 out of 10 if you won the money today, shouldn't you also be an 8 out of 10 if you won the money three months from now?

In theory, yes, but that wasn't the case. People said they'd feel a higher level of happiness today than they would in the future. Our future emotions, it seems, just feel less substantial than the ones we think we'll have today.

It's easy to see how that tendency could make it all the more likely that we'll procrastinate. We know that our future selves will find it painful to do whatever task we've put off for them, but we trick ourselves into thinking that those future selves won't find it *that* painful.

To return to my dining room table — my present self can't stomach the idea of going through those piles of paper. And yet, my present self also assumes that future Hal won't mind. He'll be a decluttering machine.

Unfortunately, I have yet to become that future Hal.

YOUR NEIGHBOR MAY KNOW BEST

We have a hard time simulating or conjuring our future feelings. What's more, most of us aren't even aware of the difficulty we have with this process; we think we're pretty good at it.

To illustrate, psychologists at Harvard created a speed-dating service. In each session, a man would first go into a room and fill out a "dating" profile, which included his photo.

One woman would then have a five-minute date with this man (the study was conducted on people who identified as heterosexual). When the date was finished, she would write up a brief report regarding how enjoyable it was. Call this the "initial dating report."

After that, other women would get a chance to have a date with the same man. But here's where things got interesting. One group of women was asked to *simulate* the experience of going on a date: the women were given the man's dating profile and asked to forecast how much they'd enjoy a date with him (before actually having the date). Another group, however, was asked to use the "initial dating report" to make a forecast of how enjoyable the date would be. You could think of this as a *surrogate* strategy. To make a forecast about the future, in other words, you can use another person as a surrogate for yourself: they've already had an experience that you're about to have, so why not trust their input?

The only difference, then—and it's an important one—is that some women made a forecast based on a simulation, and others made a forecast based on a surrogate's dating report. Imagine you were in the study. Which process would you choose: your own simulation or someone else's report?

If you're like 75 percent of the women in this study, you'd vote for simulating over surrogating. We highly value our own opinions and discount the perspectives of others.

But whose forecast was *actually* more accurate? As it turns out, surrogation won out over simulation. It wasn't even close. When it came to how much women enjoyed the date, the ones who had made their forecasts based on the surrogate's report were about twice as accurate compared to those who made their forecasts based on simulations.

Dan Gilbert, the psychology professor who led this speed-dating project, was inspired by a quote from seventeenth-century writer François de La Rochefoucauld: "Before we set our hearts too much upon anything, let us first examine how happy those are who already possess it." The point? Our forecasts about future experiences may benefit from those who have already had those same experiences.

"But other people aren't like *me!*" you might be thinking. Sure, that's true. But consider that, even though we differ from other people in many ways, we do have similar emotional responses to various things: most of us prefer to be warm rather than cold, to be full rather than hungry, and to win rather than lose. It doesn't matter if you're from New Jersey or Nebraska, Iceland or China; our basic physiological responses to stimuli in our environments are more alike than not.

Thus, the surprising power of receiving neighborly advice, or advice from surrogates: because the sources of pain and pleasure across people are similar, relying on someone else's experience—and this is especially true if they're like us—may go a long way in allowing us to anticipate what the future has in store.

In recent research, Poruz Khambatta, a postdoctoral scholar at UCLA, added a very modern twist to this insight. He and his collaborators asked thousands of people to rate how much they thought they'd benefit from reading a series of articles. He also trained an artificial intelligence algorithm to tackle this same task. Think of it as a program that first figures out what you have in common with thousands of other people, and then uses the reactions of those people to generate the best possible crowd-sourced neighborly advice for *you*.

The computer surrogate, just like the women in the speed-dating study, made superior predictions regarding how people would respond to the articles. Sure, companies already use algorithms to make predictions about what sort of material you'd like. But they don't usually make predictions about what kind of material would make you feel better off or like your time was well spent.

The algorithm, in this case, was being used to make predictions about media consumption. But the insights could easily apply to other important decisions where we rely on our simulation abilities — decisions like where to live, which college to attend, which retirement or healthcare plan would be best for our particular needs, and perhaps even whom to marry. Before dismissing this idea as a futuristic fantasy not grounded in reality, consider something Poruz told me: for any one of these big decisions, "it may be our first time at a particular crossroads, but countless others have been there before." This is why their opinions can be so valuable. What's more, our predictions about our futures — both immediate and far-off — could be vastly improved by relying on the collective experience of friends, neighbors, and strangers.

Of course, many of us may balk at this idea. As Poruz observed, "We want to think of ourselves as unique . . . we don't want to feel as if our lives are predictable. But while each of us is unique in our own way, there's a lot we can learn from the collective experience of others."

Yet, with big data — that is, a large set of data that takes advantage of the fact that there are enough similarities between you and all the people who have come before you — it should be possible to identify predictable patterns in behavior. Doing so should allow people ultimately to make more satisfying choices concerning their future selves.

Talk about neighborly advice.

We have a tendency, then, to think ahead, but not deeply enough: we simulate the future when we might benefit more from using a surrogate. Procrastination is just one mistake that arises from such instances of "poor trip planning." But it's not the only one.

By way of explanation, let me introduce you to a guy who once said yes to everything.

FROM YES MAN TO YES, DAMN

When Danny Wallace was in his mid-twenties, he found himself in a relatable twenty-something conundrum. Recently dumped by his girlfriend and in a job that wasn't inspiring, he started shrinking from society, saying no to most social invites and opportunities.

Inventing more and more elaborate excuses to avoid doing anything other than being alone, he had effectively, over a few months, become a "no man."

That is, until one evening when he was waiting for his London subway ride home. In a moment that undoubtedly brings frustration and annoyance to any regular commuter, the Tube's speaker system crackled on, informing riders that the train was out of service and that they'd all need to exit the station.

Walking outside toward a group of replacement buses, Wallace started commiserating with a fellow passenger, which turned into a general series of complaints about life itself. Well, Wallace's life.

The bearded stranger simply listened and then casually suggested that perhaps Wallace should just try saying yes more.

Which is precisely what he did. At first, he was going to do this for just one day. And it led to some awkward exchanges. Like the phone call Wallace received asking if he'd like a free quote for double-glazed windows. "Yes! Yes, I would," he replied. The only problem, however, was that his windows were already double-glazed, resulting in a very confusing phone call ("Then why did you say yes to begin with?" the salesperson eventually asked).

Before long, his little experiment turned into something bigger. Wallace decided to see what directions his life would take if he were to get serious about the three-word advice from the stranger and "say yes more" — that is, to everything! — for the next five and a half months.

Along the way, he ended up buying a thirteen-year-old mint-green Nissan ("I looked like someone put a GI Joe figure into a Smurf car"); winning — and then immediately losing — £25,000; and responding affirmatively to countless email scammers. If any of this sounds familiar to you, Wallace's memoir about his experiences, *Yes Man,* was the loose basis for the Jim Carrey movie of the same name.

It also presents a compelling, if not extreme, example of another "poor trip planning" mistake: we say yes to future time commitments, only to later rue the earlier selves who did so.

Psychologists aren't necessarily known for generating catchy names for the effects they study. But in this particular case, I think they landed on a good one. Marketing professors Gal Zauberman and John Lynch call the tendency to say yes, only to regret it later, the ... wait for it ... "Yes/Damn effect."

Yes, I'll do that thing. Damn! I wish I hadn't said yes.

In Wallace's experiment, some of his yeses resulted in what many of us would consider obvious mistakes: with "no" being off the table, he said yes in so many contexts that he ended up in massive credit card debt, nearly beaten up in a club, and the owner of antidepressant and hair-loss medicine prescriptions he didn't need.

The Yes/Damn effect, however, doesn't always rear its head in such immediate (or silly) ways. Think about the last time you were asked to make a commitment in the future. Maybe it was to give a presentation at work, or to coach your kid's soccer team, or to go to a birthday party for a friend who is more of an acquaintance.

Looking ahead and seeing an empty calendar can make "yes" seem like the obvious answer. But when the presentation, soccer season, or friend's birthday rolls around, you might find yourself wishing that you were doing anything else with the very little time you have.

That, in a nutshell, is the Yes/Damn effect.

As Zauberman explained it to me, it's not that we think that we'll have *nothing* going on in three months. It's just that we think we'll have *relatively* less than we have going on right now. And so, we get tricked into thinking that the future will be some magical land of free time.

In fact, in one of Gal's studies, research participants were asked to think about their available time on a scale from 1 (much more time available today) to 10 (much more time available a month from now). The average response? An 8.2.

Part of the reason for this tendency is that we have lots of little things that take up minutes and hours each day: the emails, the meetings, the drop-in from a coworker, neighbor, or friend. You can probably name many more. The common theme is that all of these represent minor unexpected interruptions, which consume our bandwidth and time.

The problem is that we're not particularly good at anticipating these pernicious little obligations. So, when we look to the future and see relatively massive amounts of free time, we fail to account for the commitments that will no doubt make a Tuesday in three months look a lot like a very busy Tuesday next week.

The mistake arises, then, when we commit ourselves in ways that end up adding more burden than benefit. Just like we do when we procrastinate, we are thinking ahead to the future, but not in a realistic enough way.

Clearly, though, saying yes isn't always a mistake. When I caught up with Danny Wallace to talk to him about his "Yes Man" experiment, he put it like this: "Yes is a word of opportunity to have fun and adventure and unpredictability. Because yes will lead to something else—to another yes—like knocking over dominoes." Wallace is deeply funny but became quite serious when noting that "some of the most unusual or extraordinary things that have ever happened to you—your stories and your memories—will have happened *because* you said yes to something."

You never know what will result from a yes, and that may be one of the reasons we so often lean toward saying it. As a case in point, Danny told me a story about one of the producers of the *Yes Man* film. While making the movie in LA, she got invited to a party that she just didn't feel like going to. More than an hour away, it felt a bit too far to justify leaving her house.

But, she thought, you know what? I'm making this movie about a guy who said yes to everything, so I might as well go to this thing. For most of the party, she just sat around not engaging in a meaningful way with anyone. Until the very end, that is. The way she described it, she was sitting at a table, talking about "long-dead starlets of the silver screen of the 1920s" (or something along those lines), when this gravelly voice appeared from nowhere and said, "I've been waiting my whole life to hear a woman like you say a thing like that." The meta-aspects of this anecdote aren't lost on me: it's a Hollywood-like romance that blossomed during a conversation about Hollywood clichés from a woman who was producing a movie about a guy who said yes to everything. But the two are now married with kids.

As Wallace notes, the union wouldn't have formed without that one yes. Zauberman (one of the researchers who did the original academic work on the Yes/Damn effect) echoed Wallace's sentiments. Saying yes can partially provide benefits because it commits you to doing things you might not find time for today. Maybe, he told me, the only way that you're going to attend your fourth grader's piano recital is by having that perceived abundance of time in the future. "Because if it were today, and I looked at my calendar, I might have to tell him, 'Sorry, buddy, I can't go.'"

Saying yes is tricky, though. When we say it, we keep doors open that would otherwise close. But we also open ourselves up to situations where we may overstress our future selves in damaging ways. Along those lines, "no," Wallace told me, "is a powerful word because we can use it as a shield to protect ourselves and our time." And it's not that every single "yes" results in a life-changing outcome. "You're just as likely to meet your spouse at a good party as you are at a bad one," Wallace said. The flip side of that observation is that you're just as likely—more so!— not to meet your spouse at any given party.

In recognition of these trade-offs, Dilip Soman, a marketing professor at the University of Toronto, told me that he'd implemented a "No, Yay" intervention in his life. When he gets asked to make a commitment in the future, he keeps the Yes/Damn effect in mind and says no to things that he fears will be too burdensome. Cleverly, he still puts the commitment on his calendar with a note saying "did not agree to do this." When the date of the would-be obligation rolls around, he can look at his calendar and say "Yay!" to his newfound free time.

So, how do we pick and choose between saying yes and saying no? There's no easy solution. I do like one piece of advice that Wallace offered, though: it might be a good idea to say yes to commitments to make others happy that have no obvious negative impact on your own happiness. If others' happiness is grossly prioritized over your own, or if you've developed a habit of neglecting your own schedule, then a "no" may make more sense. Clearly, the yeses and the nos need to be decided on a case-by-case basis.

———

So we keep engaging in poor trip planning: we consider our future selves, but often not quite deeply enough. Here, I've spotlighted procrastination and the Yes/Damn effect as canonical examples.

I pointed out, though, that this tendency of poor trip planning can be a mistake—especially if we end up doing, or not doing, things that we later regret. However, in the case of time commitments, this habit can occasionally be useful. The spontaneously booked duck boat tour turns out to be surprisingly fun.

The broader point of this discussion, though, is one of self-awareness. When committing our future selves to some activity, consider both sides of their well-being. How much burden and stress will they experience? But also: what opportunities could arise for them by signing up to do something later rather than now? That applies to both procrastination and the Yes/Damn effect.

In Chapter 4, I talked about times when we anchor too much on our present selves. In this chapter, I talked about times when we think about the future but not deeply enough. In the next chapter, I'll discuss times when we engage in a blend of both. When we use what's happening in the present to think about how things will be in the future, we sometimes make a specific mistake: we rely too heavily on our present emotions to make predictions about a future that we haven't fully considered. In doing so, we "pack the wrong clothes."

It's winter in Boston and we've got a suitcase full of swimsuits.

Highlights

- The second time-traveling mistake is that we think ahead to the future, but only in a surface-level way.
- Procrastination is a classic example of this mistake: in not considering the future in a particularly deep way, we fail to recognize just how much our future selves will want to avoid the same negative situations we're escaping today.
- The Yes/Damn effect presents another example: we may say yes to a future commitment but not anticipate just how much our future selves will regret it.

CHAPTER 6

PACKING THE WRONG CLOTHES

In the mid-1990s, Greg Tietz was on a professional hot streak. He was a partner in two small companies: an advertising agency and a novelty gift company that sold "off-the-wall ridiculous things." By all counts, life was going well for the Northeast Ohio native. However, he didn't enjoy the pressure that came with either of his roles, so he decided to change his entire life and move to San Francisco.

Life in the city, he told me in an interview, was just a little freer than it was in the Midwest, and he grew to love the fresh start. New friends, new job, new everything. He bartended at Bottom of the Hill, a live music club. Staying up till 2 or 3 a.m. most nights was a small price to pay for being able to see some of rock's most notable bands.

When he did have a day off, he often spent his time exploring the Mission, a centrally located San Francisco neighborhood that boasts dozens of Mexican restaurants, taquerias, and bakeries. If you've ever been in the mood for a delicious arm-size burrito that will keep you full for the rest of the day, this is the place to go.

On one of those days of wandering, Greg decided to pick up some treats and cookies for his housemates. That's when he noticed a little restaurant called Casa Sanchez, where a sign in the window caught his eye. On it was the restaurant's logo and then an arresting sentence:

TATTOO ME ON YOUR BODY AND GET FREE FOOD FOR LIFE.

He's not sure if it was the promise of a taco from a restaurant he hadn't yet tried or the sign in the window, but Greg walked right in. Was the promotion for real? he wondered. Would anyone get a tattoo of the restaurant's logo on their arm just to get... free burritos on demand? (Actually, as I write this, the idea doesn't sound all *that* crazy to me.) He asked the owner, Martha, whether the deal was still available. Sure enough, it was. "You get the tattoo," she said, "and we'll give you free food for life."

Having worked at an advertising agency, he thought the marketing behind this deal was brilliant. And truth be told, even before he landed in San Francisco, he had already been toying with the idea of getting a tattoo.

"But," as Greg explained to me, "everyone has horror stories of making a mistake with their first tattoo, and I hadn't wanted that to be the case for me." Prior to moving west, he had wanted to find something that held some meaning for him, something that mattered. So, he had resolved to wait until the perfect tattoo idea came to him.

That moment, it turned out, happened as he walked by the

ad at the taqueria. He laughed when telling me that. "It was like a lightning bolt—here's my answer to everything."

GUACAMOLE WITH A SIDE OF INK

Okay, but what exactly was the logo of the restaurant? A small boy, Greg told me, surfing into outer space on an ear of corn. "It was just such a fun graphic, and I loved the idea of the promotion anyway." He recognized that getting a tattoo was a big decision, which is partly why it had taken him so long to commit to one. On that day at Casa Sanchez, however, he was convinced.

Before running out to the nearest tattoo parlor, though, he ordered a deluxe carne asada burrito—if you're going to get free food for the rest of your life, you might as well make sure it's tasty! Deeming it pretty good, he decided that yes indeed, this was the tattoo for him. He called a friend who had several tattoos and asked if he wanted to join him.

And that is how Greg and his friend became the first people to take the tattoo-for-food deal from Casa Sanchez. By his estimate, he got free meals about forty to fifty times before the restaurant closed in 2012. (Worry not: the new restaurant that opened in the old spot continued to honor Greg's deal, and Casa Sanchez now sells its chips and salsas in grocery stores. To the best of my knowledge, though, Greg and his friend must pay for their tortilla chips like everyone else.)

It's a wild story, and when Greg related it to me, I felt a mix of admiration—I wish I could be more spontaneous—and concern. (Would Greg come to regret this tattoo? Would he always want a little boy surfing on corn etched into his skin?) Even though I used to live near the Mission and have had plenty of amazing burritos there over the years, I still felt that getting a restaurant's logo tattooed on my arm might be something I'd later question.

Regretting tattoos isn't a unique experience. Though the numbers are hard to come by, out of the millions of Americans who have tattoos, as many as a quarter regret getting at least one of them. More to the point: the global tattoo removal market is estimated to be worth about $4.7 billion and is growing at a clip of 15 percent per year.

I visited Cesar Cruz, a tattoo artist and the owner of Black Tower Tattoo Studio in Los Angeles, to ask him why, in his experience, people want tattoos removed. The two classic reasons, he told me, are when symbols cease to hold any meaning and when tattooed words no longer produce joy. Both reasons, seemingly, are the result of our expectation that tattoos might hold meaning and produce joy forever (or at least for a very long time), but when they cease to do so, we become disappointed. There are also more innocuous reasons—for instance, when tattoos simply fade or don't look good as the body ages.

Data from surveys support his observations and raise a few other possibilities: some people regret tattoos if they were impaired when they got them; some opted for ink in a place that was later deemed to be too visible to the outside world; and some chose to get a tattoo as a form of remembrance for something they later didn't want to remember.

Let me be clear: most body art doesn't produce regret or lead to laser removal. I bring tattoos up, though, because regretting them is a perfect example of the third and final time-traveling mistake, which I call "packing the wrong clothes." This mental error has potentially serious implications and can influence everything from your choice of profession to the medical care you receive at the end of your life.

SWEATERS IN MIAMI

It's February in Chicago and you are about to go on a much-anticipated trip to Florida. It's been a rough winter, and you're already clad in your warmest clothes as you pack for your South Beach vacation. Of course, the weather in Florida is much more hospitable to exposed skin than the weather in Chicago, so you decide to leave your giant winter coat at home. You know the one—it goes all the way down to your ankles and adds ten inches of circumference to your body. But, you think, it could still get a little cold at night, couldn't it?

So you go ahead and pack a sweater or two. And while you're at it, you figure you might as well throw in a long-sleeve shirt and a light jacket just in case. Sure, it will be warmer in South Beach, but it's still good to be prepared, even if it does require checking a bag or two.

Arriving in Miami, you step off the plane and find that it's eighty-two degrees with humidity levels that make the air feel drinkable. And you haven't even left the airport yet! You kick yourself as you realize that your sweaters, long-sleeve shirt, and light jacket will sit in your suitcase for the rest of your trip. If you'd packed for this weather, you could have easily gotten away with only a carry-on.

The lesson is that just because you're cold right now in Chicago doesn't mean you'll necessarily be cold in the future. When we make predictions about how we'll feel in the future, it can be dangerous to give too much weight to how we feel in the present. Humans, after all, are moody creatures — our current state probably won't last long. The mistake of "packing the wrong clothes," then, is when we rely too much on our present self's feelings, projecting them ahead to a future self who might not feel the same way.

RUNNING UP A MAGIC HILL

George Loewenstein, a professor of economics and psychology at Carnegie Mellon University, is considered to be one of the leading economists of his generation. (His name even comes up each year among the circle of people who like to speculate about who will win the Nobel Prize in Economics.) But he's also an avid outdoor adventurer, spending much of his free time climbing, running, and kayaking.

As he told me, he used to love jogging up a hill near his house in Pittsburgh — a "very big hill," he quickly added. Starting at one of the local rivers, he'd climb nearly five hundred feet, and by the time he'd arrive at the top, he would be "utterly exhausted." But within half a minute of rounding the top and starting his descent, he'd find himself thinking something along the lines of "That wasn't that big of a deal!" After a short amount of time, his pain and misery would become fleeting memories. It was as if the hill could magically create the experience of intense pain on the way up and then immediately erase its memory on the way down.

Around the same time, he'd frequently receive invitations to give seminars in different time zones. At home in Pittsburgh, he'd anticipate exciting travel abroad and the opportunity to catch up with old colleagues and meet new ones. As a result, he'd often say yes. But curiously, he told me, if he received one of those invitations during his travels, he was much more likely to say no. He'd suffer miserable jet lag on these trips, and, as he put it, "it was like I only had a perspective on the misery of jet lag when I was experiencing it in the moment."

Putting the two experiences together, George started to formulate a theory: When you're not in an emotional state, it can be difficult to appreciate how you'll feel or behave when you *are* in one. But when you are in the grip of powerful emotions it's hard to imagine *not* being in their throes—it may feel as though you always have and always will be in that same state. He put it to me succinctly: "I over-shop on an empty stomach, and when I'm depressed it feels like I'll be depressed forever."

This means that we pack the wrong clothes in two different ways: First, we use the emotional states of our current selves to make decisions for future selves who will no longer feel the same way. And second, when we are anchored on less emotional states, we fail to appreciate the strong emotions that our future selves might legitimately experience.

Consider one study conducted by George and his collaborators: people who were addicted to heroin were given the chance to have an extra dose of buprenorphine (a safe heroin substitute that helps eliminate cravings) or get some money a few days later. If they made that choice right before receiving their current dose — when they were in a state of maximum craving — they valued the extra dose twice as much compared to when they made the decision right *after* receiving it (when their craving had subsided). It makes sense to value relief from craving more when you *are* craving than when you aren't, but the addicts were making a decision that would go into effect only five days later, when their current state of craving should have been irrelevant.

Loewenstein and his collaborators Matthew Rabin and Ted O'Donoghue noticed that these observations could be applied to a range of situations in which current decisions have future consequences. They coined the term "projection bias" to refer to our tendency to make decisions for the future based on our current emotions and drives rather than on the emotions and drives we will predictably be experiencing when those decisions go into effect.

Even when we are aware that we will be in a different state of mind in the future, we don't sufficiently adjust our decisions to take that into account. We may know that we will over-shop on an empty stomach, or that our current depression is unlikely to last, but it doesn't feel that way, and we shop, and make important life decisions, based on our current, often short-lived, emotional states.

Think about how this mistake is different from the other two time-travel errors. When we "miss our flight," it's because we are too focused on the present and fail to consider the future at all. When we engage in "poor trip planning," we think about the future to some degree, but just not deeply enough. And when we "pack the wrong clothes," we are actively focusing on the future but rely too heavily on the present to do so, which often results in feelings of regret over our choices. The tattoo of the partner we are infatuated with right now, it turns out, may not look as good when they become an ex.

FROM SNICKERS TO CONVERTIBLES TO COLLEGE MAJORS

Projection bias is such a common human error that we take it for granted. We assume it's just part of life, and not a mistake we might be able to fix. Here's a mundane example that happens to me all the time. Imagine that one of your coworkers is planning a meeting for next week, and to increase the likelihood that people will attend, he smartly plans on bringing snacks. Personalized snacks, no less! So, he calls you and asks what snack you'd like to have—with your name on it—at next week's meeting.

The choices range from healthy (apples, bananas, blueberries) to less so (potato chips, Snickers, Reese's). When he offers these choices, it's late in the afternoon; the predinner hunger cravings are kicking in. What are you going to choose? When office workers in one research study made this sort of choice—late in the afternoon—they were overwhelmingly likely to opt for one of the unhealthy snacks.

Feeling the pangs of hunger, we may mistakenly think that we'll be similarly hungry when the future arrives. As a result, we choose a snack that will satisfy that imagined future craving. However, when a different group of office workers made the choice right after lunch—when they were already full—they were more likely to opt for the apple or the banana.

Consumers buying cars have been known to behave in similar ways. Namely, the weather at the time of a car purchase can have a disproportional impact on what's chosen. When the air is warmer and the skies are clearer than normal, convertible purchases increase! The flip is also true: a ten-inch snowstorm results in a 6 percent rise in sales of four-wheel-drive vehicles over the next two to three weeks.

Beyond trade-offs between apples and Snickers, and convertibles and SUVs, these patterns can be found in personal and professional contexts as well.

For instance, in 2008, South Korea implemented a mandatory cooling-off period for divorces: you'd have to wait several weeks from the date of filing for a divorce until you could actually finalize it. The practice seemed to have an impact, as divorce rates significantly decreased after the new law was adopted. Intense negative emotions and the feeling that those emotions will always be present may stoke a desire for a divorce—in fact, divorce *filing* rates never wavered. But when we give those feelings time to dissipate, that wish may wane.

Even something as trivial as the time of a required class for college undergraduates can influence important future decisions. In a study of almost twenty thousand West Point cadets over seventeen years, researchers found that cadets were about 10 percent less likely to major in a given subject area if they were randomly assigned to take an early morning (7:30 a.m.) section rather than one later in the day.

Think about why: if you were to groggily take Econ 101 early in the morning, you might incorrectly attribute your fatigue to your feelings about the subject matter, deciding that this isn't the major for you after all. You conclude economics is boring, when really you just need more caffeine and an earlier bedtime. One of the researchers on this project, Kareem Haggag, a behavioral decision-making professor and colleague of mine at UCLA, noted that the choice of college major isn't inconsequential. Rather, it holds significant weight for various life outcomes. As he told me, "Even in a high-stakes context — where the decision can influence not only the enjoyability of the next few years of college but also your lifetime earnings trajectory — people are still predictably biased by their past temporary feelings."

WHERE'S THE MISTAKE?

Let's play devil's advocate for a moment: is projection bias really a mistake? There may be many cases where we have real difficulty anticipating our future preferences. As a result, we rely on our present feelings to make predictions. Is that really so terrible?

Turns out that the mistake lies in just how dramatically we engage in this process. When an overreliance on our present circumstances leads to outcomes that our future selves consider regrettable or unfair, that's when the problems pile up. To return to those suitcases in Miami full of cold-weather clothes—the issue isn't overpacking per se. It's that we had to pay to check a bag, and maybe we underpacked swimsuits and T-shirts.

Economist Marc Kaufmann has hypothesized that in a professional context, the tendency to over-project our present circumstances forward can lead to errors in how we manage our time. Consider the feelings you have when you start a project at work that you find exciting. Maybe your old projects have been dragging. Maybe you haven't felt super motivated. The opportunity to work on something new stokes a sense of optimism; you feel like you have a lot of energy to put toward the project.

As a result, you might devote a decent amount of time to the early stages. To illustrate this, Kaufmann uses the example of a student who has a midterm the next day. Waking up feeling fresh, the student knows they have to study eight chapters. At first, the work hums along, with each chapter taking about two hours to review. "Perfect!" they might think. "I can easily make it through all of this before tomorrow!" Projection bias kicks in, however, when they mistakenly think they can sustain those early feelings of optimism and excitement until the project's completion. When evening rolls around, and feelings of boredom and hunger arise, each chapter takes longer to wade through, until the student eventually gives up.

So, we can end up expending too much effort on the early stages of an endeavor, only to run out of energy and time as the deadline approaches.

Over-projection of the present onto the future can lead to even more pernicious problems. Take a group of students who took part in research led by Loran Nordgren, a management professor at Northwestern's Kellogg School of Management. Some of the students were asked to memorize strings of numbers for twenty minutes (a tiring task!) while others were asked to commit numbers to memory for just two minutes. Immediately afterward, all of them were asked how fatigued they felt, how well they thought they could manage future fatigue, and how much of their studying they'd leave to the last week of the semester. The untired students (the group who only had to remember numbers for two minutes) were much more confident in their abilities to manage future fatigue and, consequently, opted to push off more of their studying to later.

Consider what's happening here: the students who hadn't been saddled with a tiring task had a much harder time imagining what it would feel like to be truly tired in the future. Relying perhaps a bit too much on their current, fresh state, they couldn't vividly access future feelings of fatigue, leading them to bite off more than what they'd inevitably be able to chew.

It wasn't just students who demonstrated this pattern. Over four months, reformed smokers who felt that they could better control their cravings were more likely to expose themselves to tempting situations like spending time with friends who smoke. And that, in turn, led to more smoking relapses.

We often make decisions about future courses of action when we're in "cold" states. Should we see an ex over drinks, even though we're happily married? Should we go to the office break room after receiving an email about leftover cake, even though we're on a diet? Should we leave a pack of cigarettes in the house, even though we've given up smoking? When we rely on cold feelings to make predictions about our ability to withstand temptation, we fail to fully grasp just how tempting the friendly happy hour, the slice of cake, or the cigarette will be. And so, ironically, we may overexpose ourselves to those very temptations, succumbing to them in ways we didn't anticipate.

In an interview, Loran Nordgren—the researcher who studied the "reformed" smokers—put it to me this way: "Our feelings and emotions have extraordinary power to shape our actions. But people have tremendous difficulty understanding how transformative those emotions can be. We underestimate the threat and therefore put ourselves in harm's way."

So, sometimes we "pack the wrong clothes," using our present self's feelings to make decisions that our future selves might later regret. We're cold, and we forget what it's like to be sweaty in Miami.

But there's another version of this mistake that's based less on the emotions we're having in the moment and more on the general perceptions we have about our current personalities, likes, and dislikes.

EVERYONE HAS THAT ONE BAND…

Think back to the last time there was a musical group that you were truly into. Maybe it was ten years ago, maybe more. In my early twenties, my favorite band was a Boston-based group named Guster. This admission comes with a bit of embarrassment: with their agreeable pop tunes and slightly grungy-looking album covers, Guster was quintessential late '90s fare. I couldn't imagine a world in which they wouldn't be playing on repeat in my living room (my roommate even threatened to move out if he had to listen to them one more time). And I would've paid whatever small balance was in my bank account to go to one of their concerts.

Today, my tastes have shifted a bit; Spotify informs me that I seem to play a group called the National a lot. Based in LA, they have a slightly darker, more brooding sound, and before COVID, I would try to catch their shows whenever possible. I can't wait for them to start touring again, and it's hard for me to imagine not wanting to see *them* in the years to come.

In 2020, I noticed that Guster, my old '90s favorite, was playing at the Hollywood Forever Cemetery, a half hour or so from where I live. I haven't listened to them in ages and thought this could be a fun way to revisit the past. But at forty dollars a pop, the tickets just seemed expensive. Could I justify spending eighty dollars for my wife and me to see a band that today I found kind of...cheesy?

My point? When I was a die-hard Guster fan, I was willing to spend a decent chunk of my income on their concerts and assumed I'd always feel that way. Now I feel similarly about the National, while Guster has been relegated to the dustbin of history. And it's difficult to imagine a time when I won't continue to feel this way. Even though I know my tastes changed in the past, it's hard to see how they might change in the future.

Your tastes have probably changed too as you've advanced through life. Maybe not with concert tickets, but what about that expensive skateboard you had as a kid? Are you still obsessed with Power Rangers, or Beanie Boos, or shiny black Doc Martens?

This tendency to take our general interests and preferences and project them forward is something that researcher Jordi Quoidbach and his collaborators studied in thousands of people. Consider the question that they asked visitors of a popular Belgian TV show's website: "Ten years ago, how would you have rated your personality (in terms of openness to new experiences, conscientiousness, extraversion, agreeableness, and neuroticism)?"

Now try to predict how you might score on those dimensions *in* ten years.

If you feel like you've changed more from the past to the present than you anticipate changing from the present to the future, you're not alone. Whether they were younger, middle-aged, or older, nearly twenty thousand people demonstrated a clear pattern, believing that they had changed a great deal from the past—in terms of their personalities and their values—but failing to see that they would change as much in the future.

A follow-up study found that research participants advocated paying about 60 percent more to see their current favorite band play in ten years than participants who were asked how much they'd shell out to see an old favorite band play today. It seems that people would grossly overpay for a future opportunity to indulge a currently held preference.

These effects aren't just relegated to hypothetical questions: Jordi and his collaborators also found that over a thirty-year span, thousands of Americans consistently underestimated how much their own life satisfaction would end up changing.

THE END OF HISTORY AS WE KNOW IT

This tendency has been labeled the "end-of-history illusion." The gist is that although we recognize that we've evolved from who we once were to who we are now, we fail to see that we will continue to change in the future.

One of the authors of the paper, psychologist Dan Gilbert—who also conducted the speed-dating study described in Chapter 5—told me that when he was younger, he felt that although his twenties would be different from his thirties, and his thirties a little different from his forties, from around age forty on, life would "become imperceptibly different."

His intuition was that around age forty or so, he'd somehow have "arrived" and become the full version of himself. Looking backward, though, he discovered that just hadn't been the case. "In many ways," he told me, "sixty-four is more different from fifty-four than fifty-four was from forty-four." It can be hard to see that even though we've experienced great change in the past, we will continue to experience great change in the future.

As Jordi, Dan, and their collaborator Tim Wilson eloquently put it, "Both teenagers and grandparents seem to believe that the pace of personal change has slowed to a crawl and that they have recently become the people they will remain. History, it seems, is always ending today."

We don't know exactly why this illusion occurs, but we can speculate: it may arise partly due to self-protection and partly, I suspect, due to the fear of the unknown. When people consider the ways that they've changed from the past to the present, they implicitly call to mind the ways they've improved. So, for the most part, we view our present selves in a positive light: most people like themselves, believing that their personalities are attractive to others and their values ones to be admired. It can be scary to think that if we were to change, we'd be decamping from this noble place, so we try to hold on to who we are now.

Similarly, we like to think that we know ourselves well, and anticipating that our personalities, values, and preferences might change can produce a measure of existential anxiety. If we don't know how we might be different in the future, how well do we actually know who we are today?

There are some important implications here.

In our professional lives, for instance, we may draw too much on our current circumstances when making future career plans, neglecting to see how our values and interests have changed in the past and might change moving forward. A survey of public service officials pointed to just this conclusion. One group of employees assessed how their values had changed moving from the past to the present and acknowledged that being able to work independently and help others were values that grew dramatically in importance over the prior ten years.

A different group, however, was asked to predict what values would be important to them in the years to come. As it turned out, this second group—the "predictors"—anticipated far less change in their work motivations than the "reporters" experienced.

Here's the problem: when faced with new career directions or job prospects, if we make mistakes in considering what we think will matter, we may opt to take (or not take) paths that we'll later regret.

In a conversation with me, Jordi raised another compelling outcome: "Could the end-of-history illusion cause us to pass on opportunities that we would have otherwise enjoyed?" Take traveling to an exotic location as an example. Imagine that at this point in your life, you can only afford a bare-bones trip; think buses and hostels. On the plus side, you'd get to go to another part of the world, though not necessarily in a high-end way. On the negative side, you also place a good amount of value on life's niceties and enjoy a fancy hotel bed. Based on this calculus, you might incorrectly assume that that's exactly what your future self will value, too. "Oh, I'll wait until I'm older, until I have the money to do it right," Jordi suggested. But what if that's a mistake? What if when you become that older version of yourself, you'd rather spend time with your family than travel to the Australian bush? Would you regret your decision to skip the adventure when younger? Sometimes, seizing the day means embracing the interests of your present self, because your future self might not be interested in a Guster concert.

There's an additional nefarious consequence that can arise,

and it concerns the far-off future: end-of-life planning. This is a topic that B. J. Miller, a cutting-edge palliative care doctor in San Francisco, has spent much of his life considering.

THE END CAN BE DIFFERENT

"One Man's Quest to Change the Way We Die." That's the title of a 2017 *New York Times* profile of B. J. Miller. Though it sounds like a lofty description, it's right on the mark.

Dr. Miller's first encounter with death came on a November night in 1990. A sophomore at Princeton, Miller was horsing around with some friends as they walked to a local convenience store at about four in the morning. To get there, they had to cross over train tracks for the Princeton commuter line, which takes passengers on a short ride from campus to the Amtrak station. For whatever reason, Miller and his friends thought it would be fun to climb the tiny train (locals call it the "Dinky") that sat dormant on the tracks.

Miller went first, climbing the ladder on the back of the train. But when he stood up, his arm got too close to the electrical wire, and eleven thousand volts of currency arced to a metal watch on his wrist, rocketing through him. Although he survived, one arm needed to be amputated at the elbow and both legs at the knees.

That single event put him on a course to try to better understand and ultimately change the way that patients experience healthcare. Telling the story, Miller sometimes laughs as he reflects on how his life was changed by something named the Dinky.

Though he received excellent treatment at Saint Barnabas Medical Center's burn unit, he recognized that so much of the medical world is designed to treat diseases and not necessarily people. From his perspective, nowhere is this clearer than in end-of-life care, where the default is to keep patients alive at all costs.

Until recently, Miller was a professor of medicine and palliative care physician at the University of California, San Francisco, and the director of San Francisco's Zen Hospice Project, an organization that uses the tenets of Buddhism to care for the dying. In 2020, he started Mettle Health, an organization dedicated to helping patients navigate their way through the healthcare system, especially at the end of life. It's a sort of "living-with-death" consultancy.

His goal in this work is to make death less something that is pushed aside until the very end, as is often the case with traditional care, and more a life-cycle event to be celebrated. The modern medical model, replete with bright lights, blinking machines, and sterile rooms, treats death as an outcome to be "gotten over": when a patient dies, they are swiftly taken out of the room, leaving little trace that they were ever even there.

By contrast, Miller aims to infuse more of a sense of humanity into palliative care. His goal is to make death—as he put it to me—"more of a part of life." In past talks, he's brought up the example of a patient whose lungs are failing due to ALS. She wants a cigarette—not to hasten death but to "feel her lungs filled while she still has them." Another patient wants, rather than more chemotherapy, her dog to be in the room with her, nuzzled against her skin.

Neither wish would be granted at a traditional hospital. In promoting this more empathic approach, Miller is now, as the *New York Times* profile described him, the "pioneer of a new model of palliative care."

How do we implement this model? First, we need to have more, and deeper, conversations about death.

Death, of course, is the ultimate downer; it's not a topic that comes up naturally, nor is it something that people want to discuss. Layered on top is a problem that has its roots in the end-of-history illusion. Namely, when we think ahead in time, we naturally call to mind aging and the end of our lives, which—at least in many cultures—are typically not viewed in positive ways. I suspect that to exert some control over the aging process, we may believe that we'll stay the people we are now, which causes us to ignore the inevitable. It's hard enough imagining our future selves. It's even harder imagining a world in which our future selves don't exist.

Perhaps it's not surprising, then, that many adults don't have end-of-life plans in place. Recent estimates suggest that only about one in three Americans have completed an advance directive. And among those who have, it's possible that the plans haven't been updated to reflect wishes that have changed. As a case in point, when healthy respondents in a research study were asked if they'd ever want a grueling course of chemotherapy that could extend their lives by three months, only 10 percent agreed. But when cancer patients were asked that same question? Fully 42 percent said yes. It seems that as the end approaches, life's value increases.

As we've discussed, the conundrum with these types of choices—and the conundrum that's at the core of projection bias and the end-of-history illusion—is that even though our tastes and preferences are always evolving, we often make decisions with our current selves in mind. Only later do we grapple with the fact that our previous selves—who no longer share the same viewpoints as those of the people we've become—made important decisions that affect us now.

I asked Dr. Miller, When it comes to making choices for the end of our lives, when do we get it right? He spent a while turning the question over, before explaining how it often goes wrong. Things fall apart, he told me, when there's a feeling of "Oh shit, I thought it was going to be this one way and it turns out that's not it at all." That element of surprise, when piled on top of all the other emotional burdens that surround death, can be devastating.

His answer for when it goes right, though, represents a nice antidote for the times when we "pack the wrong clothes." The people who have had the best deaths, he told me, aren't the ones who experience a pain-free end. Rather, they're the ones who hold a mature view of time, recognizing that they can plan for a given future but can also feel differently about those plans as time progresses.

Part of this maturity comes from an awareness of fluidity: the patients who understand that they are "works in progress" are the ones who can more actively maintain the conversation about end-of-life wishes. They're the ones most comfortable with changing preferences, values, and even personalities. I suspect that part of the reason many of us resist such shifts is that change is entangled with loss; we have to admit that our past self is gone, vanished. The wisest patients, though, grapple with these little losses head-on and, along the way, embrace their own mortality. As Miller put it, "By realizing what you've lost, you almost invariably realize all that you still have."

In his practice, Miller is a fan of the expression "Man plans, and God laughs." There's some truth to that, he told me, especially to the extent that we can never know how the end will play out. "And yet," he exclaimed, "you still plan!" Those plans — whether they're for tomorrow, the very end of life, or something in between — need to be made thoughtfully, and not in a dogmatic way. (From a practical standpoint, planning may take the form of appointing a "healthcare proxy," or someone who can make plans for you as the end approaches.) He emphasized the importance of holding "loose assumptions about what the end will be like." Doing so helps you recognize that you can control some outcomes, but of course not all of them.

To Miller, adopting this kind of mindset will land you in a good place, no matter what's coming.

BACK TO THE BOY ON THE CORN ROCKET SHIP

When it comes to relying on our current selves to make projections for the future, there are plenty of instances in which we make mistakes and pack the wrong clothes. Like the times when we fail to appreciate how the feelings we're having in the moment won't be the ones we'll continue to experience indefinitely. We won't always be this hungry, or cold, or anxious. Or the times when we don't acknowledge how our future selves differ from the people we are now. My most-played list on Spotify won't always feature a surplus of heavy songs by the National.

Returning to Greg Tietz, the man who got the Casa Sanchez tattoo in exchange for free burritos: Did his decision fall under one of these categories? Did he, in other words, end up regretting his tattoo?

When I asked him just this question, his answer was clear: "No way. I don't regret it for an instant."

The tattoo, he told me, "captures a specific moment in time" — a time when things were a little more carefree for him. While he certainly feels like his life now is good, he's nonetheless more a part of the corporate world and can't stay up until two or three in the morning, serving drinks, listening to great bands, and eating giant burritos on his days off. He takes comfort, though, in knowing that whenever he wants, he can look at his arm and be connected back to that particular time in his life.

Greg, like Dr. Miller's wisest patients, saw that the younger version of himself was just one patch in his quilt of selves. Just as he's changed from who he was to who he is, he'll certainly continue to change as the years unfold. Greg hasn't gotten any other tattoos, but he has thought about it. Maybe he's just waiting for another offer of free food that he'll want to eat for the rest of his life.

Highlights

- Our final time-traveling mistake: we fail to recognize the ways in which the future may be different from the present.

- Projection bias is one example of this mistake: we take our present-day emotions and *over*-project them onto our future selves.
- The end-of-history illusion is another example: we think that our current personalities and preferences won't change that much in the years ahead.
- As a result of both projection bias and the end-of-history illusion, we may make decisions we'll later regret, from what we eat to the careers we pursue.

PART III

THE LANDING

*Solutions for Smoothing the Path Between
the Present and the Future*

CHAPTER 7

MAKING THE FUTURE CLOSER

The scene opens in a nondescript office building. The clock on the wall ticks closer to 5 p.m. With a Christmas tree displayed in the background, it's clear that a holiday break is right around the corner.

Three twentysomethings kill time by throwing a ball back and forth, chatting about silly things.

Suddenly, the building shakes. A flash of light erupts, and three older men appear in the room, standing in front of the water cooler and copy machine.

Dramatically, the older man in the center of the pack says, "We're you, from the future."

He and his friends have come back to deliver a grave warning about the dangers of climate change.

But before he can continue his sentence, his younger counterpart interrupts. "First of all...hello. It's nice to meet you," the young man says. Laughing, he and his friends blast off a flurry of questions. How are our lives going? Are we rich?

The older men answer dejectedly, noting that they are actually in a lot of debt.

"Okay, okay," one of the younger guys responds, "but family life is good? We're all married, right?"

Again, the answers fail to produce optimism: "No," the leader reports, "I went through a really bad divorce. But if you can act now, we can avoid total human extinction!"

Looking deflated, one of the young guys cuts him off and says, "I . . . I don't care." And then comes the punch line of this ridiculous *Saturday Night Live* skit: "If you're what I'm working toward," the younger man says, "I don't want any part of it."

After repeatedly trying to turn back to climate change, the interaction between present and future selves devolves into an argument about who is to blame for their older selves' misfortune.

This scene, written by the improv trio Please Don't Destroy, harks back to the Ted Chiang science fiction story I mentioned in the introduction to this book. Both pose the same intriguing question: if you were able to sit down and have a conversation with your future self, what would you say, and what would happen as a result?

Hopefully, the meeting wouldn't be quite as dark as it is in the *SNL* bit. Hopefully, you'd find out something more important than the warning given by the future self shown in the following *New Yorker* cartoon. With any luck, the meeting would be a lot more positive and educational. Would it, however, change anything about the way you live your life today? This is the question I started exploring several years ago with some cameras, lights, and futuristic-looking goggles.

"I'm you from the future. I came back to warn you not to order the scallops—the sauce is a little too creamy."

MIND THE GAP

In her decades-long career, Jane Fonda has worn many hats. From movie star to political activist, workout guru to champion of social justice, she's managed to remain at the cultural cutting edge. Several years ago, I worked with her as she tried out a completely different role.

Standing in front of me, she donned a somewhat clunky-looking virtual reality mask and waited patiently as I attached a few camera sensors to her shoulders. The room we were in contained a long, two-by-four gymnastics beam laid out on the drab carpet. But, thanks to those VR goggles, this wasn't what she saw.

Instead, she saw a hayfield with an enormous pit in the middle. The hole was so deep it looked almost as if the ground had been struck by a comet. And stretching from one end of the pit to the other was a solid wooden plank.

Through the sensors on her shoulders, cameras positioned around the room tracked her movements. Each step Fonda took was relayed to a central computer, which used that information to redraw the world she saw on her screen. With each step she took in real life, it looked—in her virtual world—as though she were inching closer and closer to the pit. Although she knew that she was in a standard room, what she saw through her virtual reality goggles was much scarier. Her task was simply to walk across the beam, knowing that, in reality, it rose only two inches above the well-cushioned carpet.

Having watched other research subjects try to navigate "the plank," I was used to seeing people fearfully refuse to walk across it. That wasn't the case, though, with Fonda. I stood behind, spotting her in case she fell off the beam, and watched as she impressively tiptoed her way across, landing safely at the end. The exercise she had just completed was part of a demonstration meant to showcase the realism and "immersiveness" of virtual reality.

Fonda was there to promote, among other things, a more positive approach to aging. In the middle of writing a book focused on wellness during life's later years, she had become interested in the work that a host of researchers and I had been conducting. For the last several months, I had been putting research participants into a different type of virtual reality room. In it, people would come face-to-face, via a virtual mirror, with older, grayer, and more wrinkled versions of themselves.

The idea arose from a meeting where I described my research on future selves. I had been talking about the relationships we have with our future selves and why they matter: with weaker bonds came more regrettable long-term decisions. If only, I had lamented, there was some way to have people interact with a hologram or some other version of their future selves. Some of my colleagues pointed out that even though a hologram might be a bit far-fetched, other possibilities existed. Only a few feet down the corridor from the psychology building, they told me, was the communications department. And inside, one of the most up-to-date immersive virtual reality rooms in the world could be found.

My thinking went like this: If you could see and talk to your future self in a virtual setting, would you feel a stronger emotional bond with Future You? And would that strengthened connection make you more likely to do things today—like saving money, eating healthier, and so on—that would improve your life in the future?

It might sound implausible, but there was a good reason why we thought it might work.

THE POWER OF ONE

Late in August 2015, Abdullah Kurdi, a Syrian refugee, arranged to leave Turkey with his family on a small boat headed to Kos, a Greek island. The goal was to sail to Canada, where the Kurdis had relatives.

Tragically, the trip ended almost as soon as it started: the boat capsized five minutes after leaving the shores of Turkey, and in the process, Kurdi's wife and two sons drowned. Turkish journalist Nilüfer Demir was nearby and captured an image of the younger child, three-year-old Alan, lying facedown on the beach. A day later, that shocking photograph landed on the front pages of international newspapers and was viewed by more than twenty million people on social media.

It did more than capture the world's attention, though. Shortly after the incident occurred, changes in refugee policies were implemented as far away as the United States. And donations to a Swedish Red Cross fund, explicitly aimed at helping Syrian refugees, increased one hundredfold in the week after the photograph was published. But, as psychologist Paul Slovic—an expert in the study of risk assessment—and his colleagues have pointed out, the Syrian crisis had been raging for more than four years at the time of Alan Kurdi's death. Conservatively, when the photo was taken, the death toll was already at 250,000. Yet, the world's response had been relatively muted.

Singular, identifiable victims like Kurdi tend to produce headlines that last for weeks or even months at a time.

As Deborah Small, a marketing professor at Yale and lead researcher on several "identifiable victim effect" papers, pointed out to me, it's not just singular humans who generate such attention. When Cecil the lion, an adult male lion from Zimbabwe, was hunted and shot, the reporting of his killing stoked international outrage. Statistics about many such instances, by contrast, do very little to pull at heart- or purse strings. Indeed, Small observed in one of her papers that more than a billion children live in poverty, but stories about mass poverty rarely produce media coverage or donations from private citizens.

There's an obvious irony here: we are more motivated by the singular victim than the suffering of many. We pour out our hearts (and open our wallets) for an individual but bury our heads in the sand when faced with statistics detailing similar tragedies on much larger scales. It's a tendency that's been well-documented not only in cases like Kurdi's, or Cecil the lion's, but in tightly controlled scientific experiments as well.

In one clever study conducted by Small, for instance, mall patrons were asked if they would like to donate to a local Habitat for Humanity home. Some respondents were told that the family who would get the home "had been selected" and others were told that the family "will be selected." Consider what's happening here: describing the family as having already been selected made them more identifiable. It was easier, in other words, to picture a given family receiving the donation knowing that they had already been chosen than if they hadn't yet been picked. And in fact, such framing led to higher contributions.

Similarly, Small and colleagues found that when users of the microfinance lending site Kiva.org chose between donating to single entrepreneurs and donating to groups of entrepreneurs, people preferred to lend to individuals.

Whether for Habitat for Humanity or microfinance lending, donors are more likely to reach for their wallets when potential charity recipients are singled out. Of course, you don't have to search far and wide to see charitable organizations regularly employing this sort of strategy.

Consider *why* one invokes more sympathy than many. Think about what happens when you watch a professional sport on TV. When the camera pans over the stadium — whether football or baseball, basketball or soccer — the faces are blurred, and the colors tend to blend. Any single person is obscured by the larger crowd. Yet, when the camera crew decides to spotlight one fan, it's much easier to see their facial expression and the specific outfit they're wearing, and even imagine the life they lead; it's that much easier to feel like we might know them.

Similarly, when a potential charity recipient is singled out, it's easier to identify with them, feel like them, and take their perspective, seeing the world through their eyes. Recent research has even indicated that when people view an identifiable charity recipient, regions of the brain associated with positive emotions become active. That activity, in turn, predicts donation behavior.

A single target person, then, generates a sense of closeness, and closeness matters when it comes to our desire to help others.

It's a psychological mindset I was hoping to produce in the virtual reality room. By *showing* people their future selves — by making those distant selves more identifiable — I aimed to reduce the distance between the people we are and the people we will be. Of course, our future selves aren't the same as unknown charity recipients. We share more with the people we will one day become than we do with strangers in philanthropy campaigns. And yet, common ground can be found: just like the targets of a Habitat for Humanity drive, the well-being of our future selves ultimately depends on the decisions we make today.

IS THAT GRANDPA?

Altering someone's image to make them look older was once the stuff of FBI artists and Hollywood special effects teams. To see what you'd look like older, your best bet was probably to spend time with an elderly relative. However, by the time I started on my quest to introduce people to their future selves, technology had given us a few more possibilities.

These new techniques weren't perfect, but they seemed to work well enough. The basic procedure for "age progression" was that we'd first have to take a picture of a person while they were making a neutral expression — no smiling, frowning, and the like. Having practiced this on myself hundreds of times, I came to the unfortunate conclusion that my "neutral" face looks downright scary. You can see what I mean in the images that follow. But I digress.

After snapping a neutral photo of a research participant's face, my collaborators and I would run the picture through a computer program to create an avatar. In simple terms, that's a virtual version of the face. It's still an image of you but more "digitized." That's the middle picture — of me.

The fun part came next. After creating the digital avatars, my colleagues and I ran the images through an "age progression algorithm." Essentially, the algorithm attempts to do to a picture what time does to a real face. It sags the skin slightly, adds some fatty deposits under the eyes, makes the ears a little bigger, creates some age spots, thins out and whitens the hair, narrows the face, and lengthens the nose. That's the picture on the right. And, as my wife has reminded me several times, the older version of me might be a little forgiving. I have to agree with her — I'll most likely have way less hair and way more wrinkles by the time I'm in my seventh or eighth decade.

To be fair, the available age progression techniques we used were in their relative infancy. Now, of course, several readily available apps can make your face look older in a quick, cheap, and realistic way. Nonetheless, the image certainly looks like it could be a version of what I'll look like when I'm older. Once, in fact, when I was toying around with my aged image, my daughter walked by and asked why I had a funny-looking picture of her grandpa up on my screen.

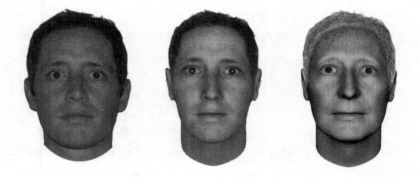

Rather than just show these images to people, however, we decided to up the ante a bit. In the same virtual reality room where Jane Fonda gingerly tiptoed across "the plank," my collaborators and I created a different sort of digital world. Instead of a field with an imaginary pit, this one looked like a room you'd see in any office building, with plain white walls and a neutral carpet. But on one of the walls was a mirror. Or rather, a virtual mirror. If you were to walk up to that mirror, you would see — staring back at you — either an image of yourself today *or* an age-progressed version of yourself.

With the virtual reality setup, the experience realistically mimicked that of looking into any mirror in your house. If you shifted your body to the right, the aged image in the virtual mirror would move *its* body to the right. And if you turned your head, so too would the image in the mirror. To make sure our participants were fully engaged, we prompted all of them to spend a few minutes talking to themselves — that is, talking to the same-age or older version of themselves — in the mirror.

Afterward, we removed their virtual reality goggles, brought them into an adjacent room, and had them fill out a series of questionnaires. Crucially, one of them contained a question about financial decisions: If you were to receive $1,000 right now, how would you allocate that money? Would you invest for the short term to reward your present self? Or would you seek out long-term savings to ensure your future self is taken care of?

MEETING FUTURE YOU

What happened when people could stand across from, talk to, and meet the older version of themselves? Just as when charity recipients were singled out and made more vivid, seeing one's future self tended to make people more charitable toward those distant selves. Namely, those who interacted with their age-progressed images allocated significantly more money to long-term savings than those who simply saw a picture of themselves today.

Admittedly, this was a small study, and our participants were undergraduates who were decades away from retirement. So, we ran a similar experiment but without the virtual reality context. Instead, in an online setting, working adults were asked to consider how much they'd hypothetically like to put aside from their paychecks toward a 401(k) account (that is, a tax-sheltered, employer-sponsored retirement account), using a little slider bar that ranged from 0 percent to 10 percent. The catch? After uploading a photo of themselves, some participants would see a picture of their future self hovering over the slider bar, while others saw an image of their current self.

Grayer hair, wrinklier skin, and age spots again won the day: those who saw their future selves put aside a significantly higher portion of their income toward retirement (about 6 percent of their paychecks) than the people who simply saw their present selves (who set aside about 2 percent of their wages).

I still want to be cautious here: we asked people about *hypothetical* money. It's possible, of course, that we wouldn't see such differences when it comes to behavior with real dollars and cents. Decisions about retirement savings, after all, are big ones, and on top of that, 401(k)s can be confusing. (One Twitter user comically demonstrated such confusion: "I signed up for my company's 401k, but I'm nervous because I've never run that far before.")

And so, for several years, one of my collaborators, Dan

Goldstein, and I sought opportunities to run a well-controlled study in the "real world." Our chance arrived in the form of a partnership with a behavioral science think tank called Ideas42, the Mexican finance ministry, and a large Mexican bank. The setup was relatively simple: We emailed or texted approximately fifty thousand banking customers, asking them if they'd like to contribute to their personal pension plans, which are sort of like American 401(k)s. Although all customers were encouraged to save more for the future, half of them were allowed to "meet" their future selves.

As it turned out, seeing those older selves increased not only the number of customers who made contributions to their accounts but the amount they saved as well.

Extending this work, behavioral scientist Tamara Sims and her collaborators introduced community college students to their future selves during a semester-long Transitioning to College course. Students were confronted with images of their same-aged or digitally aged avatars every few weeks as they responded to check-in surveys. Those who met their future selves displayed a higher motivation to learn about financial planning and greater confidence in their financial abilities, which ultimately translated into increased financial knowledge (or what researchers call "financial literacy"). It's worth noting that these students were socioeconomically diverse, and most were the first in their families to attend college; their financial literacy scores fell below the median of other Americans their age. Nevertheless, envisioning and meeting their future selves every few weeks produced a measurably positive change. Along similar lines, a future-self visualization exercise increased preventive health behaviors, as well as savings, among several thousand women in rural Kenya.

These types of interventions even seem to impact small children: preschoolers who drew images of their future selves (a day into the future) and described the experiences of those future selves showed improved planning abilities. For instance, they did a better job of recognizing what sort of items they'd need to pack for an overnight trip. Sure, the sort of planning you'd need for a successful overnight trip is on a shorter time scale than the planning required for a wealthier retirement. But as anyone who has ever interacted with a toddler can tell you, a tool that helps a three- or four-year-old plan for the near future is a valuable tool indeed!

Given these results, major companies have begun implementing versions of our intervention. Merrill Lynch, for instance, created a Face Retirement website where users could upload pictures and see their very aged selves sixty years into the future, replete with the projected price of gas at that time (on the off chance that we'll still be driving fossil fuel–powered cars then). The thinking was that doing so would prompt users to contribute or contribute more to their retirement accounts.

Prudential introduced "Future You" aging booths at employee benefits fairs in the hopes of increasing benefit participation. They've even gone so far as to take out retirement billboards by major highways that read, "Make Future You Proud."

Other companies, though, have taken a less direct approach. Rather than *showing* people aged images, Nationwide, a UK bank, partnered with comedian Sunil Patel to conjure up a notion of a specific future self. "I get the idea of saving—you're supposed to make good decisions now for your future self," Sunil observes. After a pause, though, he exclaims, "But like, I just don't think that guy deserves it! What's he done for that money? He hasn't earned that money; I have! He's done nothing for it, so I'm gonna keep it because I like nice things." When Patel finishes his bit, Nationwide spells out the real meaning: "A Message from Your Future Self: it's easier to save if you do it the day you're paid."

These are just a few of my favorite examples, and other financial firms have followed suit. But the impact of actively thinking about and envisioning future selves goes beyond the realm of dollars and cents. Take, for instance, Anmol Bhide, a college student from Northern California. A year into the COVID-19 pandemic, his diet had become spectacularly unhealthy, consisting mostly of Cinnamon Toast Crunch cereal and Chick-fil-A sandwiches. Over just three months, the combination took its toll, and he gained almost thirty pounds. Traditional diets, unfortunately, weren't helping him reverse course. But, as he related to me in an email, after reading about some of our research, he decided to take a different tack: he used an online tool to create an image of his ideal-looking future self.

To put the brakes on eating binges, he taped a copy of that image to his bathroom mirror and on the door of his refrigerator. "Whenever I would go downstairs to grab a Häagen-Dazs bar, I would see that visualization and walk back upstairs," he wrote. As he put it, the image gave him something to look forward to, and, with the help of a lower-calorie diet, some cardio, and a weight-lifting routine, he was able to shed much of the weight over time.

Adding some scientific heft to Mr. Bhide's anecdotal account, Sarah Raposo and Laura Carstensen found that adults who "met" their future selves via age-progressed images subsequently reported exercising more compared to adults who had not snuck a peek at the wrinkled future face.

And, in the domain of ethics, my colleagues and I found that exposure to vivid age-progressed images led people to take the more righteous path when faced with opportunities to cheat in games we created in the lab. In a more real-world setting, when high school students befriended their forty-something future selves on Facebook for a week, they were slightly less likely to act in delinquent ways that week.

These studies about ethical behavior contained small samples, and the effects were relatively modest. This shouldn't be too surprising: lots of factors go into the decision to act ethically or not, and seeing one's future self may be just one piece of the puzzle. It may nonetheless be an important piece: Jean-Louis van Gelder, my collaborator on this work, has begun introducing convicted Dutch offenders to their future selves via age-progressed images. Preliminarily, he's found that doing so has reduced the self-defeating behaviors (such as drinking and engaging in drug use) of former convicts on parole.

From savings to ethics to health, visualizing your "future you" can help change behavior for the better. Such images aren't necessarily a panacea, though, and context matters. For example, in the summer of 2019, celebrity influencers, and then more than a hundred million social media users, took part in a face-aging craze. They downloaded FaceApp, which allowed them to upload a photo and then, in a matter of seconds, see what they'd look like when they were much older. Some were horrified ("I look like Moses on his 584th birthday," one commented), while others were amused (Gordon Ramsay observed that this was what he'd look like hosting the fiftieth season of *MasterChef*). But did tens of millions of people suddenly increase their retirement savings rate and swap out their doughnuts for salads?

I suspect not. Social psychologists are fond of noting that water travels in the most straightforward path carved out for it, and people are no different, meaning that we often take the path of least resistance. If we want some undesirable behavior to change (like spending too much on frivolous purchases and not saving enough for the long run), the process for doing so has to be easy. By contrast, the FaceApp images weren't partnered with any readily available savings tool, healthy eating program, or the like, making behavior change unlikely.

More importantly, even though these images introduced a sizable portion of the world to their older selves, introductions alone may not be enough. Indeed, researchers Dan Bartels and Oleg Urminsky have found that to change behavior, we must know that our future selves exist *and* care about the outcomes that will befall them. With the appropriate context, seeing older versions of ourselves may help on both fronts: just like glasses help with seeing, and cochlear implants help with hearing, age-progressed images serve as aids to our imagination, making our future selves more top of mind and enhancing our ability to empathize with them. In that way, they perfectly represent the first strategy for improving our time-travel capabilities: making the future self feel closer to who we are now. *Seeing* age-progressed images, though, is just one way to go about it.

DEAR FUTURE ME

Ann Napolitano, author of the *New York Times* bestseller *Dear Edward,* grew up a voracious reader. She still is—when you're a novelist, reading comes with the territory—but as a child, she was extremely voracious. After having read all of L. M. Montgomery's Anne of Green Gables series, Napolitano wanted more. So, she turned to Emily of New Moon, another series written by Montgomery.

As Napolitano told me, Anne of Green Gables might be the more famous fictional character, but Emily was a spunky and charismatic orphan. She was also bookish, introverted, and shy. "As a fourteen-year-old," Napolitano said, "I was all of those things, so I resonated with Emily."

In the novels, Emily finds herself in a particularly lonely situation. To connect with someone—anyone—she decides to write a letter. Unfortunately, she's soon faced with the sad reality that she has no one to send it to. And so, she writes a letter to herself... in ten years' time.

Napolitano found the idea of writing to her twenty-four-year-old self very cool. Late one night, she decided just to do it. After crafting her letter, she carefully wrote, "To Ann at 24" on the outside of the envelope.

"The real miracle," Napolitano recounted, "was that I didn't lose that letter!" Over the ten years from age fourteen to age twenty-four, she finished high school, started and graduated from college, moved to her first apartment in Manhattan, and began graduate school. All the while, the letter traveled with her. When she was nineteen, she felt a strong urge to open it up — the remaining five years she had to wait seemed like an impossibly long time to hold out. But wait she did, and on the morning of her twenty-fourth birthday, she sat down to read the letter from her teenage self.

Its contents were predictably adolescent, full of angst and romantic yearnings. In an op-ed, Napolitano detailed how she was mortified to find that her fourteen-year-old self was mainly concerned with the shape of her body and whether she'd find love. Disappointed, she decided to reprise the exercise and write another letter, this time to herself at age thirty-four.

Napolitano is fifty now, and every ten years she writes (and reads) a "Dear Future Self" letter. She always starts by telling her ten-years-later self what her life is like. She includes basic things like where she's living and what she's doing but also explores deeper topics, like whom she loves, the quality of her friends, and the worries that consume her. The second half of the letter, however, tends to focus on where she'd ideally like to be in ten years. She told me that she tries to stay realistic: she lives with her husband and two kids in Brooklyn and eventually wants to have a writing room with an actual door!

As she said, she often can't remember what she wrote down when she reads the letters. She wrote her last one six years ago and has few memories of what's in it. But the experience of reading each ten-year-old letter, and finding out about her past hopes and anxieties, has been eye-opening. Some of the letters have an element of sadness: none of the things she wanted as a twenty-four-year-old ever happened. But some are hopeful and take a bigger-picture perspective on her life. The one thing she recalled from her thirty-four-year-old letter before she opened it was a wish to be less disappointed in what she's done and more curious about what happens next. In fact, reading that letter, she told me, was the first time she didn't feel anxious opening one. As she put it in her op-ed, it was the first time she felt "fully embedded in her life."

The novelist in Napolitano is genuinely interested in the stories that characterize our individual lives. Writing and reading letters to and from herself over time has allowed her to see more of a narrative arc in her own life as well. But an additional benefit comes from the letters' ability to prompt her to think in more specific ways about her distant self. The act of communicating with her future self every decade compels her to think about where she'll be in ten years, what her children's lives will be like, and what she wants her own life to look like. She considers the pieces already in place and how they could eventually add up to the idealized version of who she wants to become. The value in doing that, she told me, is that it forces her to live more intentionally. "It also," she observed, "makes me stay focused on living the fullest life that I can because I don't know how many more letters I'll get."

HIGH SCHOOL TIME CAPSULES

Napolitano isn't, of course, the only person to have engaged in this sort of exercise. Every year since 1994, Richard Palmgren, a teacher from New Jersey, has asked his sixth-grade students to write letters to their senior-year selves. He, like Napolitano, works hard to ensure that the notes are eventually read. Once the envelopes are sealed, he stores them in his office and then mails them when the students are in their final year of high school. (Smartly, after grappling with post office inflation for too many years, he now has the students affix three stamps to the envelopes.)

In the letters, students write about what middle school life is like, describe some current events, and list some wishes for their future selves. When they ultimately read the letters, Palmgren told me, it's "as if they are having a conversation with their past selves." Indeed, he contextualizes the exercise as a way for the students to think about where they exist along their timelines. As sixth graders, they were in kindergarten only six years ago, and in six years, they'll have their driver's licenses, ready to graduate from high school. To Palmgren, the project forces young students (like Napolitano) to think more deeply about their goals and where they want to be when the letters are opened.

Over the decades, Palmgren has remained blind to the contents of the letters. In 2020, however, filmmakers made a short documentary entitled "Dear Future Me" about Palmgren, his students, and the letter-writing exercise. During the filming, he witnessed his former students opening letters from their past selves. The publicity surrounding the short movie also prompted past students who'd never received their letters (because they'd moved or otherwise couldn't be reached) to return to their hometowns to pick up their little time capsules. The oldest class of letter writers is now in their late thirties.

Anecdotally, a common theme emerged: reading the letters from their past selves prompted many of Palmgren's students to rethink their current paths and revisit the goals they'd set for themselves all those years ago. "Seeing their past selves reflected back helps move the needle — one way or the other — to the person they are," Palmgren told me. They readjust, realign, and look forward to the ensuing years in a more realistic way.

The school ritual of "Dear Future Me" letters, perfected by Palmgren, is certainly one that other schoolteachers have adopted, too, and it's the motivation behind the website FutureMe, which I spotlighted in the introduction to this book. These stories are all suggestive of the power of such letters. But stories are just that. Is there any better evidence that communicating with our distant selves can help make our current and future lives better?

Growing evidence suggests that the answer may be yes. For instance, in a project led by Abe Rutchick, we discovered that when hundreds of college students wrote letters to themselves in twenty years (compared to a group who wrote letters to themselves in just three months), they were more likely to exercise, and exercise for a longer amount of time, over the subsequent week. Because they thought concretely about their distant future selves, they were motivated to take care of their bodies.

However, it can be challenging to figure out what to put in such letters or how to even go about writing them. And so, in a collaboration with Ideas42, my colleague Avni Shah and I used a Mad Libs–style app with a series of fill-in-the-blank questions to help Mexican banking customers write notes to their retirement-aged selves. Hundreds of financial advisers prompted thousands of customers to consider—in detailed fashion—who they would be at retirement. The app asked them, for example, to think about where they'd live, whom they'd spend time with, and what they'd be doing in their later years. Doing so mattered: customers who wrote such letters were significantly more likely to sign up for an automatic savings account compared to those who did not.

Recently, psychology professors Yuta Chishima and Anne Wilson found that when COVID-19 first struck, adults who wrote letters to (or from) their future selves one year into the future experienced an immediate drop in negative emotions, relative to adults who hadn't gone through such an exercise. The letter-writing exercise helped people step outside of the here and now and gain some perspective on how their negative feelings about COVID might wane as they grew closer to their distant selves. And, in drawing that connection, the participants were able to shed the shackles of an anxiety-producing period.

These particular interventions I've just discussed are one-way "conversations": people wrote letters either to or from their future selves. Better would be conversations where there's some back-and-forth between parties. Who, after all, wants to go on a date with someone who talks only about themselves? Recent work has found that a conversation between current and future selves may have an even bigger impact than a simple letter to (or from) a future self. For example, Chishima and Wilson asked hundreds of high school students to write letters to and from their future selves in three years. Compared to students who sent letters only one way, those who engaged in a send-and-reply reported feeling a stronger sense of connection to their distant selves. They subsequently reported that they were more likely to engage in career planning and study for exams, even when faced with other temptations.

———

Outside of letter writing and age-progressed images, there are other powerful ways to bring the future self closer. For instance, my former student Kate Christensen, now a professor at Indiana University, came up with one clever idea: start in the future and mentally travel back to the present. Most of the time, when we think about the years that lie ahead, we begin our mental journey today and travel forward to some point in the future. But nothing is forcing us to travel in that particular direction.

In fact, in several studies, Kate, Sam Maglio, and I have found that starting at the end and moving backward through time increases the sense of closeness that we feel toward our future selves. We've even found that this sort of "reverse time travel" leads people to take action today to take care of tomorrow. For example, in one experiment, we collaborated with a college savings app, UNest. We reached out to more than twenty-five thousand people who had started but never finished their sign-up process. One group saw a message that read, "The Year is 2031. Rewind back to 2021." Another group saw something more traditional: "The Year is 2021. Move forward to 2031." Even though overall conversion rates were low, traveling in reverse was powerful: the users who started at the end and traveled back to the present were more than twice as likely to input their personal data and enroll in a college savings account.

Why? Consider what happens when you drive to a new restaurant. What seems to take longer: the trip there or the trip home? If you're like most people, coming home seems to take less time than traveling to a new spot (psychologists have a smart name for this phenomenon: the "going home effect"). There's uncertainty involved in going to a new destination, and we don't feel "there" until we've parked the car and arrived at the front door. The return trip is different: we feel like we're home when we've reached the first landmark—the convenience store, stoplight, or schoolyard—that marks the geographic circle we think of as "home." And the same may be true for mental time travel. Traveling backward in time—from an uncertain future to a more certain present—makes the trip feel shorter, shrinking the distance between now and later.

Here's one final suggestion for making the future closer: rather than think about the time that lies between now and later in terms of years, consider it in terms of days. Researchers Neil Lewis and Daphna Oyserman asked thousands of research participants to do just this, and to great effect. When people were asked to think about retirement starting in 10,950 days, they planned to start saving four times earlier than those asked to think about retirement starting in 30 years. Thinking about the days rather than the years ahead impacted other out-comes, too — like the likelihood of planning for college savings. There's a compelling reason: days feel short, and years feel long, and mentally journeying through days instead of years enhanced the bond people felt toward their distant selves.

Whether it's reframing the calendar years into days, travel-ing backward in time, fostering conversations between present and future selves, or interacting with an aged selfie, these solu-tions for making the future closer share a common theme. We are naturally focused on the present, myopically absorbed in the here and now. But these tested tricks help to grease the wheels of our time-traveling machines, ultimately bringing our future selves nearer to the people we are now.

Highlights

- To bridge the gap between present and future selves, you can "make the future closer."
- You can do this by visualizing the future self with age-progressed images or by writing letters to *and* from your future self.
- But context matters. Simply seeing your aged self or writ-ing letters to or from them may not be enough to change

behavior. Instead, pair these "vividness" exercises with situations where you can make an immediate choice (like an online investment platform).

- Other methods might work as well: travel backward from the future to the present or think about the time that lies ahead in terms of days rather than years.

CHAPTER 8

STAYING THE COURSE

The pill looks like any other you'd get from a pharmacy: small and white, with a slash through the middle. Around the edges, there are some cryptic-looking letters. One morning, right after he had had his coffee, James Cannon washed one down with a glass of water.

But then he did something slightly unusual. He grabbed a bottle of vodka, carefully poured a shot into a tumbler, and topped it off with seltzer.

Despite the early hour, James drank half, went into his bedroom, and watched some TV.

After about fifteen minutes, the sense of loosening inhibitions that usually goes hand in hand with a cocktail was noticeably absent—no euphoria or mild buzz. He just felt a weird pressure building in his neck.

He dragged himself out of bed, walked to the kitchen, and finished his vodka soda.

Ten minutes later, the mild pressure intensified and spread to the rest of his head. He felt uneasy on his feet. His eyes were scratchy and bloodshot—so much so that up close, "the capillaries in the whites were so engorged that they resembled ivy growing on a wall."

It was almost as if he'd bypassed the fun part of drinking and skipped straight to a hangover of epic proportions.

That, in fact, was exactly what James Cannon had done. And it was entirely due to that little white pill. When we drink alcohol, our liver breaks it down, first into acetaldehyde, which is poisonous, and then into acetate, which is not. But Antabuse — the pill that Cannon took with his first cup of coffee — puts the alcohol train on a different track. In essence, it stops your body from processing alcohol properly. It blocks the metabolism of the acetaldehyde so that all that's left in your system is the part of a drink that'll give you a wildly unpleasant hangover.

It's also a perfect example of another solution for our time-travel difficulties. As I will explain, Antabuse is a form of a tool known as a commitment device: something that makes the journey harder to screw up but the hoped-for outcome easier to obtain. Like the bumpers used in bowling lanes, commitment devices aim to keep us on track. To understand exactly how that process works, let's go back to James Cannon.

FOUR KIDS AND A TWELVE-PACK

In the years leading up to his at-home experiment with Antabuse, Cannon gradually developed a drinking problem that kicked into full gear after he and his wife had their fourth daughter. Every day, starting around 2 p.m., he'd crack open his first beer and then have between eight and twelve more until he went to sleep. For a light or social drinker, that quantity of beer would surely result in some out-of-control drunkenness and debilitating morning-afters. But for Cannon, the twelve-pack-a-day habit never resulted in any real issues. He rarely got drunk and maintained a functional existence at home and work. The amount he drank became easy to justify precisely because he didn't have any problems with it.

However, all that changed when his wife became increasingly uncomfortable with his drinking, especially when their young children were around. Rather than scale back, the marital tension led him to consume more and periodically go on days- or even weeks-long binges where all that mattered was finding the next drink. The only thing that ended these benders was the realization that his health was failing. As he put it, "I did not want to deal with my life, but I also did not want to die."

After one nasty bender in the 1990s, he decided to seek help from a physician-friend.

That friend was Dr. Alexander DeLuca. At the time, DeLuca was the director of the Smithers Center for Drug and Alcohol Treatment. The Smithers Center, which is now a part of Columbia University's psychiatry department, is at the cutting edge of addiction treatment.

DeLuca prescribed various treatments to patients with alcohol problems, including Antabuse. As he told me in an interview, this was a drug he was particularly fond of in large part because he had experienced its effectiveness firsthand.

DeLuca was himself an alcoholic. He traced his problematic drinking back to trauma he'd experienced during childhood.

After trying just about every other treatment option to stop drinking, and finding all of them ineffective, he decided to see if Antabuse would perform any better. It did. Within days, DeLuca had dramatically cut back his drinking.

Why was Antabuse so effective? DeLuca credits its simplicity. Having a drink while on Antabuse, DeLuca explained to me, is quite awful: "Even the mildest reactions are terribly unpleasant." And it's not as if you can drink enough to push past that initial unpleasantness, because the more you drink, the worse the reaction gets. But maybe the most important aspect of Antabuse is its ability to remain in the bloodstream for several days after it's been consumed. For DeLuca, it would often last for about ten days. So, it was much harder to "cheat" and take the Antabuse on a Thursday only to skip it on Saturday morning in preparation for a weekend party.

In DeLuca's words, "It was really so much easier to make one decision a day rather than twenty-five." One decision, that is, to take the Antabuse, compared to twenty-five instances of needing to say no to a tempting drink. In truth, because Antabuse remained in the body for so long, it was more like one decision every few days.

Now retired in Boise, Idaho, DeLuca no longer drinks, nor does he feel the urge. But in the 1990s, he took Antabuse for about six years, a period, he told me, when he did his best academic and professional work.

Like DeLuca, James Cannon had experimented with many different treatment options for his alcoholism. Only when all of them failed to put the brakes on his drinking did he engage in the Antabuse trial.

THE VOICE OF A PILL

For Cannon, just as for DeLuca, the days before Antabuse represented a series of decisions about when to drink, how much to consume, or whether to abstain altogether. Taking the little pill every morning muted these sorts of internal dialogues.

But the pill also gave Cannon the freedom to explore a different set of issues. Because he was no longer fixated on the mechanics of drinking, Cannon was able to reckon with the triggers in his life that would typically prompt the desire to numb the edges with a beer or three. In writing about his experience with Antabuse, he recounted a moment on a Saturday afternoon when he was trying to fix a glitch on the family computer — a glitch that resulted from one of his daughters accidentally downloading a virus-laden file. After about an hour of work, just when he was about done, his youngest daughter walked into the office, sat down on the keyboard, and undid Cannon's repairs.

He recalled thinking that even though this was infuriating, he should just bite his tongue and power through. What was the use in getting angry at the kids, anyway? He thought about the party he'd be going to on Tuesday — he could relax and have a few drinks there.

But then the voice of Antabuse kicked in: "That party sounds great, but as long as you have me along, the drinking is not going to be too much fun, and you can't get rid of me by Tuesday." Reflecting upon that moment later, Cannon realized how his normal response to any sort of frustration was to figure out when he could consume his next drink. Going deeper, though, it made him appreciate just how much he'd been bottling up, and how, rather than confronting the everyday stressors of parenthood and working through them, he'd simply keep quiet and plan his next binge.

By removing alcohol from the menu of coping strategies, the Antabuse shone a light on Cannon's state of mind before he went on a bender. The little white pill forced him to develop new coping tools, none of which could be chugged from an aluminum can.

Antabuse can be an effective tool for a specific problem that affects about 6 percent of the American population over age twelve. However, excessive drinking shares similarities with many other problematic behaviors, like overeating, overspending, or spending too much time on our screens. Any problem, in other words, where we have an ideal image of our future selves, but then a present self who will undoubtedly mess things up.

We may want our future selves to be healthy, financially stable, and more present. We hope that they will have a low body mass index, a full bank account, and family and friends who will enjoy their company. Yet, we know that there is going to be a present self who will order chili fries at lunch (especially when the alternative is a side salad!), succumb to the free shipping offer from a clothing company whose products we don't need, and ignore our family in favor of finding out what that little ping was on our phones (but it could be an *important* social media alert!).

There will be present selves, in other words, who will—despite our best wishes—make our lives look different from our hoped-for ideal.

KEEP THE BALL ROLLING

In the case of problematic drinking, Antabuse makes it rather difficult for our present selves to fall off the proverbial wagon. I'm sure you're familiar with some other strategies that fall under this umbrella. If you've ever bought a one-hundred-calorie snack pack, that is a commitment device: you are committing to eating only one hundred calories' worth of those small, delicious Chips Ahoy! chocolate chip cookies. If you've ever signed up for a work-out class or made a plan to go on a walk with a friend, you're committing—in advance—to not being a couch potato. These are mild forms of "pre-commitment"—at least certainly milder than taking a pill that commits you to a raging headache and severe nausea if you have a vodka tonic.

The idea of pre-committing to a particular course of action didn't originate with people trying to limit the number of Twinkies in their cupboards. Pre-commitment was first formally discussed by Thomas Schelling, an economist who won the 2005 Nobel Prize, in the context of preventing the escalation of the Cold War. Back in 1956, he suggested that nations could lessen the likelihood of an all-out conflict by committing to a course of action in advance.

Here's how it could work: Imagine that Canada's maple syrup factories were the target of an imminent heist by some maple syrup–hungry nations. If Congress passed a bill stating that the United States would defend Canada's maple syrup factories at all possible costs in the event of an attack, it would make it less likely that foreign thieves would attempt to steal syrup by the truckload. Why? Because the threat of a definite and already committed-to response from the United States would make an attack on Canada that much less appealing.

It's an insight that speaks to a critical aspect of commitment devices that we try to enact on a personal level: to come up with an effective one, you have to possess a healthy ability to take the perspective of others, and specifically, our future selves. In my silly maple syrup example, members of Congress must be able to take the perspective of leaders of other nations (with pancake-eating, syrup-starved citizens!) who will be deterred by the United States' commitment to action. Like potentially warring nations, when we take a pre-commitment approach, we must engage in perspective taking and figure out what exactly will tempt future versions of ourselves.

Although Schelling put a name to this strategy, commitment devices have been around for centuries. In 1519, for instance, upon arriving in Mexico, explorer Hernán Cortés deliberately sunk eleven of his twelve ships to ensure that his army of men was forced to march onward and not turn back. And similarly, nearly seventeen hundred years earlier, when deciding where to position his men for a particular battle, Chinese general Han Xin placed them with their backs to a river, cutting off their ability to retreat.

In the 1980s, Schelling switched gears and started thinking

about how these sorts of strategies could be extended to the conflicts we face within ourselves. He generated some creative possibilities and inspired subsequent economists to come up with their own. Let's say, for instance, that you need to get some work done but are constantly being distracted by other tasks and errands. You might consider asking a friend to drop you off at a coffee shop for several hours and take your phone away, so you can finally cross those items off your to-do list. (A similar strategy was used by the poet Maya Angelou: although she owned a large house, she would regularly go to a hotel with no art on the walls just so that she could write in a focused state — a café with no Wi-Fi may be a cheaper alternative!) Or you could brush your teeth immediately after dinner to make it that much harder to consume late-night snacks. Or how about this wacky one that I haven't yet tried: if you have a hard time waking yourself up in the morning, you could drink plenty of water at night, which should force you out of bed when your alarm goes off (if not before).

These examples raise a larger question about commitment devices. In order to create one that works for you and helps you achieve those goals you've set for your future self, it's important to understand what kind of commitment devices are most effective, and why.

COMMIT TO A COURSE OF ACTION

I'm sure you know people who take pictures of their food, or maybe you do so yourself. My friend Craig, however, is not one of those people. In fact, in the almost ten years that I've known him, I can't say I've ever seen him whip out his phone to take a picture of anything.

That is, until one day at lunch, when I saw him carefully lay out an apple, a small bag of chips, and a sandwich on the table and then snap a pic.

"Oh, sorry," he said, noticing my skeptical expression, "I need to let my nutritionist know what I'm having for lunch."

After gaining weight in recent years, Craig had decided to make some changes, and his chosen strategy was quite simple. Any time he was about to eat something—whether it was breakfast, a snack, lunch, or dinner—he would text a picture of his food to a nutritionist. Her job was to make a rough assessment of his calorie intake and the diversity of his diet. She could quickly tell him to add more protein to his next meal or cut back on the carbs.

Sure, Craig was committing, in advance, to taking pictures of his food. But, by creating a diet with his nutritionist—and promising her that he'd share photos of his meals—he was also committing to eating healthier foods. You could think of this as a *psychological commitment:* by stating in advance that you are going to do—or not do—a behavior, you are making a commitment that is strictly psychological in nature. Some economists call this a "soft commitment."

Notice that nothing was stopping Craig from eating whatever he wanted. It's not as if his nutritionist could magically appear and scold him were he to load up on chocolate cake. Heck, she wasn't even based in the United States!

And yet, even though there were temptations to cheat (I did once catch him holding an extra pack of nuts just out of the camera frame), the program worked quite well for him: he lost fifteen pounds and felt healthier day to day.

Craig's experience with this psychological commitment wasn't unique. A growing number of research studies have found that, under certain circumstances, a soft commitment device can be pretty successful. Perhaps the most well-known bit of evidence comes from a colleague of mine, Shlomo Benartzi. Along with Nobel Prize–winning economist Richard Thaler, Benartzi introduced the Save More Tomorrow savings plan to employers. The program features automatic contributions from paychecks to 401(k) accounts, and contributions that increase in amount over time. Fancy as it may sound, it is nonetheless a simple psychological commitment: employees are automatically signed up for it, but they can opt out at any time. And it's worked. At the first company in which this popular plan was implemented, employees enrolled in the program quadrupled their savings rate over roughly four years.

Similar psychological commitment plans—that is, soft commitment plans—have been used successfully to increase other behaviors such as donating to charities and attending and completing weight loss classes.

It's worth noting, however, that these sorts of commitment plans can backfire if not carried out carefully. One recent study, for example, found a drop in savings rates when employees were asked if they'd like to sign up for the plan now *or* commit to signing up in a few months. In seeing the two options simultaneously, employees may have gotten the wrong message: "My employer is saying that I can do this now or I could just do it later? Maybe it's not that important to begin with!"

There's a fix, however. If someone declines participation in a program, only then should they be offered the chance to commit at a later point in time. Indeed, in an experiment in which thousands of adults were asked if they wanted to take a free financial well-being assessment, those who were given a chance to take it now, followed by the option to take it in a week if they said no, were far more likely go through with the assessment compared to people who were given the opportunities simultaneously to sign up now or later.

The point? If psychological commitment plans — or any sort of commitment plans — are offered in a way that doesn't signal urgency, they most likely won't be adopted.

Reflecting on his dieting program, Craig told me that a big reason for its success boiled down to the accountability he felt toward the nutritionist. Knowing he would be sending a picture of his meal forced him to be more mindful about what he chose to eat. As he put it, taking those photos "put a mirror to what I was eating," and he worried that he'd be letting his nutritionist down if he frequently chose unhealthy options.

Some initial research backs up this idea that accountability matters. For instance, in a study conducted in Chile, entrepreneurs saved about three and a half times as much when they publicly committed to saving in a "peer savings group" compared to those who did not have such accountability partners.

However, the costs of failing when we make such commitments go beyond letting others down. When we go against our plans, *psychological* costs may be incurred as well. Think about it this way: we like to be consistent in our actions. If I've told myself that tonight will be the night when I keep the pantry closed after dinner but then find myself mindlessly munching M&M'S, I've let my past and future selves down. And I don't want to think of myself as the type of person who lets others down.

With these sorts of psychological commitments, we commit future versions of ourselves to act a certain way. But there are no material punishments if we *don't* act that way: it's not as if we'll get fined or locked up for failing to follow through. If we do stray from our plan, what we primarily lose — as economists Roland Bénabou and Jean Tirole have pointed out — is a sense of faith in ourselves.

Surely, though, there are more extreme ways of "staying the course." Rather than the simple commitments I just discussed, we can go a step further and commit ourselves to taking away tempting options.

TAKE AWAY OPTIONS

When Dave Krippendorf was an MBA student at MIT, he lived in an apartment in Boston's Beacon Hill, conveniently located within walking distance of a Whole Foods. Convenient for Krippendorf's daily desire to eat snacks while he completed his coursework. Not convenient, though, for his equally strong desire to snack less.

In an interview, Krippendorf told me that after this conflict repeatedly played itself out, he started wondering if there was a way to put the brakes on his snacking obsession. He knew he couldn't effectively stop himself from strolling over to Whole Foods and buying yet another small pack of cookies. And he knew that limiting his trips and simply purchasing a larger package wouldn't work either. Finding all other strategies lacking, he recognized the need for a heavier hand.

Perhaps because he was at MIT, surrounded by some of the world's top engineers and aspiring entrepreneurs, the solution he arrived at involved inventing a new product. But this wasn't some newfangled app or high-tech device. Rather, it was an old-fashioned safe. Or rather, a "Kitchen Safe."

It's just what it sounds like: a locked box that sits in your kitchen. But instead of a clunky metal contraption with a bolted lock, this one is more like a plastic Tupperware container with a lid fitted with an electronic keypad. The lock can be programmed for times ranging from one minute to ten days. No matter the amount of time, its central function is to remove temptation from everyday life.

Krippendorf originally came up with the idea as a final project for one of his business school classes. It turned into a side project and then, eventually, a real company when Krippendorf left his Wall Street job to go all in. A few articles in the popular press and a winning appearance on *Shark Tank* later, his small start-up is now a thriving, self-supporting business. Every year, tens of thousands of consumers — consumers with admitted self-control problems — choose to buy lockboxes so they can resist the desires of their present selves.

Although some consumers use the product for its intended purpose—locking away chocolates, cookies, and candy—a number use the Kitchen Safe to address much more severe problems. Some have put alcohol or other drugs in it, including prescriptions. Krippendorf, for example, told me about a letter he received from a user who suffers from a sleep disorder. A prescription medication helps her achieve deeper periods of sleep but can only be taken safely every four hours. After finding herself "cheating" and taking the drug after shorter periods, she started locking the pill bottle into the Kitchen Safe with a four-hour timer set.

My favorite case study might just be that of the young man who reported on Reddit that he'd used the Kitchen Safe to help him deal with internet distractions. His extreme solution required a padlock, his physics books, and a closet. By putting the key to the padlock in the Kitchen Safe and setting the timer to four hours, he effectively turned his closet into a forced study chamber.

Personally, after finding myself distracted by screens one too many times during family time (did I really need to check Twitter as I got up from the table to refill my water glass?), I've started using Krippendorf's contraption to lock up my phone in the evening... at least until the kids go to bed. The version I use is designed for just this purpose: the box is opaque, so you can't see any pop-ups or alerts, and there's a space in the back for a charger.

Clearly, the product is helping people cope with problems that extend far beyond the kitchen. Because of the wide variety of uses people have found for the device, Krippendorf recently changed the name of his company and product to KSafe.

The driving force behind this particular commitment device is that it *takes away options*. It removes the cookie, the phone, the prescription drugs, and, yes, even the ability to get out of a closet. In fact, the only way to open the KSafe once it's been locked is to break it open with a hammer or other blunt object! Elaborating on the "taking away options" strategy, neuroscientist Mark Lewis, who has struggled with his own addiction issues, describes a dog who has seen a steak placed in the refrigerator. Knowing there's a juicy piece of meat just behind the fridge door, the dog paws at it repeatedly. But if its owner could demonstrate that the fridge door was now locked, the dog's pawing—and maybe even its desire—would cease.

In more ways than one, I can certainly relate to this feeling. After I lock up my phone at night, I've noticed that my incessant urge to check each ping lessens in intensity. Similarly, several years ago, I was having lunch with the psychologist Walter Mischel and noticed that I was the only one eating all the bread that was served before our meal. When I asked him if he wanted a piece, he told me that the bread was—for him—completely off-limits. As someone with celiac disease, the pre-meal carb basket posed no strong temptation for him. Do you know the feeling of eating several rolls before your meal arrives—all the while recognizing that you should stop and save room for your entree? It wasn't one Mischel regularly experienced after he was diagnosed. In an interview with his former student, author Maria Konnikova, Mischel described this reality eloquently: celiac disease created "a sudden change where the things I've adored all my life — Viennese pastries, pasta Alfredo — have been mentally transformed into poison."

When he told me about his experiences, I remember thinking that I could be healthier if I could only convince myself that an undesirable food simply wasn't a possibility. A few years after that lunch meeting, I was unfortunately granted my wish. I found out I also had celiac disease and, suddenly, bread products became just like the locked phone: off-limits.

It turns out that prohibiting temptations has benefits far beyond the realm of tasty carbs. Economist Nava Ashraf, for instance, partnered with a rural bank in the Philippines to create a new type of savings product they called a SEED account. That is, a Save, Earn, Enjoy Deposits account. The defining feature of the account is that it worked a bit like the KSafe: once a customer made a deposit into their savings account, they wouldn't be able to access their money until a specified time that they selected (say, August for school supplies or December for holiday purchases). Or they could elect to have their funds held hostage until some goal amount was reached.

After a year, customers who had SEED accounts increased their savings balances by 82 percent, or about eight dollars, compared to those who didn't. That may sound like a small amount of money, but it's consequential in this setting: when the field experiment was conducted, it cost a family of five about twenty dollars to buy rice for the month. Slightly different products have met with some success in rural areas of Kenya and Malawi, too.

Despite their relative effectiveness, people fail to adopt these sorts of "take away the option" products in large numbers. For example, only 28 percent of the banking customers in the Philippines who were offered the locked savings account chose to adopt it. Part of the issue, plain and simple, might be that it's difficult to restrict our access to resources we need and enjoy (like money and our favorite foods).

The psychologist Janet Schwartz may have arrived at a clever solution to this problem. Her insight arrived during a summertime visit to Coney Island. You can't go to Coney Island without stopping by the famous Nathan's hot dog stand. Schwartz and two of her friends happened to visit Nathan's right after restaurants in New York started listing calorie counts on their menus. In an interview, Schwartz told me how shocked she was to see that the side of fries she typically ordered clocked in at a whopping eleven hundred calories.

Instead of three hot dogs and three orders of fries, she and her friends decided to split one side of fries. Note that it's not as if they opted to split the fries *and* the hot dog—who would go all the way to Coney Island just to have a third of a hot dog? No, rather than restricting their options when it came to the central item of interest (the hot dog!), they chose instead to limit their options for something on the side (the fries).

If the overall goal was to eat at least somewhat healthily— that is, not to consume more calories than you need in a day— then for Schwartz, the solution of "cutting down on the sides" seemed to work: she and her friends could just as easily have gone back and ordered another side or two of fries, but they stuck with their full dog plus third-of-a-fries combo. They still left Nathan's happy and full, but they also felt good about their self-control.

An expert in commitment devices, Schwartz and some of her research collaborators later put this insight to the test. They did so in conjunction with a Chinese fast-food restaurant where main courses came with four side-dish options: steamed vegetables, steamed rice, fried rice, and chow mein. If diners ordered one of the high-calorie, high-starch choices—all of which were at least four hundred calories—they were given the option to downsize it to half the amount.

Consider that, before the experiment, about 1 percent of diners spontaneously requested a smaller portion of one of the high-calorie side dishes. But when the "half the side" offer was given to diners, about one in three said yes. Now, it's not as if diners were somehow making up for the smaller side dish by ordering higher-calorie entrees; the customers who accepted the offer ordered entrees with no more calories than the entrees ordered by those who rejected it. Nor did the diners who ordered the full-portion side dish leave more of it on their plates at the end of the meal.

Part of the reason that the intervention was successful, Janet told me, was "because we targeted the peripheral parts of the meal, not the focal parts." As she pointed out, when you go to a fast-food restaurant, something usually draws you there, whether it's the fried chicken sandwich, the cheeseburger, or the orange chicken. You most likely would be reluctant to give up half of one of those dishes. But half the rice? Half the fries? That might be slightly more palatable.

ADD APPROPRIATE PUNISHMENTS

There is, however, a major issue with these strategies, and it's well illustrated in a children's tale by Arnold Lobel. In "Cookies," one in a series of short stories about Frog and Toad, two best friends, Toad has just baked chocolate chip cookies for them to enjoy.

They each have one and declare that it is the tastiest cookie they've ever eaten. So, they have another. And . . . another. They continue shoveling more and more in their mouths, even as they say, "We must stop!" Both a cookie connoisseur and a crafty amateur psychologist, Frog decides to develop basic commitment devices to help them end their cookie binge.

But with every creative possibility he generates, Toad sees an easy workaround.

The cookies, Frog thinks, could go into a box! Sure, but you could simply open the box, Toad points out.

The box could be tied up with string! Sure, but then you could cut the string, notes the always practical Toad.

The cookies, in the tied-up box, could go all the way up on top of the cupboard, only accessible by a ladder! Sure, but then you could climb the ladder, cut the string, open the box, and devour what's left, Toad pessimistically observes.

Frog comes up with a better idea. After climbing the ladder, cutting the string, and opening the box, he takes it outside. Shouting in his loudest voice, he screams, "Hey birds, here are cookies!" In moments, birds fly in from the trees and gobble up the box's contents.

Frog, finally satisfied that he will be tempted no more, happily concludes that he and his buddy have exerted a hefty dose of willpower.

It's a feeling, however, that Toad doesn't share. You can keep your willpower, he tells Frog, "I am going home now to bake a cake."

Like these two amphibious best friends, within ourselves, we may get into similar battles over commitment devices. Just like Frog, we have the best intentions in committing to a course of action and taking away future options. But our present selves — the Toads — may sneakily figure out ways to thwart those plans.

To create the greatest harmony between these warring selves, commitment devices must strike the right balance between being strong enough to limit objectionable behavior but not so strong that the devices become undesirable.

Simply put, these strategies can work only if they're adopted. And they won't be adopted if they are too harsh. Thomas Schelling, the economist who theorized about commitment strategies, wrote about the case of an addiction clinic in Denver. As part of the program, patients would write "self-incriminating letters" and hand them over to the medical staff, with the promise that those letters would be delivered to their recipients in the event of a failed drug test. If, say, a doctor with a cocaine addiction were to randomly test positive for that drug, a letter would be sent to the state medical board confessing to violations of state law. That seems quite extreme, and it promises effectiveness but may fail to be adopted in large numbers.

The solution, then, might be to introduce the possibility of future punishments that are *appropriate*. The punishment for straying from the course, in other words, needs to be painful enough to act as a deterrent but not so painful that no one will want to risk having it enacted.

Consider, for instance, a strategy that author Nir Eyal calls his "burn or burn" technique. In an interview, he told me that he keeps a calendar in his dresser. Taped to today's date is a one-hundred-dollar bill, but on top of the dresser is a Bic lighter. Every day, he has a decision to make: "I can either burn some calories, or I can burn the hundred-dollar bill." It's "loss aversion" in action: in certain contexts, potential losses have an extra emotional oomph that can be motivating. Eyal, in other words, might not want to sweat, but he *really* doesn't want to lose his money.

That calorie-burning activity can be anything—taking a walk, going to the gym, doing sit-ups...anything that gets him to move. The threat of having to burn one hundred dollars has been enough to force him not to fall into the inactive state in which he so often found himself before he introduced this choice to his daily routine. It's a threat that's painful enough to prompt action but not so painful as to make him want to abandon ship. Three years on, he still makes his burn-or-burn decision every day. Eyal, who was once clinically obese, is now, at the age of forty-four, the healthiest he's ever been.

The "add an appropriate punishment" strategy has been tested in more formal settings. Janet Schwartz and her colleagues worked with grocery-store shoppers already enrolled in a healthy-foods incentive program. The shoppers were given a chance to receive a discount on their bills, but only if they committed to increasing their healthy purchases by 5 percent each month for six months. If they failed to do so, they would lose the discounts they had already accrued over that period. Not exactly burning hundred-dollar bills, but pretty close. About a third of shoppers signed up for this decently strong but not overly extreme commitment device. And the program worked: for those who enrolled, there was a 3.5 percent increase in healthy food items purchased. (To be fair, this wasn't the 5 percent goal that shoppers committed to, highlighting just how challenging it is to change our habits over time.)

Success for these sorts of "punishment-style" commitment devices has also been found outside of the food and exercise contexts. For example, one quit-smoking program offered smokers the chance to deposit money into a savings account for six months. After that time, if a urine test detected that they had had cigarettes, the savings would be forfeited and donated to a charity. About one in ten smokers signed up, and, compared to a group that wasn't offered the program, they were three percentage points more likely to pass the urine test after six months. (They were also more likely to pass a surprise urine test a year later.) Along similar lines, in a series of research studies, economist John Beshears and his colleagues found that investment accounts with early withdrawal penalties attracted more deposits than accounts that promised the same interest rate but with no early withdrawal punishment attached. (This is the logic behind 401(k) plans and other accounts where an interest rate is guaranteed, but penalties are enacted if you want to pull your money out before some specified future date.)

The common theme in these commitment devices—whether they are aimed at promoting healthy eating, smoking cessation, or better saving habits—is that a third party is putting the punishments into place, and those punishments occur *automatically*. You can probably see why that might matter: if you were to be the one to dole out your punishments—or set up an otherwise weak system—it would be easy to sweet-talk your way out of getting punished for failing to do the thing you said you were going to do.

Having a third party as the punishment enactor may also be the driving force behind the success of a site called Stickk.com, founded by Northwestern University behavioral economist Dean Karlan and his colleagues. There, you can put these sorts of punishment strategies into practice. If, for example, you wanted to walk for thirty minutes daily, you would go to the site and set a goal of walking thirty minutes a day. But you'd also give the site your credit card details. At day's end, if you've failed to get in your half hour of walking (as reported by you or by an accountability partner), some painful amount of money (decided by you) will be charged to your credit card and donated to a political campaign you don't support.

However, not all commitments on Stickk.com have to be tied to a punishment. You could simply commit to walking thirty minutes a day without any threat of a donation to an undesirable political campaign. Based on the work I covered earlier in this chapter, I'd speculate that doing so is most likely better than not committing to any sort of plan at all. But the most effective strategy may be to add in a punishment. A recent analysis of almost twenty thousand Stickk.com users found that although only a third of users opted for an account with monetary stakes, the ones who did were more than four times as likely to follow through with their commitments.

———

There's something enticing about the commitment device strategy. Whether through introducing a simple psychological commitment, removing tempting options, or putting into place a future punishment, commitment devices prompt us to stay faithful to our future selves. But they may be most effective for people who are aware of their tendencies to succumb to temptations. It's ironic but true: before we can boost our self-control we first need to recognize our failings.

After only three months, James Cannon decided to end his trial with Antabuse—he felt, at that point, that he no longer needed the drug to maintain sobriety. It did help him successfully identify some of the triggers that would lead to benders. Still, his decision to end the trial was perhaps premature, as he eventually relapsed. Dr. DeLuca, who treated Cannon, noted that in his own experience with Antabuse, he'd often stop taking the drug after a sustained period of sobriety, only to go back on it later.

Along these lines, preliminary evidence from the banking study in the Philippines I discussed earlier suggests that the most self-aware consumers—that is, those most aware of their tendency to succumb to temptation—were the ones who got more use out of the locked accounts. Other work, conducted in better-controlled laboratory settings, has arrived at similar conclusions. These findings add nuance to the adage "If it ain't broke, don't fix it": we must recognize that something is broken before attempting a solution.

Before we set out to constrain our future courses of action, in other words, we must first appreciate that there are things in our environment that tempt us and then identify what those things are. But as Cannon's experience demonstrates, we probably can't stop there. Initial success with commitment devices can be seductive; after some early wins, we can fool ourselves into thinking we no longer need them. If this happens, we'd be wise to keep past failures in mind when debating whether to retire a commitment device.

Beyond "staying the course," there's another fix for our time-travel woes, though, and it doesn't involve taking pills that simulate a hangover or setting hundred-dollar bills on fire. In the final chapter, I focus on our present-day sacrifices and how we can make them easier to undertake.

Highlights

- To better ensure that you arrive at the future you want, consider "commitment device" strategies that make it harder to fall prey to temptation.
- The weakest form is known as a "psychological commitment": make a plan to commit to a course of action. Try to

recruit an accountability partner—someone who can make sure that you do the thing you said you were going to do.

- Stronger yet are commitment devices where tempting options are removed from your environment (for example, check out the KSafe).

- More extreme still are commitment devices where punishments are enacted if you veer off track. If possible, make the punishments automatic so that you leave no room for negotiations with yourself.

CHAPTER 9

MAKING THE PRESENT EASIER

Mitch Hedberg was a comic beloved by comedians. Hedberg, active in the 1990s and early 2000s, was famous for his one- and two-liners, the deadpan way he delivered them, and his chilled-out demeanor. Usually sporting a pair of tinted glasses, a floppy hat, baggy clothes, and a sparse beard, he certainly looked the part of the "stoner" comedian. Most of his sets avoided raunchy or dirty jokes. Instead, he focused on absurd, almost surreal observations about daily life. Consider his take on shaving: "Every time I go and shave, I assume there's someone else on the planet shaving. So I say, 'I'm going to go shave, too.'"

But it was a joke he made about junk food that's stayed with me over time: "That would be cool if you could eat a good food with a bad food and the good food would cover for the bad food when it got to your stomach," he observed. "Like you could eat a carrot with an onion ring, and they would travel down to your stomach, then they would get there, and the carrot would say, 'It's cool, he's with me.'"

Hedberg, who died in 2005, was tapping into a feeling familiar to many people who have tried to maintain a healthy diet.

Who, after all, hasn't wanted an extra scoop of ice cream or piece of chocolate to simply "not count"? Shouldn't the carrot in carrot cake cancel out the cake part?

The joke speaks to a profoundly human desire: to make our present-day sacrifices and struggles seem less painful. After all, from the perspective of your present self, optimizing for your future is mostly downside: Current You makes the sacrifice but Future You reaps the (uncertain) benefits. Of course, these tugs-of-war in time apply to many of our saving versus spending and exercising versus lounging-around problems, but they're relevant in other contexts, too.

Think about confrontations — or rather, potential confrontations — with loved ones or coworkers. As anyone close to me could tell you, I'm a chronic avoider of conflict. I know, though, that when I avoid it, what I'm steering clear of is the possibility of an unpleasant conversation. And at the extreme, the possibility of a relationship unraveling. But while conflict avoidance allows me (or you) to skirt feelings of discomfort and fear, it also serves to make things worse in the long run. Tensions that were once minor grow into something much worse, until a conversation that could have been calm ends up being anything but.

In case it's not clear, the present-day sacrifice here is the sacrifice of your in-the-moment comfort in service of better relationships moving forward. In this scenario — as with saving money and exercising — the "unpleasant" action occurs now for the promise of something better at a later point.

The tension inherent in these trade-offs was perfectly captured in a quote attributed to Groucho Marx: "Why should I care about future generations—what have they ever done for me?"

So, what can we do about it? In this final chapter, rather than focus on our distant or near-distant selves, I want to spotlight our current selves and discuss ways to make our present-day "sacrifices" feel subjectively easier. The first strategy—"taking the good with the bad"—is best illustrated through a radical experiment conducted in the halls of the Stanford School of Medicine.

TAKING THE GOOD WITH THE BAD

In the 1970s, when David Spiegel was a young psychiatry professor at Stanford, he was invited to colead a series of "supportive-expressive group therapy" sessions for women with metastatic breast cancer. At the time, the idea was novel: normally, conversations between doctors and patients occurred in a one-on-one context (with the occasional family member present). And yet, Spiegel and his collaborators proposed that benefits could be reaped from having small groups of women with breast cancer meet regularly to communicate with and support one another.

However, other doctors—and oncologists, in particular—weren't optimistic about these sessions. As Dr. Spiegel told me in an interview, they thought he was crazy for wanting to run such an experiment. The worry was that having eight women sitting in a room talking about their experiences with cancer and watching one another get sicker over time (and eventually die) would only demoralize them. It was as if the group sessions would somehow introduce them to the idea of dying, like "they hadn't already thought of this?" Spiegel told me.

Despite these criticisms, he pressed on, much to the advantage of the women who ended up being part of his sessions. Yes, they often faced powerful and challenging situations, especially when they witnessed the loss of some of the other group members. But they also learned to grapple with the stressors—both large and small—that they were all facing. As Spiegel points out, the group therapy didn't make the negatives of cancer disappear. Rather, the patients simply became more adept at confronting these negative experiences and traumas. As one woman put it, "Being in the group is sort of like looking into the Grand Canyon when you're afraid of heights. You know if you fell down, it would be a disaster, but you feel better about yourself because you can at least look at it. I can't say I feel serene, but I can look at it."

Like this patient, many of the other women in Spiegel's sessions also faced negative topics head-on. For instance, in one of his research studies, Spiegel and his coauthors analyzed the emotional expressions and content of the group sessions on a minute-by-minute level. When bad news came up—and it inevitably did—the tone of the conversations shifted. The discussions took on a more serious tone, yet not a demoralizing one. In being able to express negativity alongside the positive support of others, the women in Spiegel's sessions were more fully able to process information that might have otherwise been ignored or brushed aside, creating anxiety without resolution.

Learning how to confront and process the bad news led to better outcomes. Spiegel and his collaborators found that the more expressive women were over time, the less anxious and depressed they became. Those going through group therapy even saw improvements in the lengths of their lives. For example, in one early study, compared to women who didn't participate in the group therapy sessions, those who did lived approximately eighteen months longer. Subsequent studies suggest that that amount of life extension may be extreme. But recent reviews of the relevant research have found that women who have undergone such sessions—especially when provided to older patients with less social support—not only live longer but also live better: the women reliably report feeling less anxiety and depression as well as a heightened quality of life.

There are several mechanisms at work here, but one was most likely a shift in perspective. Namely, the women began recognizing that they could experience the negative with the positive and vice versa. One of Spiegel's patients, for instance, was a fan of opera but after being diagnosed with breast cancer stopped visiting her beloved Santa Fe Opera house. How could she attend something as beautiful, peaceful, and cheerful as the opera while cancer raged inside? She figured she'd just wait until she felt better. After supportive discussions with her group therapy partners, however, she realized that that time might never arrive. As she reported to Spiegel, she eventually decided to go to the opera: "I brought my cancer with me and put it in the seat next to me. It was there, but I had a wonderful time."

A PEACEFUL COEXISTENCE

This woman, and many of the others in the group therapy treatment, realized, as Spiegel put it, that "happiness and sadness were not two poles of one dimension," but rather could peacefully coexist. The concept of these sorts of mixed emotions is one that Jeff Larsen, a psychologist at the University of Tennessee, has spent most of his career studying. With papers like "Can People Feel Happy and Sad at the Same Time?," "The Case for Mixed Emotions," and "Further Evidence for Mixed Emotions," Larsen has used cutting-edge techniques to demonstrate that we can experience different flavors of emotions simultaneously, whether happiness and sadness, rage and pride, or excitement and fear.

Why does the ability to experience competing emotions matter? From a practical standpoint, there's a reason these findings are essential.

To Larsen and his collaborators, being able to experience positive emotions alongside negative ones—like the women in Spiegel's therapy groups—may produce certain benefits that you can't get from experiencing just one emotion on its own.

The idea is simple, but the implications are profound. Think for a minute about the last time you grappled with a stressor or obstacle. It could've been something relatively minor, like the weeknight feeling of not wanting to cook a healthy meal when you could just as easily order delivery (but knowing, all along, that you'll feel better afterward were you just to cook). Or it could have been something more significant, like dealing with the pain of a layoff and the subsequent logistical challenges that go along with it.

When we face such stressors, one option is to wallow in the negative, spending our time beating ourselves up for the things both in and out of our control. Or we can act like ostriches, burying our heads in the ground, attempting to avoid any unpleasant feelings altogether. There's a third way to respond, though, and it's the one that the opera fan employed: do our best to experience joy alongside the things that bring us discomfort. Could doing so improve the lives of our future selves?

Several years ago, my collaborator Jon Adler and I put this idea to the test. Jon, a clinical psychology professor at Olin College, had previously conducted research examining people's psychotherapy experiences. For three months, he tracked outpatients as they attended weekly therapy sessions. And at the end of each session, the patients recorded what they were thinking and feeling in short journal entries. Each week, the patients also reported their "psychological well-being."

Jon's setup presented a perfect opportunity to explore just how useful it would be to "take the good with the bad." Perhaps adding a dose of hope or joy to otherwise negative experiences would allow for better outcomes in the long run.

To find out, we asked research assistants to code the journal entries. Some were "one note" in nature, dominated by a single emotion like sadness, fear, or even happiness. But others, it turned out, were rife with mixed feelings. Check out this one, for instance, which contains a blend of happiness and sadness:

> This has been a difficult couple of weeks. My wife and I celebrated the good news of a healthy pregnancy report at nine weeks (the time when we lost our pregnancy last January). But I also feel the sadness of still looking for a job and for my wife's and my pending loss of my wife's grandmother. It feels as if "what more can I take." But in reality I also feel reasonably confident and happy. Not that I don't feel down, but I also feel happy with my marriage.

After three months of therapy, people's mental health—that is, their psychological well-being—improved. That's in line with decades of psychotherapy research.

But mixed emotions mattered, too: the patients who experienced more of a mingling of happiness *and* sadness from one session to the next were also the ones who showed the most significant improvements in psychological well-being. And that was true even when we stripped away the impact of experiencing happiness or sadness on its own. The heavy lifting, in other words, was being done by the combination of the positive and the negative, not just one emotion or the other by itself. This suggests that well-being isn't only about chasing happiness—it's about learning to find glimmers of joy and pleasure even in our more difficult moments.

What was even more surprising was that the influence of

mixed emotions on well-being wasn't felt immediately. Sprin-
kling in a dash of joy, happiness, or hope to an otherwise anxiety-
producing event didn't magically zap away the negative. On
the contrary, mixed emotions experienced during one therapy
session were linked to improved psychological well-being the
following week. The true benefit from taking the good with
the bad, in other words, may not be instantaneous but rather
something that unfolds gradually over time.

Other work has also highlighted the advantages of taking
the good with the bad. For example, bereaved adults who express
positive emotions when talking about their deceased spouse
show lower levels of grief over time. Similarly, reliving happy
memories alongside feelings of sadness results in a healthier
course of bereavement. Finally, experiencing mixed emotions in
the face of conflicting goals (say, a desire to eat healthier but also
to have an extra doughnut in the office break room) is linked to
more effort spent resisting temptations. The larger lesson is that,
by adding a measure of positive emotion to the negative, we
make it easier to cope with life's stressors and push through difficult times in the present to better times in the future.

On a more practical level, when we're working through
something painful in the present, we might have better luck if
we pair the struggle with something that makes us smile. That's
an insight that underlies the popularity of something known as
"prize-linked savings accounts." The idea? Get people to save
more money (the painful sacrifice) by pairing the act of saving
with something potentially more fun: the chance to win lottery-
like payouts.

It's also an insight that Katy Milkman, a behavioral economist at the University of Pennsylvania's Wharton School, hit on
to deal with obstacles she faced in her own life. In the early days
of her PhD program, she dealt with two separate struggles: motivating herself to go to the gym and staying on top of a particularly challenging computer science class. Where she didn't have
trouble, however, was in the relaxation department. She loved
spending her nights reading engrossing fiction—books like
Harry Potter or the latest James Patterson thriller. While we typically think of the pleasurable pursuit as the enemy of the challenging work goal—just think how productive we'd be if it
weren't for Netflix—Katy wondered if there was a way to turn
the pleasure into an ally. Could her desire for a good narrative
make her more productive?

FROM GOING TO THE GYM TO BRUSHING YOUR TEETH

Katy, a friend and collaborator, is an extraordinarily creative scientist. Some of that creativity, I suspect, is bred from a sense of
necessity: she constantly tries to engineer solutions to obstacles
in her own life (as well as the lives of countless others). Once,
when we needed to meet but were both pressed for time, she
proposed that we schedule a call ten minutes before we each had
another obligation—that way, she suggested, we wouldn't waste
time and could get down to business. It was this same degree of
resourcefulness that she applied to her inability to work out.
What if, she thought, she only read the next chapter of a thriller

when she was at the gym exercising? Or what if she tackled some of her coursework while she was indulging in a pedicure?

This strategy, which she's labeled "temptation bundling," helped her better accomplish the things in her life that were difficult and stressful. Research she's conducted has found that it works for others as well. For instance, in one study, Katy and her collaborators partnered with the gym on the University of Pennsylvania's campus. They encouraged groups of students to exercise at the start of the fall semester. One group was simply encouraged to work out. Another was told to do their best to pair their workouts with something tempting—namely, a compelling audiobook that the researchers loaded onto the students' personal iPods. But things were more extreme for a third group: students could only access the next bit of content in their chosen audiobooks—which were loaded on iPods locked at the gym—*when* they showed up to work out.

Over the first several weeks of the study, relative to the students who were simply encouraged to work out, the more extreme form of temptation bundling led to a 51 percent increase in workouts. And the intermediate form of temptation bundling—where people were encouraged to listen to audiobooks while they worked out—led to a 29 percent increase.

In a different field experiment conducted with 24 Hour Fitness, Katy and her colleagues found that over the course of a four-week intervention and up to approximately four months afterward, when gym goers were given a free audiobook as well as the encouragement to bundle their temptations, the likelihood of gym visits increased.

When I talked to Katy about this work, she stressed that part of the beauty of temptation bundling is that you might constantly modify the tempting treat—it could always be a book, but every few weeks, of course, that book will be different. What matters is that it's something *you* find fun.

It's a strategy that has potential far beyond the gym. Allie Lieberman, a marketing professor and colleague at UCLA, recently examined another behavior in this context: toothbrushing. As Allie is quick to mention, most of us don't brush our teeth for nearly as long as we're supposed to; I feel compelled to say that she talks about other topics as well, but as someone who used to work in public health, she is passionate about time spent brushing. Dentists recommend two minutes (twice a day—but hopefully, that's obvious). Sure, two minutes may not seem that long when you're streaming a show, scrolling through social media, or mindlessly eating a bag of chips. But standing in your bathroom, brushing your teeth? Those can be two interminable minutes.

To get over this obstacle, Allie proposed something she calls "tangential immersion." If we're at risk of cutting short a boring but important endeavor—like brushing our teeth, washing our hands, or even going on a walk—we may have better luck if we simultaneously engage in something else that takes up some, but not all, of our attention. Indeed, in one study Allie and her colleagues conducted, research participants who watched a relatively immersive documentary video clip about bears and wolves while brushing their teeth brushed for about 30 percent longer than people who watched a less engaging clip of nature scenes.

The nuance here, and where this work goes beyond the classic temptation bundling research I mentioned earlier, is that the engaging task has to be only *slightly* more interesting than the boring one. If you go too far and try to pair your tedious activity with something significantly more complex — say, a challenging word game on your phone — you may abandon your task sooner than you meant to. There's one other key difference: temptation bundling helps you get *started* on a behavior (say, going to the gym), whereas tangential immersion gets you to do a task for a longer time.

It's a tactic that can also be applied to our professional lives. For instance, as Allie has suggested, if a company wants to encourage its employees to thoroughly wash their hands, daily news stories could be displayed on bathroom mirrors for them to read. Or do you have any tedious work tasks you could do while listening to an audiobook, podcast, or even a new album from a favorite artist?

So, taking the good with the bad can be enormously helpful in various situations, from toothbrushing to taxes to vacuuming. But I should be clear: a life where we are constantly trying to kill two birds with one stone may be one that prevents us from being genuinely present for some of our indulgences. We needn't *only* pair pleasurable activities with less desirable ones; there should be times when we "just" read an engaging book, watch the next binge-worthy series, or go to the salon. And one can go too far with these sorts of strategies: a McDonald's in China recently made headlines when a picture surfaced of a customer eating a Big Mac while using an exercise bike inside the restaurant. I don't think that's the kind of "good covering for the bad" that Mitch Hedberg called for. But occasionally pairing indulgences with the things we know we should do — and creating a good match between the two — may help us grow into the people we want to become.

Yet, this isn't the only way to make sacrifices in the present *feel* easier to undertake. Another solution comes from what I'd consider an unlikely source of inspiration: the typewriter industry.

MAKE THE BIG…SMALL

If you had opened Salt Lake City's *Deseret News Salt Lake Telegram* on August 26, 1960, you would've seen a short article detailing the strengths and weaknesses of US presidential candidates John F. Kennedy and Richard Nixon, an editorial about the benefits of going back to school, and a cartoon about the end of the dog days of summer. And in the bottom corner, next to some other ads, you would have seen a promotion for a state-of-the-art Olympia typewriter. A Precision Portable model, to be exact.

Just below a grainy picture of the typewriter, large text screams out: "IT'S YOURS … for just pennies a day!" More than six decades later, I'm sure you've seen other campaigns that have used this sort of approach. For instance, one Chicago mattress firm has claimed that for only ten cents a night, you could enjoy the best sleep of your life. And, back in the 1980s, magazine publishers started to reframe their subscriptions in terms of price per issue rather than price per year.

Does this advertising tactic seem a little...obvious? Perhaps, but it's also been met with success in specific contexts. Those magazine publishers in the '80s? They claim that their price-per-issue ads were 10 percent to 40 percent more effective than the price-per-year ones.

Why might that be the case? When advertisers use a "pennies per day" strategy, what they're doing on the surface is taking some bigger expense and making it feel smaller. Deeper down, though, as economist John Gourville has found, they're making you think of other similar, trivial expenses.

A mattress for $1,000? That's a lot of money! It's probably hard to think of other things — apart from maybe your rent or mortgage — that might fall into the category of "big" expenses. But if you were to keep that mattress for seven years, your costs would amount to roughly forty cents per night. That *feels* a lot less expensive, and it's probably easier to imagine parting with forty cents a day. (For me, the first thing that comes to mind in that pricing ballpark is a stamp...which I rarely use, making it that much easier to think that I'd happily give up forty cents a day in exchange for better sleep!)

This strategy of "making the big small" is yet another way to make present-day sacrifices feel easier. And it's something I put into practice with my collaborators Steve Shu, Shlomo Benartzi, and a financial technology firm in Southern California called Acorns, a savings and investing app primarily aimed at novice investors.

At the time of our project, a few thousand people a day were signing up to invest money with the company. Even though it was good news that so many were starting an initial investment, their accounts would fare better if they continued to save over time. As behavioral economists have found, one way to achieve that goal is to make the act of saving automatic. That is, make it something you don't have to think about or take any action to do.

But how to do *that*? We decided to get a little tricky with how we asked users to join such an automatic savings plan. We asked one group if they'd like to save $150 a month, another if they'd like to save $35 a week, and another if they'd want to save $5 a day. Even though the three approaches add up to roughly the same amount on a monthly basis, the psychological pain associated with each one may be different.

You'll probably agree that five bucks a day feels like an easier sacrifice: we can quickly come up with $5 expenses that we'd be willing to give up. When I talk about this research with others, many point to a single item: a Starbucks coffee. In fact, in annual terms, $5 a day adds up to more total money ($1,825 a year) than

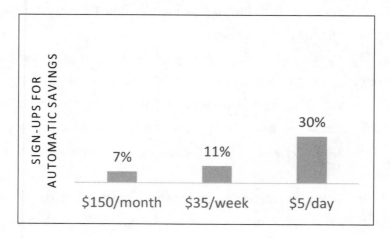

either $150 a month ($1,800 a year) or $35 a week ($1,820 a year). And yet, as you can see in the chart, four times as many users signed up for the savings plan when it was framed in daily rather than monthly (or weekly) terms.

But the daily framing did more than just increase sign-ups. It also helped address something known as the "income savings gap," where less wealthy people have a harder time socking money away simply because they have less of it. Despite this strong tendency, we found that when the plan was framed in terms of dollars per day (compared to dollars per week or month), the income savings gap closed: lower-income and higher-income consumers signed up at the same rate.

You don't have to look far to see this strategy in action, for smaller purchases as well as bigger ones. Although they've been available for years, so-called buy now, pay later payment schemes—in which consumers can spread out the cost of a purchase over several installments—exploded in popularity during the COVID-19 pandemic as more and more people shopped from the comfort of their homes. There's a danger here, though: whether it's a new purse, kitchen gadget, or home sound system, we can get suckered into buying things we can't afford. In fact, at the time of this writing, with almost four out of five American consumers regularly using such payment plans, some economists suggest that there may eventually be a buy now, pay later bubble.

Making the big small isn't just about purchasing consumer goods, however; there are other areas in which this strategy will help. For instance, when it comes to paying off debt, people have an easier time following through on a debt repayment plan where they start by paying off smaller accounts. And asking people to donate four hours of their time per week — or eight hours every two weeks — results in more success than asking for two hundred hours annually.

Generally speaking, breaking a larger goal into its smaller components can help make present-day challenges feel easier, even if there's some nuance to the strategy. As researcher Szu-chi Huang and her colleagues found, breaking things down is especially effective when you are at the starting point of pursuing a goal. You'll be more motivated to burn two hundred calories climbing stairs if you think of the workout in chunks of fifty calories, for example. But once you get close to the end of your goal, it may be better to keep that bigger picture in mind (that is, thinking about that larger overall goal and how close you are to burning all two hundred calories).

When we add up the evidence, the benefits of making the big small outweigh the costs. Yet, we should carefully consider when this approach will benefit us over time compared to when it will make our lives harder. Here are two rules of thumb to simplify things: use the "make the big small" strategy when you are (1) building up your resources versus spending them (for instance: when you're saving for a big trip, think about the amount in broken-down terms, but when you're considering buying a brand-new stereo system, think about the overall cost); and (2) when you are starting an undertaking versus coming close to finishing it (for example, if you are planning on going for a thirty-minute run, at the beginning just think about it in five-minute chunks, but when you near the end, keep in mind how close you are to the thirty-minute mark).

Let me provide just one final strategy for making the present feel easier: celebrate today and skip the sacrifice altogether.

CELEBRATE THE PRESENT

Several years ago, Carl Richards and his family moved to New Zealand. Because they were from the United States and a long way from their friends, Carl and his wife found it hard to spend time away from their kids. Eventually, though, after they made connections in their community, they felt comfortable leaving town without the children in tow. Carl told me that they started to plan a trip—specifically, a sea-kayaking adventure in Nydia Bay, a beautiful, remote part of the world off New Zealand's northeast coast.

The three-day adventure, however, wasn't going to be cheap. Between the kayak rental, the meals, and a stay at a small inn, the whole trip would cost somewhere north of $1,000. Richards, a Certified Financial Planner, is used to weighing the pros and cons of these sorts of financial decisions, and this one was starting to feel overly expensive. He's also the creator of the "Sketch Guy" column, a weekly cartoon that has appeared in the *New York Times* since 2010. In it, he takes complicated financial concepts and conundrums and, in single-panel sketches, distills them into easy-to-grasp ideas.

At first, the sea-kayaking trip seemed like a simple math problem. A thousand bucks was a lot of money! If Richards invested it smartly, with an average return of 7.5 percent, he'd have $4,461 after twenty years! He could make a sacrifice here — possibly by choosing a less expensive trip or skipping it altogether. After all, wasn't it wildly irresponsible to spend all that money just for three days away?

You could argue that, on the surface, Richards's initial instinct was in line with the wishes of his future self. By saving rather than spending, he would put Older Carl in a better place financially.

What if, however, that wasn't the right move? What if there are times when acting in *what we think* are the best interests of our future selves won't make the future any better after all?

Like Richards, we might either skip or put off some experience for later. If that doesn't sound like you, consider how many tourist attractions you've visited in your local area. If you're in Chicago, think about the Art Institute, the Field Museum, and the Willis Tower. Or, if you're in New York City, there are countless examples, from the Empire State Building to the Statue of Liberty. Chances are, you probably haven't been to most of those sites recently (if at all). In fact, as my collaborator Suzanne Shu has found, people who visit Chicago and New York for a few weeks average seeing nearly six sites during their stay. But the residents who live there? They typically only visited three attractions their first year in town.

Sometimes, we save such experiences for the *right* time. If you're just visiting a place, the right time is now; when else would you have an opportunity to do so? If you live there, though, you can see the museums, monuments, buildings, and historical sites at your convenience. You can save them for your future self to enjoy. But just as tomorrow seems to never come when you need to start a diet or clean out the attic, it might also not come for some of the more *pleasurable* things in life, too, like visiting a famous museum, making a reservation at a fine restaurant, or purchasing a nice bottle of wine to celebrate a special day or achievement.

In putting experiences off for too long, we may diminish their value entirely. A perfect illustration of this idea comes from one of my favorite memes. It's a picture of what looks like a Venetian gondola, and while the driver is smiling wide, his two elderly passengers are slumped together, sleeping soundly. As one Twitter user commented, "Don't wait till you're this old to retire and travel the world."

If you've ever rushed to use frequent-flier miles before they expire—taking a less than ideal trip solely to use up those miles—you'd be guilty of the same behavior. Or perhaps you've waited for the perfect occasion to use a restaurant gift card only to find the restaurant closed.

These examples may seem relatively trivial. But this same tendency to put things off for tomorrow—perhaps with the best intentions—can result in much more severe consequences.

To illustrate, let me introduce you to a movement called FIRE, whose members devote themselves to achieving a life of *financial independence*, allowing them to *retire early*—in their twenties or early thirties. To accomplish such a seemingly impossible goal, they cut their expenses to the bone and save intensely (as much as half or more of their income).

Now, there are certainly folks who thrive on this austere life-style. And I should note that some principles of the movement make sense. Clearly, if you want to have more resources later, figuring out which expenses you can cut now is a wise exercise.

But others who have tried it have realized that the herculean effort to make the future work-free can come at a cost they aren't willing to pay. Lisa Harrison, who was part of the movement for two years, is one example. She used to love watching "HGTV before bed, going out for pizza on Friday, and having coffee at our favorite downtown spot every Sunday." Sure, these things cost money, she realized, and by removing them from her budget, she and her husband were saving more toward early retirement. "But cutting these things out came at the price of our day-to-day happiness." As her net worth increased, her well-being plummeted. And that realization eventually led her to exit the movement.

Her experience with FIRE demonstrates the dangers of living excessively for tomorrow. Researchers have labeled this sort of behavior "hyperopic," and it occurs when we are so farsighted that we later regret our choices.

I've spent most of this book preaching the importance of knowing and befriending our future selves. It might seem strange that I'm suddenly discussing times when we should skip sacrifices and . . . just go for joy in the present. But I don't think so: living too much for tomorrow may make life worse for both our present and future selves.

Harrison navigated this tension by introducing more balance into her family's life. Although she and her husband abandoned the idea of retiring early, they did retain one aspect of their time with the FIRE movement. Namely, they now more carefully consider their values when spending money. Things like subscription TV, pizza on Friday, and coffee outings are back on the table. But so is a more intentional budget and approach to financial decisions.

As a result, Harrison has come a long way from her happiness free fall. Her more balanced financial approach has helped create "a life of options that we want...both now and later."

Unfortunately, there's no guidebook to figuring out the so-called right balance between now and later. What worked for Harrison and her family might be different from what works for you. Yet, thinking through when it makes sense to indulge versus restrain, and when it makes sense to prioritize our current or our future selves, may go a long way toward creating harmony over time.

———

Ultimately, Carl Richards and his wife decided to spend the money and go on their kayaking trip. Roughly a half hour after paddling out to sea, they floated by a small cove full of starfish, stingrays, and sea urchins. As he explained, he and his wife looked at each other and incredulously asked how they ever considered *not* going on that trip.

We're regularly reminded that we need to save for tomorrow. To some extent, that's a central message of this book. But as Richards put it, that's only one side of the coin: "Don't forget about the other side: Spend for tomorrow. Because it's not just money you're going to need off in the distant future." If we live only for tomorrow, we'll deprive our future selves of the very memories and experiences and friends and family that help make life worth living.

Richards's insight, of course, doesn't apply to just monetary expenses. In the past year, I've been spending more and more of my time on work projects. As with most everyone else, COVID took a toll on my productivity, and I've convinced myself that working harder now will help me get back on track, ultimately providing benefits for my future self.

Several months ago, though, I decided to take a morning off and walk my son to his preschool. Although it's a long walk, I knew it would give me a chance to hang out with him one-on-one, something that almost never happens. But about twenty minutes after leaving our house, we noticed a little commotion starting to take place. Two cars had slowed to a stop, and an Animal Control truck idled near them. As we got closer, we immediately realized why: a small and confused chicken was running through the street. We live in Los Angeles, so the number of times that we had seen live poultry in the neighborhood before this moment was exactly...zero. I was amused, but my son was beside himself, happily screaming at the top of his lungs that there was an actual "CHICKEN IN THE ROAD!" For the rest of the walk, it was all he could talk about, and it was the first thing he told his teachers when I dropped him off. Six months later, the chicken story has become part of our family lore and continues to be a tale my son gleefully tells strangers and friends alike.

Had I spent that morning working, I certainly would have made more progress on my projects. But it's also abundantly clear what I would have missed.

The final way, then, to make the present easier is to give in occasionally. To skip the sacrifice and indulge in the experiences that cost money and time but bring a different sort of wealth. That may be a way not only to make tomorrow better, but to make today better, too.

Highlights

- Tension exists when Current You has to sacrifice for the benefit of Future You. But you can improve future outcomes by making those present-day sacrifices easier to undertake.
- One category of strategies is to "take the good with the bad": Experiencing positive emotions in the face of negative events may provide a buffer of sorts, allowing better insight into stressors big and small. "Temptation bundling," where you pair tempting positive activities with the things that feel like sacrifices, can be effective. And "tangential immersion," where you pair the boring task with something that's *slightly* more interesting, can help you stay on track.
- You can also "make the big small" and break sacrifices down into smaller, easier-to-accomplish pieces.
- We must also find ways to celebrate the present. Recognize that if we live only for tomorrow, we may arrive at a future that's devoid of the memories and experiences that make life worth living.

EPILOGUE

As I've been researching and writing this book, the world has experienced a series of catastrophic events. It's a list that sounds like it could come from a bad summer blockbuster: warring nations, a shape-shifting virus, rising inflation, sociopolitical upheaval, climate disasters, and so on. (All that's missing is an imminent asteroid.) Some—or perhaps a lot of—anxiety about our present circumstances certainly seems warranted! In fact, the World Health Organization announced that in 2020 alone, cases of major depression and anxiety disorders increased by more than 25 percent.

Given these uncertainties and disruptions, it can feel pointless to make plans for the future. A recent report from Fidelity, for instance, found that almost half of adults between eighteen and thirty-five don't see a point in saving for the future "until things return to normal." Stand-up comedian Hannah Jones, twenty-seven, explained it this way: "I'm not going to deprive myself some of the comforts of life now for a future that feels like it could be ripped away from me at any moment...No, I'm not saving for retirement. I'm going to spend my money *now*, while we still have a supply chain at all."

These observations capture our collective weariness. However, I see reasons for hope amid all the gloom and doom. Although we never should stop planning for the future entirely, taking a pause can allow for more reflection on what matters. As an analogy, milestone birthdays often create little breaks in our lives, offering us a chance to take stock of what we've accomplished (or not) in the previous decade and what we hope to tackle in the next one. In the same way, the great global pause that COVID inflicted may have prompted many of us to focus on what we truly value. As my collaborators Adam Galinsky and Laura Kray put it, the pandemic created a sort of "universal midlife crisis," forcing us to reconsider how we spend our precious resources of time and money.

And yet, the current state of affairs doesn't mean that we can ignore our distant or very distant futures altogether. The march of time is blind to the strife of the present, and the future will arrive whether we've planned for it or not. After all, this isn't the first time that rampant uncertainty has made planning feel pointless. Consider, for instance, how people felt at other precarious historical moments like the Great Depression, the Cuban Missile Crisis, or the 2008 financial crisis. Surely, just like now, it must have been difficult to think about the years ahead during those angst-filled periods. What would have happened, though, if plan making had come to a screeching halt then?

Zander Rose, the executive director of the Long Now Foundation, a nonprofit dedicated to long-term thinking, elegantly summed up these tensions: "Many of our present problems," he told me, "are because of a lack of long-term thinking in the past."

Present-day problems should of course demand the lion's share of our attention. But solely focusing on in-the-moment problems may mean that those same issues could appear again and intensify in pernicious ways in the years, decades, and centuries to come.

Given these competing demands — the stressful present versus the distant future — how should we allocate our mental resources? It's a hard question that begets an even harder question, as many of our plans for the future must now take into account periods that are much longer than our own lifetimes. In essence, we're being asked to make choices that will benefit people who will live long after we are gone.

Nowhere is this topic more relevant than in the context of the environment. Between rising temperatures and rising tides, and an increase in catastrophic weather events worldwide, the impact of climate change is now being felt. Yet many of the severely negative consequences — some of which have already begun occurring — will impact future generations. Future generations, I might add, whom we don't know and whom we can barely even fathom. It's difficult to imagine and relate to our own future selves, but it's far harder to relate to our unborn descendants. They're not just strangers — they don't even exist yet.

What can we do, then, to change the perilous future? Given the psychological challenges, should we just give up and burn more fossil fuels? We can't even motivate ourselves to go to the gym; changing the modern economy seems like a daunting ambition.

But I'm not ready to surrender — I think there are practical steps we can take to make it easier for us to act on behalf of the planet and our descendants, even if we'll never inhabit that future Earth or meet those future people. Recent work by my colleagues and me points to one initial approach: to increase the chances that people will take action for the distant future, have them pay attention to the *past*. Sensing deeper roots in one's community—feeling a part of what has been and what will come to be—for instance, is linked to a greater likelihood of adopting solar panels. And focusing on the long and rich history of one's country makes it that much easier to look farther ahead to the future and subsequently invest in the environment.

This work is preliminary, but it raises an interesting possibility: rather than thinking forward to more vivid futures, if we want to save our great-grandchildren from a broiling planet, perhaps we should consider the people who came before us and the sacrifices they made on our behalf. Just as we are a chain of separate selves over our own lives, on a larger scale, we are part of a chain of human beings that extends back hundreds of thousands of years. Those early humans didn't know us and could never have imagined today's world, but we exist only because they were able to consider the future in some rudimentary way. Isn't it our duty to do the same, both to give ourselves a brighter tomorrow and to ensure that people we'll never meet will continue to thrive?

These questions are just scratching the surface, though, and more work certainly needs to be done. One thing, however, is clear. Whether we're on a timeline of 15 years or 150, whether we are focused on our future selves or our future grand-children, and whether the seas of the present are smooth or choppy, we'll have a better shot at improving our lives once we come to understand, know, and love the people we will one day become.

ACKNOWLEDGMENTS

A huge thank you to the team that worked with me tirelessly to make this project a reality. Tracy Behar, when I considered my ideal editor, I wanted someone with your sharp eye but hadn't banked on how much I'd appreciate and value your warmth and generosity as well. Thank you, also, to my astute agent, Rafe Sagalyn; I am grateful for the guidance and strong encouragement you provided from the very beginning. To Karina Leon, Talia Krohn, Juliana Horbachevsky, Katherine Akey, Betsy Uhrig, Lucy Kim, Pat Godefroy, Travis Tatman, and Dave Nussbaum, thank you for doing all that you did to make sure more people got to know and improve their future selves.

This book represents research and thinking that have taken place over many years with the support of some truly wonderful mentors. Laura Carstensen, thank you for giving me the freedom to think about big ideas and always pushing me to consider the big problems we might solve with our work. Brian Knutson, I'm grateful to you for making me a more careful researcher and thinker. Martha Shenton, I appreciate how you taught me to make space for a rigorous academic life as well as a rich personal one. Keith Maddox, thank you for fueling my first interest in social psychology. And Adam Galinsky, thank you for helping me learn how truly fun the research process could be.

Throughout my writing journey, a number of friends and colleagues read earlier drafts and helped me express my ideas more clearly. Thank you to Adam Alter, Eugene Caruso, J. D. Lopez, Sam Maglio, and Kathleen Vohs for your critical eyes, open ears, and practical advice. I can't believe my good fortune that I get to know and spend time with each one of you. And thank you to Jonah Lehrer; your editing superpowers made my rough edges smoother.

I've been lucky to have a group of colleagues from UCLA whom I can safely call my close friends. To Craig Fox, Noah Goldstein, Cassie Mogilner Holmes, Allie Lieberman, Suzanne Shu, and the rest of the marketing and BDM areas Franklin Shaddy, Sanjay Sood, Stephen Spiller, you make meaningful work a daily pleasure. Having spent the first few years of my academic career at NYU, I'm fortunate to have a similarly loved group of colleagues from there: thank you to Geeta Menon, Tom Meyvis, Priya Raghubir, Yaacov Trope, and Russ Winer, for helping me get my footing in the academic world.

None of the work I've undertaken could have been possible without so many dedicated collaborators, all of whom have pushed my thinking further and made the experience of conducting research much more enjoyable than I could ever imagine. In particular, for work related to this book, thank you to Jennifer Aaker, Jon Adler, Dan Bartels, Shlomo Benartzi, Debbie Bocian, Bryan Bollinger, Chris Bryan, Dan Goldstein, Cassie Mogilner Holmes, Derek Isaacowitz, Sue Kerbel, Jeff Larsen,

Sam Maglio, Joe Mikels, Katy Milkman, Loran Nordgren, Mike North, Jordi Quoidbach, Abe Rutchick, Greg Samanez-Larkin, Anuj Shah, Avni Shah, Marissa Sharif, Bill Sharpe, Steve Shu, Abby Sussman, Diana Tamir, Jean-Louis van Gelder, Dan Walters, and Adam Waytz for spending so many of your precious hours with me.

To my doctoral students and postdocs—Steph Tully, Adam Greenberg, Kate Christensen, Elicia John, Joey Reiff, David Zimmerman, Malena de la Fuente, Taylor Bergstrom, Poruz Khambatta, Megan Weber, Ilana Brody, and Eitan Rude—thank you for always helping me stay on the cutting edge of science and for making my research family feel more like an actual family.

I've benefited tremendously from a dedicated team of research assistants who helped me get the details right. I'm grateful to the students in my Fiat Lux class, Anmol Bhide, Zoe Curran, Celia Gleason, Audrey Goman, Haley Karchmer, Elizabeth O'Brien, and Hannah Zhou, for all the hours they spent working with me. Beyond details, though, I was lucky to be able to talk to many colleagues, friends, and people I've never met who had interesting stories to tell. To Eve-Marie Blouin-Hudon, Cesar Cruz, Rodica Damian, Alex DeLuca, Utpal Dholikia, Michael Dukakis, Liz Dunn, Eric Eskin, Alex Genevsky, Dan Gilbert, Dave Krippendorf, George Loewenstein, Meghan Meyer, B. J. Miller, Sarah Molouki, John Monterosso, Tim Mueller, Ann Napolitano, Daphna Oyserman, Tim Pychyl, Jordi Quoidbach, Brent Roberts, Michael Schrage, Janet Schwartz, Marissa Sharif, Fuschia Sirois, Deborah Small, Nina Strohminger, Oleg Urminsky, and Gal Zauberman: I am so appreciative of your willingness to answer my questions as well as the invaluable insights you've given me.

The process of working on this book—during a pandemic, no less—had its predictable ups and downs. I am fortunate to have a robust community of friends who were there for both, and several of who provided treasured advice throughout. To Mike Ashton, Sarah Ashton, Mike Champion, Annie Cox, Danny Cox, Brad Dakake, Daniel Farag, Perry Farag, Tori Fram, James Myers, and Laurel Myers: thank you for your regular support as well as your opinions on everything from the cover font to the number of exclamation points I should use. And to Adam Alter and Nicholas Hengen Fox, thank you for listening to my thoughts on an almost daily basis and for providing me with deep perspectives that range far beyond my own.

Apart from my friends and colleagues, I couldn't have written this book without the support of my family. To my parents, Robin and Seth Ersner-Hershfield: I always said that our family didn't need another psychologist, but in this case, imitation is truly the highest form of flattery. I can't tell you enough how much I appreciate all that you've done for me, from instilling in me a love of learning when I was little to helping with childcare now. In many ways, you both represent my own future self, and that gives me a great deal of hope. To my grandmother Deenah Ersner, who turned ninety-nine while I worked on this project: I count myself among the luckiest of people to have you, your wisdom, and your warmth in my life.

I've also had the great fortune of having an amazing second family in the form of my warm and caring in-laws. Thank you to

John Heil, Nancy Heil, Whitney Abramo, and John Abramo for adding so much joy to my days.

There's an academic debate surrounding the well-being benefits of having children, with many data points suggesting that post-kid happiness levels aren't exactly what they were pre-kid. When I was months away from becoming a father, I ran into a wonderful colleague, Yaacov Trope, and told him I was excited about having our first child but also anxious that the research findings might ring true in my life. Stop worrying, he told me; once you have children, happiness is no longer one color but instead becomes a many-colored phenomenon. How right he was. Hayes and Smith, you add so much meaning, laughter, and insight to my life every day. Hayes, whether it's been your witty sense of humor or your loving approach to friendship, I've loved watching you grow into yourself. Smith, I'm not offended that you prefer your mother over me — who wouldn't? — but I still cherish the time we spend together. In the years to come, I'll walk you wherever you need to go, whenever you want, whether there's a chicken in the road or not. And of course, I can't forget Oliver, the original loving "child" in our life, whose bark regularly interrupted me but also warded off many imaginary intruders.

Finally, thank you to Jennifer. When we first met, I saw my future self as an older man surrounded by one giant question — who would be my partner in life? I couldn't be happier that the answer is you, with your clever wit, your fierce passion for helping others, and your desire to do right in the world. I feel lucky that I get to travel through time by your side. I appreciate all that you do to make sure that our family is content now and will be in the years that lie ahead. And whether it's come in the form of reading every word I write, listening to me talk excitedly about my latest research, or doing more than your half of the parenting, thank you for giving me immeasurable love and support over the years.

NOTES

Introduction

x: *The scenario I've just described*...T. Chiang, *The Merchant and the Alchemist's Gate* (Burton, MI: Subterranean Press, 2007).

xi: *what's now known as the "default network"*...M. E. Raichle, A. M. MacLeod, A. Z. Snyder, W. J. Powers, D. A. Gusnard, and G. L. Shulman, "A Default Mode of Brain Function," *Proceedings of the National Academy of Sciences of the United States of America* 98, no. 2 (2001): 676–682.

xi: *"the defining property of human intelligence"*...S. Johnson, "The Human Brain Is a Time Traveler," *New York Times,* November 15, 2018, https://www.nytimes.com/interactive/2018/11/15/magazine/tech-design-ai-prediction.html.

xii: *"ability to contemplate the future"*...M. E. P. Seligman and J. Tierney, "We Aren't Built to Live in the Moment," *New York Times,* May 19, 2017, https://www.nytimes.com/2017/05/19/opinion/sunday/why-the-future-is-always-on-your-mind.html.

xii: *Rahbar was one of more than eighteen thousand people*...C. Yu, "A Simple Exercise for Coping with Pandemic Anxiety," *Rewire,* November 27, 2020, https://www.rewire.org/a-simple-exercise-for-coping-with-pandemic-anxiety/?fbclid=IwAR3jRvJFN98AXg998P3UCI3mRaO583uhUSf7Pr-dXJENkD0n7ZUqXHiHzeI.

xii: *Some are riddled with anxieties*...Anonymous, letter, May 5, 2017, FutureMe, https://www.futureme.org/letters/public/9115689-a-letter-from-may-5th-2017?offset=0.

xii: *Some offer encouragement*...Anonymous, letter, September 11, 2016, FutureMe, https://www.futureme.org/letters/public/8565331-a-letter-from-september-11th-2016?offset=7.

xii: *some are just funny*...Anonymous, "Read me," October 24, 2009, FutureMe, https://www.futureme.org/letters/public/893193-read-me?offset=3.

xv: *there are lots of future selves along the way*...Previous researchers talk about this idea in terms of the "possible identities" of our future selves, some positive and some negative. Although negative future selves can also be motivating in certain circumstances, in this book, I focus on the positive, ideal, and realistic future selves we wish to become. For a deeper dive into possible selves, see the work of Daphna Oyserman and her colleagues, especially D. Oyserman and L. James, "Possible Identities," in *Handbook of Identity Theory and Research,* ed.

S. Schwartz, K. Luyckx, and V. Vignoles (New York: Springer, 2011), 117–145; and D. Oyserman and E. Horowitz, "Future Self and Current Action: Integrated Review and Identity-Based Motivation Synthesis," *Advances in Motivation Science* (forthcoming), https://psyarxiv.com/24wvd/.

xvi: *Those who confronted their future selves*...H. E. Hershfield, D. G. Goldstein, W. F. Sharpe, et al., "Increasing Saving Behavior Through Age-Progressed Renderings of the Future Self," *Journal of Marketing Research* 48, special issue (2011): S23–S37.

xvi: *I've since tested this same sort of intervention*...J. D. Robalino, A. Fishbane, D. G. Goldstein, and H. E. Hershfield, "Saving for Retirement: A Real-World Test of Whether Seeing Photos of One's Future Self Encourages Contributions," *Behavioral Science and Policy* (forthcoming).

Chapter 1: *Are We the "Same" over Time?*

5: *This doesn't excuse his violence*...For details about Pedro ex-Matador's life, see "Case 127: Killer Petey," *Casefile*, February 4, 2021, accessed July 13, 2022, https://casefilepodcast.com/case-127-killer-petey/.

9–10: *Plutarch discussed such issues through the story of the Greek hero Theseus*...Plutarch, *Plutarch's Lives*, trans. B. Perrin (Cambridge, MA: Harvard University Press, 1926).

11: *Jerzy Bielecki and Cyla Cybulska, who met*...D. Hevesi, "Jerzy Bielecki Dies at 90; Fell in Love in a Nazi Camp," *New York Times*, October 11, 2011, https://www.nytimes.com/2011/10/24/world/europe/jerzy-bielecki-dies-at-90-fell-in-love-in-a-nazi-camp.html. I first came across this anecdote in R. I. Damian, M. Spengler, A. Sutu, and B. W. Roberts, "Sixteen Going on Sixty-Six: A Longitudinal Study of Personality Stability and Change Across 50 Years," *Journal of Personality and Social Psychology* 117, no. 3 (2019): 674–695.

12: *"We marry," de Botton writes*...A. de Botton, "Why You Will Marry the Wrong Person," *New York Times*, May 28, 2016, https://www.nytimes.com/2016/05/29/opinion/sunday/why-you-will-marry-the-wrong-person.html.

13: *published a paper that looked at personality continuity*...Damian et al., "Sixteen Going on Sixty-Six."

14: *most people change in terms of*...Growth in conscientiousness and emotional stability doesn't occur simply as a result of getting married or having children. Rather, it seems that growth in these traits is something that happens organically over time. Even adults who were imprisoned for part of their younger years show similar levels of growth to those of their non-incarcerated peers after they've finished their sentences. J. Morizot and M. Le Blanc, "Continuity and Change in Personality Traits from Adolescence to Midlife: A 25-Year Longitudinal Study Comparing Representative and Adjudicated Men," *Journal of Personality* 71 no. 5 (2003): 705–755.

15: *whether we are the same person over time*...When talking about the sameness of identity over time, philosophers often refer to "qualitative" and "numerical" identity. Qualitative identity means that two things share all the same properties.

Numerical identity implies that two things are in fact the same thing. If, for example, we are eating at a restaurant together, and we both order a slice of pepperoni and mushroom pizza, those two slices are qualitatively identical. They both contain the same ingredients. But they are clearly not numerically identical—there are two slices of pizza! And if you eat yours, it has no impact on mine. In terms of people, when we ask about "sameness" or "identity," we are really asking about qualitative identity, recognizing that an earlier self and a later self are not numerically identical.

16: *Sure, your face might have aged*...E. Olson, *The Human Animal: Personal Identity Without Psychology* (Oxford: Oxford University Press, 1997); B. A. Williams, "Personal Identity and Individuation," *Proceedings of the Aristotelian Society* 57 (1956): 229–252.

16: *what persists over time is the physical*...For accessible and short overviews of the philosophy of identity, see E. T. Olson, "Personal Identity," in *The Stanford Encyclopedia of Philosophy,* ed. Edward N. Zalta (Stanford University, summer 2022), https://plato.stanford.edu/archives/sum2022/entries/identity-personal/; and "Personal Identity: Crash Course Philosophy #19," CrashCourse, June 27, 2016, YouTube video, 8:32, accessed July 13, 2022, https://www.youtube.com/watch?v=trqDnLNRuSc.

16: *He ups the ante*...Williams, "Personal Identity."

17: *You'd remain living, but your memories*...P. F. Snowdon, *Persons, Animals, Ourselves* (Oxford: Oxford University Press, 2014).

17: *what makes you the same person over time*...J. Locke, *An Essay Concerning Human Understanding* (Philadelphia: Kay & Troutman, 1847).

19: *people were roughly three times more likely*...S. Blok, G. Newman, J. Behr, and L. J. Rips, "Inferences About Personal Identity," in *Proceedings of the Annual Meeting of the Cognitive Science Society,* vol. 23 (Mahwah, NJ: Erlbaum, 2001), 80–85. There's a second experiment in this paper where Blok and his colleagues change things up even more. People in the study still read about Jim the accountant who needs a brain transplant. But now some of them read that the contents of his brain are transferred to a computer, which is then placed inside a robot. Others, however, read that the brain itself is transplanted into the robot (just like the first study I talked about in the text). Again, Jim's memories are preserved or they are deleted. Now the robot is only considered to still be Jim if it has the physical brain *and* the memories. If just the memories are transplanted to the robot via a computer (and without a physical brain), then people are much less likely to vote that the robot can still be thought of as Jim. From a layperson standpoint, then, it may be the case that there's a mix of the body theory and memory theory that wins out. What matters is not only the memories, but the brain that houses them.

20: *These are disorders where the brain has changed fundamentally*...N. Strohminger and S. Nichols, "Neurodegeneration and Identity," *Psychological Science* 26, no. 9 (2015): 1469–1479.

21: *frontotemporal dementia was seen as having*...This result wasn't simply because of any differences in disease severity—daily functioning was similar among the three disease types.

22: *these sorts of moral traits, when changed*...L. Heiphetz, N. Strohminger, S. A. Gelman, and L. L. Young, "Who Am I? The Role of Moral Beliefs in Children's and Adults' Understanding of Identity," *Journal of Experimental Social Psychology* 78 (September 2018): 210–219.

Chapter 2: *Is Future Me Really...Me?*

25: *studies have shown that the lagoon*...J. H. Ólafsson, B. Sigurgeirsson, and R. Pálsdóttir, "Psoriasis Treatment: Bathing in a Thermal Lagoon Combined with UVB, Versus UVB Treatment Only," *Acta Derm Venereol (Stockh)* 76 (1996): 228–230; S. Grether-Beck, K. Mühlberg, H. Brenden, et al., "Bioactive Molecules from the Blue Lagoon: In Vitro and In Vivo Assessment of Silica Mud and Microalgae Extracts for Their Effects on Skin Barrier Function and Prevention of Skin Ageing," *Experimental Dermatology* 17, no. 9 (2008): 771–779.

26: *"Imagine that you have a onetime opportunity"*...For a full discussion of the vampire problem and the concept of transformative experiences more generally, see L. A. Paul, *Transformative Experience* (Oxford: Oxford University Press, 2014).

29: *between the ages of six and nine, children*...W. Damon and D. Hart, "The Development of Self-Understanding from Infancy Through Adolescence," *Child Development* 53, no. 4 (1982): 841–864.

30: *Hume argued that there is no such thing as a self*...D. Hume, *A Treatise of Human Nature,* ed. D. F. Norton and M. J. Norton (Oxford: Oxford University Press, 2007).

31: *he even had the same meal each morning*...For a profile of Parfit's life, see L. MacFarquhar, "How to Be Good," *The New Yorker,* September 5, 2011, https://www.newyorker.com/magazine/2011/09/05/how-to-be-good.

31: *He starts by asking that you imagine a tele-transporter machine*...D. Parfit, *Reasons and Persons* (Oxford: Oxford University Press, 1984).

33: *what matters is the sense of connection*...D. Parfit, "Personal Identity," *Philosophical Review* 80, no. 1 (1971): 3–27.

34: *89 percent of adults over sixty-five were fully vaccinated*...B. Wallace-Wells, "An Uncertain New Phase in the Pandemic, in Which Cases Surge but Deaths Do Not," *The New Yorker,* July 31, 2021, https://www.newyorker.com/news/annals-of-inquiry/an-uncertain-new-phase-of-the-pandemic-in-which-cases-surge-but-deaths-do-not. Vaccination statistics derived from https://data.cdc.gov/Vaccinations/Archive-COVID-19-Vaccination-and-Case-Trends-by-Ag/gxj9-t96f/data.

34: *one of the main benefits of vaccination*...T. Lorenz, "To Fight Vaccine Lies, Authorities Recruit an 'Influencer Army,'" *New York Times,* August 1, 2021, https://www.nytimes.com/2021/08/01/technology/vaccine-lies-influencer-army.html?action=click&module=Spotlight&pgtype=Homepage.

35: *"This boy," writes Parfit, "does not identify with his future self"*...Parfit, *Reasons and Persons,* 319–320.

36:   *"So, you get up in the morning..." Seinfeld,* season 5, episode 7, "The Glasses," written by T. Gammill and M. Pross, produced by J. Seinfeld, P. Melmanand, M. Gross, and S. Greenberg, directed by T. Cherones, aired September 30, 1993, on NBC.

37:   *the future self looks as if it is another person*...E. Pronin and L. Ross, "Temporal Differences in Trait Self-Ascription: When the Self Is Seen as an Other," *Journal of Personality and Social Psychology* 90, no. 2 (2006): 197–209. In the original study I've described, there were three additional conditions, where participants pictured a meal from the very distant past (from their childhood), yesterday, or tomorrow. For the yesterday and tomorrow images, a first-person perspective was overwhelmingly likely to be used. But, just like the distant-future condition, a third-person perspective was more likely to be adopted for the distant past. I should also cautiously note that this particular study contained a small sample of people (about twenty per condition). However, there are six other studies in this paper that show converging evidence for the idea that future selves are seen as "other" people, most of which use larger samples.

38:   *When it came to assigning the disgusting liquid*...E. Pronin, C. Y. Olivola, and K. A. Kennedy, "Doing unto Future Selves as You Would Do unto Others: Psychological Distance and Decision Making," *Personality and Social Psychology Bulletin* 34, no. 2 (2008): 224–236.

38:   *we treat them as others, too*...Other research has also found, indirectly, that the future self is viewed as an other. When describing others, we can use either broad-level categories (for example, female, Black) or more concrete and specific ones (for example, female executive at General Motors, a Black activist at the forefront of the Black Lives Matter movement). We tend to use the more abstract categories when talking about our future selves—just as we are likely to do when talking about others—but are more likely to use specific categories when referring to ourselves, today. C. J. Wakslak, S. Nussbaum, N. Liberman, and Y. Trope, "Representations of the Self in the Near and Distant Future," *Journal of Personality and Social Psychology* 95, no. 4 (2008): 757–773.

40:   *this region was more active when people thought about themselves*...W. M. Kelley, C. N. Macrae, C. L. Wyland, S. Caglar, S. Inati, and T. F. Heatherton, "Finding the Self? An Event-Related fMRI Study," *Journal of Cognitive Neuroscience* 14, no. 5 (2002): 785–794.

42:   *activity in the brain that arises when thinking about the future self*...H. Ersner-Hershfield, G. E. Wimmer, and B. Knutson, "Saving for the Future Self: Neural Measures of Future Self-Continuity Predict Temporal Discounting," *Social Cognitive and Affective Neuroscience* 4, no. 1 (2009): 85–92.

42:   *Other studies have since come to similar conclusions*...See, for example, K. M. Lempert, M. E. Speer, M. R. Delgado, and E. A. Phelps, "Positive Autobiographical Memory Retrieval Reduces Temporal Discounting," *Social Cognitive and Affective Neuroscience* 12, no. 10 (2017): 1584–1593; and J. P. Mitchell, J. Schirmer, D. L. Ames, and D. T. Gilbert, "Medial Prefrontal Cortex Predicts Intertemporal Choice," *Journal of Cognitive Neuroscience* 23, no. 4 (2011): 857–866.

42: *TMS is currently being used*...L. L. Carpenter, P. G. Janicak, S. T. Aaronson, et al., "Transcranial Magnetic Stimulation (TMS) for Major Depression: A Multisite, Naturalistic, Observational Study of Acute Treatment Outcomes in Clinical Practice," *Depression and Anxiety* 29, no. 7 (2012): 587–596.

43: *When the mind-traveling region of the brain was shut off*...A. Soutschek, C. C. Ruff, T. Strombach, T. Kalenscher, and P. N. Tobler, "Brain Stimulation Reveals Crucial Role of Overcoming Self-Centeredness in Self-Control," *Science Advances* 2, no. 10 (2016): e1600992.

44: *people see a clear separation*...S. Brietzke and M. L. Meyer, "Temporal Self-Compression: Behavioral and Neural Evidence That Past and Future Selves Are Compressed as They Move Away from the Present," *Proceedings of the National Academy of Sciences* 118, no. 49 (2021): e2101403118.

44: *just an analogy*...In the most direct examination of this analogy, Sarah Molouki and Daniel Bartels asked research participants to divvy up a hypothetical allocation of money toward others or to their future selves. Were future selves truly treated as others? In important ways, yes. Four characteristics dictated allocation decisions—need, deservingness, liking, and similarity—and the influence of these four factors was similar regardless of whether allocations were made to the future self or to others. However, people consistently chose to donate more money to their future selves than they did to others, suggesting that the "future self as other" analogy goes only so far. Yes, the future self may be treated as another person, but it's probably a special type of other, one whom we're more willing to help. S. Molouki and D. M. Bartels, "Are Future Selves Treated Like Others? Comparing Determinants and Levels of Intrapersonal and Interpersonal Allocations," *Cognition* 196 (2020): 104150.

45: *what truly matters is what sort of other people they are*...This perspective was captured eloquently by philosopher Jennifer Whiting. Noting that we often make sacrifices on behalf of close others, the same "goes for our future selves; benefits to them can compensate for burdens imposed on our present selves, if our present selves care about them in ways analogous to those in which we care for our friends." J. Whiting, "Friends and Future Selves," *Philosophical Review* 95, no. 4 (1986): 547–580; quote, 560.

Chapter 3: *Relationships with Our Future Selves*

47: *Franklin wasn't satisfied with abstract wishes*...B. Franklin, *Mr. Franklin: A Selection from His Personal Letters,* ed. L. W. Labree and J. B. Whitfield Jr. (New Haven, CT: Yale University Press, 1956), 27–29.

51: *attendees at an "Undoing Aging" conference*...B. M. Tausen, A. Csordas, and C. N. Macrae, "The Mental Landscape of Imagining Life Beyond the Current Life Span: Implications for Construal and Self-Continuity," *Innovation in Aging* 4, no. 3 (2020): 1–16.

52: *in one of my first attempts at measuring relationships*...On a seven-point scale ranging from 1 (I don't like my future self at all) to 7 (I like my future self very much), they scored an average of roughly 6.

52: *Aron was desperate to find a research topic*... UC Berkeley, "The Science of Love with Arthur Aron, February 12, 2015, YouTube video, 3:17, https://www.youtube.com/watch?v=gVff7TjzF3A.

53: *best known for generating thirty-six questions*... A. Aron, E. Melinat, E. N. Aron, R. D. Vallone, and R. J. Bator, "The Experimental Generation of Interpersonal Closeness: A Procedure and Some Preliminary Findings," *Personality and Social Psychology Bulletin* 23, no. 4 (1997): 363–377.

53: *that's a form of including your partner in your self*... A. Aron, E. N. Aron, M. Tudor, and G. Nelson, "Close Relationships as Including Other in the Self," *Journal of Personality and Social Psychology* 60, no. 2 (1991): 241–253. Other researchers have also talked about "self-expansiveness" in different contexts, such as H. L. Friedman, "The Self-Expansive Level Form: A Conceptualization and Measurement of a Transpersonal Construct," *Journal of Transpersonal Psychology* 15, no. 1 (1983): 37–50.

53: *Aron and Aron came up with a simple drawing*... A. Aron, E. N. Aron, and D. Smollan, "Inclusion of Other in the Self Scale and the Structure of Interpersonal Closeness," *Journal of Personality and Social Psychology* 63, no. 4 (1992): 596–612.

54: *Specifically, we asked about a future self who was ten years out*... H. Ersner-Hershfield, M. T. Garton, K. Ballard, G. R. Samanez-Larkin, and B. Knutson, "Don't Stop Thinking About Tomorrow: Individual Differences in Future Self-Continuity Account for Saving," *Judgment and Decision Making* 4, no. 4 (2009): 280–286. Notably, earlier work also looked at the link between similarity toward one's future self and behavior on a laboratory financial decision-making task, but found no relationship. In that particular paper, researcher Shane Frederick asked people to report the similarity they felt toward their future selves on a 100-point scale. And, rather than a series of simple financial choices between smaller amounts of money now versus larger amounts of money later, Frederick asked his research participants to report how much money they would need in one, five, ten, twenty, thirty, or forty years in order to be indifferent to receiving one hundred dollars tomorrow. It's possible that either task—the similarity measure or the financial questionnaire—was too abstract for participants, making it difficult to produce meaningful results. S. Frederick, "Time Preference and Personal Identity," in *Time and Decision,* ed. G. Loewenstein, D. Read, and R. Baumeister (New York: Russell Sage Press, 2003), 89–113. Additionally, around the same time I was working on this research with my collaborators, Dan Bartels was also independently investigating the links between connection to future selves and decision-making. In a rigorous series of studies, he asked research participants to judge different levels of connection between other people's current and future selves. The more connection people perceived, the more patient they were in making financial choices for those characters. D. M. Bartels and L. J. Rips, "Psychological Connectedness and Intertemporal Choice," *Journal of Experimental Psychology: General* 139, no. 1 (2010): 49–69.

55: *the more similarity you feel that you share with a stranger*...D. Byrne, "Interpersonal Attraction and Attitude Similarity," *Journal of Abnormal and Social Psychology* 62, no. 3 (1961): 713–715.

55: *We also gave our research participants a set of financial choices*...The time frame for the future-self circles scale was on the order of ten years, and yet the time scale for the financial decisions ranged from tonight to up to six months from now. It may seem strange to have such different timelines for the two tasks, but note that if we had chosen a future-self scale that was very short, we might have found what are known as "ceiling effects," with everyone choosing very high scores. Or, if we had chosen a financial task where the payouts didn't occur for another ten years, we might have found "floor effects," where everyone opts for the smaller, earlier reward.

55: *we're more likely to forgo money for ourselves*...B. Jones and H. Rachlin, "Social Discounting," *Psychological Science* 17, no. 4 (2006): 283–286.

57: *the more of a connection people felt with their future selves*...Just to give a sense of the numbers here: if you're a millennial, making around $60,000 a year, those who have a strong connection to their future selves have about a 10 percent differential on financial well-being. If you're a boomer making around $100,000, those who have a strong connection have around a 7 percent differential on financial well-being...and this applies to everyone in between as well. H. E. Hershfield, S. Kerbel, and D. Zimmerman, "Exploring the Distribution and Correlates of Future Self-Continuity in a Large, Nationally Representative Sample" (UCLA working paper, July 2022).

57: *This correlation held up*...Our results were strong even in the face of personality characteristics like the propensity to plan and the degree to which someone considered future consequences in their daily lives. This particular study, however, did not measure classic personality variables like extraversion, neuroticism, openness to new experiences, agreeableness, and conscientiousness. Notably, other work by Dan Bartels and Oleg Urminsky has found that links between future-self connection and patient behavior still hold up in the face of these "Big Five" variables. See D. M. Bartels and O. Urminsky, "On Intertemporal Selfishness: How the Perceived Instability of Identity Underlies Impatient Consumption," *Journal of Consumer Research* 38, no. 1 (2011): 182–198.

57: *if you were to think about someone very similar*...J. P. Mitchell, C. N. Macrae, and M. R. Banaji, "Dissociable Medial Prefrontal Contributions to Judgments of Similar and Dissimilar Others," *Neuron* 50, no. 4 (2006): 655–663.

58: *the "otherness" of the future self was linked to*...One thing to note — almost all our research participants returned to the lab to take part in the financial decision-making task. But two did not. And they happened to be the two who had the biggest gap in brain activity between thoughts about their current and future selves. H. Ersner-Hershfield, G. E. Wimmer, and B. Knutson, "Saving for the Future Self: Neural Measures of Future Self-Continuity Predict Temporal Discounting," *Social Cognitive and Affective Neuroscience* 4, no. 1 (2009): 85–92.

58: *the more connected people are to their future selves*...For the link between future-self relationships and ethical decisions, see H. E. Hershfield, T. R. Cohen, and

L. Thompson, "Short Horizons and Tempting Situations: Lack of Continuity to Our Future Selves Leads to Unethical Decision Making and Behavior," *Organizational Behavior and Human Decision Processes* 117, no. 2 (2012): 298–310. For the link with exercise and health, see A. M. Rutchick, M. L. Slepian, M. O. Reyes, L. N. Pleskus, and H. E. Hershfield, "Future Self-Continuity Is Associated with Improved Health and Increases Exercise Behavior," *Journal of Experimental Psychology: Applied* 24, no. 1 (2018): 72–80. For the link to high school GPA, see R. M. Adelman, S. D. Herrmann, J. E. Bodford, et al., "Feeling Closer to the Future Self and Doing Better: Temporal Psychological Mechanisms Underlying Academic Performance," *Journal of Personality* 85, no. 3 (2017): 398–408; and for college GPA, see M. T. Bixter, S. L. McMichael, C. J. Bunker, et al., "A Test of a Triadic Conceptualization of Future Self-Identification," *PLOS One* 15, no. 11 (2020): e0242504.

58: *the most impressive outcome of our relationships with our future selves*...Over the years, different researchers have devised different ways to measure and define the relationships that people have with their future selves. For example, in my own research with my students and collaborators, I have primarily focused on perceptions of similarity with a future self, for a reason stated earlier: when we feel a shared sense of similarity with someone else, there's a higher likelihood that we will like them (and, presumably, do things on their behalf). I have also measured a related construct: "connectedness," or a sense of connection that people feel to their future selves. There are theoretical differences between similarity and connectedness, but in practice, they produce similar results when you look at the link between future-self relationships and important outcomes (like saving). Recently, a set of researchers has attempted to define the relationship to one's future self more precisely, using the term "future self-identification," which is comprised of similarity and connectedness, ease of vividly imagining one's future self, and positivity toward that future self. The most concrete outcome the researchers examined — college GPA — was positively related to similarity and connectedness, but not to vividness and positivity (Bixter et al., "A Test of a Triadic Conceptualization"). There may be important links between how similar I feel to my future self, how positive I feel about them, and how vividly I can imagine that self. I focus here, however, on similarity (and connectedness) to the extent that those two aspects of future-self relationships seem to have been the most commonly tested ones, and the easiest to grasp. For a more complete description of these different aspects, and the links between them, see H. E. Hershfield, "Future Self-Continuity: How Conceptions of the Future Self Transform Intertemporal Choice," *Annals of the New York Academy of Sciences* 1235, no. 1 (2011): 30–43; and O. Urminsky, "The Role of Psychological Connectedness to the Future Self in Decisions over Time," *Current Directions in Psychological Science* 26, no. 1 (2017): 34–39.

59: *the degree of overlap between selves*...These findings remained strong even if we took into account initial levels of life satisfaction in 1995, as well as standard demographic factors and socioeconomic status. J. S. Reiff, H. E. Hershfield, and

J. Quoidbach, "Identity over Time: Perceived Similarity Between Selves Predicts Well-Being 10 Years Later," *Social Psychological and Personality Science* 11, no. 2 (2020): 160–167. For an accessible summary of this work, and an intriguing set of questions that it raises, see J. Ducharme, "Self-Improvement Might Sound Healthy, but There's a Downside to Wanting to Change," *Time*, May 3, 2019, https://time.com/5581864/self-improvement-happiness/.

60: *Researchers Sarah Molouki and Dan Bartels have found...* S. Molouki and D. M. Bartels, "Personal Change and the Continuity of the Self," *Cognitive Psychology* 93 (2017): 1–17.

61: *and split them into two groups...* Technically, you'd also need a third group of people to be in a "control" condition, whom you'd just track over time, without any sort of intervention. To make the example a little easier to understand in the text, however, let's keep our mad scientist to just two groups of people.

61: *as people grow older and they experience more stability...* See J. L. Rutt and C. E. Löckenhoff, "From Past to Future: Temporal Self-Continuity Across the Life Span," *Psychology and Aging* 31, no. 6 (2016): 631–639; and C. E. Löckenhoff and J. L. Rutt, "Age Differences in Self-Continuity: Converging Evidence and Directions for Future Research," *Gerontologist* 57, no. 3 (2017): 396–408.

62: *compared to adults who haven't been so lucky...* E. Rude, J. S. Reiff, and H. E. Hershfield, "Life Shocks and Perceptions of Continuity" (UCLA working paper, July 2022).

62: *when it came to choosing between small gift certificates...* Bartels and Urminsky, "On Intertemporal Selfishness."

67: *Doing so has allowed patients to more completely express...* V. S. Periyakoil, E. Neri, and H. Kraemer, "A Randomized Controlled Trial Comparing the Letter Project Advance Directive to Traditional Advance Directive," *Journal of Palliative Medicine* 20, no. 9 (2017): 954–965.

67: *that clear and well-documented end-of-life plans lead to "better" deaths...* A. A. Wright, B. Zhang, A. Ray, et al., "Associations Between End-of-Life Discussions, Patient Mental Health, Medical Care Near Death, and Caregiver Bereavement Adjustment," *Journal of the American Medical Association* 300, no. 14 (2008): 1665–1673.

68: *"between my present experiences and future experiences"...* D. Parfit, *Reasons and Persons* (Oxford: Oxford University Press, 1984), 281–282.

Chapter 4: *Missing Your Flight*

77: *that you're a fan of scratch-off lottery tickets...* This lottery ticket example is adapted from an example that Madden and Johnson bring up in their approachable review on temporal discounting and its link to impulsivity. G. J. Madden and P. S. Johnson, "A Delay-Discounting Primer," in *Impulsivity: The Behavioral and Neurological Science of Discounting,* ed. G. J. Madden and W. K. Bickel (Washington, DC: American Psychological Association, 2010), 11–37.

79: *"discounting the value of a future reward"...* Specifically, economists and psychologists refer to this tendency as "temporal discounting." There is a rich literature that tries to best characterize the nature of such discounting, not just for academic reasons, but so that we might be able to better predict how people will behave when faced with different choices in their lives, over different time periods. To draw out the example that I've been discussing, you might require less and less money now if the larger reward was placed farther and farther out in time. That is, if the $1,000 were to be given to you in, say, one year rather than six months, then maybe you'd be okay with $950 right now (as opposed to $990). This sort of behavior takes the form of what's known as "exponential discounting," and the idea is that you'd be devaluing a later reward at some constant rate the farther in the future it occurred. A whole book could be written about the different forms of discounting and all the research that's been conducted over the last fifty or so years on this topic, not only on people but on other species, like pigeons, as well. In this chapter, I try to cover the key insights that are most related to our discussion of present and future selves, and in doing so, I necessarily leave out some of the intricacies that have been uncovered by a slew of dedicated researchers. If you want to read more, a short, accessible summary of "intertemporal behavior" can be found here: G. Zauberman and O. Urminsky, "Consumer Intertemporal Preferences," *Current Opinion in Psychology* 10 (August 2016): 136–141.

81: *"If someone gives you a whole bunch of ice cream"*...Josh Eels, "Night Club Royale," *The New Yorker,* September 23, 2013, https://www.newyorker.com/magazine/2013 /09/30/night-club-royale.

82: *we often see evidence of these sorts of preference reversals*...To put it more technically, hyperbolic discounting, in contrast to exponential discounting, implies that people discount future rewards at a steeper rate when the delays between two rewards are shorter (that is, when the smaller of two rewards is available closer to the present moment, as I explain in the text). Discount rates, however, become more shallow (that is, the future is not discounted as steeply) when there is a delay between two available rewards. Hyperbolic discounting models can be traced back to R. H. Strotz, "Myopia and Inconsistency in Dynamic Utility Maximization," *Review of Economic Studies* 23, no. 3 (1955): 165–180.

83: *and people opt for the smaller, immediate reward*...This particular study had a small number of research participants in it, but I spotlight it here because it represents one of the most straightforward research paradigms used to examine hyperbolic discounting (K. N. Kirby and R. J. Herrnstein, "Preference Reversals Due to Myopic Discounting of Delayed Reward," *Psychological Science* 6, no. 2 [1995]: 83– 89). In another typical study, when the smaller reward was available in twenty-six weeks, sightly more than a third of research participants chose it over the larger reward. When that same smaller reward was available immediately, however, four out of five participants chose it over the larger one (G. Keren and P. Roelofsma, "Immediacy and Certainty in Intertemporal Choice," *Organizational Behavior and Human Decision Processes* 63, no. 3 [1995]: 287–297).

83: *Most of them...switched course*...D. Read and B. Van Leeuwen, "Predicting Hunger: The Effects of Appetite and Delay on Choice," *Organizational Behavior and Human Decision Processes* 76, no. 2 (1998): 189–205.

83: *went for the junk food over the healthy food*... It is important to note that despite the intuitive appeal of this concept of hyperbolic discounting, it is something that's relatively difficult to pin down in laboratory settings. In one rigorous test of the idea, research participants weren't just asked to consider rewards with smaller and longer delays; they actually made choices at one point in time, and then again in another, in what's known as a longitudinal test. Specifically, research participants were asked if they would rather have some amount of money within a day or a larger amount after a week (for example, twenty dollars in one week or twenty-one dollars in two weeks). The following week, they were again given a series of choices, which mapped onto the ones they made a week prior. For example, they were asked to choose between twenty dollars they could get within the day and twenty-one dollars in one week. In this particular test of hyperbolic discounting, the researchers did not find evidence for preference reversals (D. Read, S. Frederick, and M. Airoldi, "Four Days Later in Cincinnati: Longitudinal Tests of Hyperbolic Discounting," *Acta Psychologica* 140, no. 2 [2012]: 177–185). The important takeaway from the current research may be that we don't *always* see people reversing their preferences when smaller rewards become available. And at times, as discussed in Chapter 9, there may be instances where, if anything, people show *too* much of a preference for larger, later rewards in a way that brings about less optimal outcomes.

83: *extreme discounting of future rewards*... J. M. Rung and G. J. Madden, "Experimental Reductions of Delay Discounting and Impulsive Choice: A Systematic Review and Meta-Analysis," *Journal of Experimental Psychology: General* 147, no. 9 (2018): 1349–1381.

84: *pigeons acted like the junk food–eating humans*... L. Green, E. B. Fisher, S. Perlow, and L. Sherman, "Preference Reversal and Self Control: Choice as a Function of Reward Amount and Delay," *Behaviour Analysis Letters* 1, no. 1 (1981): 43–51.

84: *Rats have been shown to behave the same way*... For a review of the similarities and differences in discounting behavior between humans, rats, and pigeons, see A. Vanderveldt, L. Oliveira, and L. Green, "Delay Discounting: Pigeon, Rat, Human—Does It Matter?," *Journal of Experimental Psychology: Animal Learning and Cognition* 42, no. 2 (2016): 141–162.

85: *"A sheep's foot in thine own hand"*... F. C. Conybeare, J. R. Harris, and A. S. Lewis, *The Story of Ahikar from the Syriac, Arabic, Armenian, Ethiopic, Greek and Slavonic Versions* (London: C. J. Clay and Sons, 1898), 6.

85: *it may be wise to go for what's available in the present*... John Monterosso, a neuroscience professor at the University of Southern California, and expert in the study of addiction and self-control, pointed out to me that to some extent, there are cases when it is "rational" to quickly opt for the certain bet now. Switching preferences to opt for a smaller but immediate reward demonstrates flexibility, which may have been—and continues to be—adaptive for many species.

85: *the tendency to overemphasize the present*... This caveat—that hyperbolic discounting is determined by multiple causes—is one that Zauberman and Urminsky ("Consumer Intertemporal Preferences") make in their review. It's a point that I think is particularly important to consider: just as there are no easy explanations for behaviors that we find maladaptive, there are also no easy solutions. On the bright side, the fact that there are multiple possible explanations gives rise to multiple possible ways to intervene (a point I return to in the final section of the book).

87: *"seems to be viewed under an emotional magnifying glass"* ... E. W. Dunn, D. T. Gilbert, and T. D. Wilson, "If Money Doesn't Make You Happy, Then You Probably Aren't Spending It Right," *Journal of Consumer Psychology* 21, no. 2 (2011): 115–125; quote, 121.

88: *"visceral factors"* ... G. Loewenstein, "Out of Control: Visceral Influences on Behavior," *Organizational Behavior and Human Decision Processes* 65, no. 3 (1996): 272–292.

88: *The prefrontal system* ... For a more detailed discussion of these systems, see S. M. McClure, D. I. Laibson, G. Loewenstein, and J. D. Cohen, "Separate Neural Systems Value Immediate and Delayed Monetary Rewards," *Science* 306, no. 5695 (2004): 503–507.

89: *Dr. Lhermitte took one of his patients to his apartment* ... F. Lhermitte, "Human Autonomy and the Frontal Lobes. Part II: Patient Behavior in Complex and Social Situations: The 'Environmental Dependency Syndrome,'" *Annals of Neurology* 19, no. 4 (1986): 335–343. (I originally discovered this paper through watching lectures by Samuel McClure, a psychology professor at Arizona State University.)

89: *they were the ones most likely to pick the cake* ... B. Shiv and A. Fedorikhin, "Heart and Mind in Conflict: The Interplay of Affect and Cognition in Consumer Decision Making," *Journal of Consumer Research* 26, no. 3 (1999): 278–292.

90: *even an incidental distraction in the form of* ... Along these lines, recent work has found that the mere presence of one's phone can reduce the enjoyment of social interactions. Research participants who were randomly assigned to place their phones in front of them (versus put them away) reported being more distracted and thus less able to fully enjoy interacting with a social partner. R. J. Dwyer, K. Kushlev, and E. W. Dunn, "Smartphone Use Undermines Enjoyment of Face-to-Face Social Interactions," *Journal of Experimental Social Psychology* 78 (2018): 233–239.

91: *a slight burn on his left butt cheek* ... S. Mirsky, "Einstein's Hot Time," *Scientific American* 287, no. 3 (2002): 102.

92: *Blocks of time feel compressed* ... G. Zauberman, B. K. Kim, S. A. Malkoc, and J. R. Bettman, "Discounting Time and Time Discounting: Subjective Time Perception and Intertemporal Preferences," *Journal of Marketing Research* 46, no. 4 (2009): 543–556.

92: *consider your feelings about a long flight or drive* ... A. Alter, "Quirks in Time Perception," *Psychology Today,* April 13, 2010, https://www.psychologytoday.com /us/blog/alternative-truths/201004/quirks-in-time-perception.

92: *if a span of time feels like it lasts a long time* ... B. K. Kim and G. Zauberman, "Perception of Anticipatory Time in Temporal Discounting," *Journal of Neuroscience, Psychology, and Economics* 2, no. 2 (2009): 91–101.

94: *our research participants identified three clear blocks* . . . In the previous chapter, I mentioned research that focused on future selves that exist three months out from today. That, indeed, is one period of relevant time for discussing future selves. When we talk about the present, though, the key insight may be that there are a variety of ways to think about how to define that present period. In my research with Sam Maglio, we deliberately kept things neutral and open-ended by asking our research participants to tell us about the present "in general." But, as I mentioned in the book's introduction, when we are pursuing long-term plans, there can be multiple present periods (housing our present selves) that feed into multiple futures (housing our future selves). What's most important is the specific decision-making context in which you find yourself, and the various "presents" and "futures" that go along with it. For more on the research behind these questions regarding when the present ends, see H. E. Hershfield and S. J. Maglio, "When Does the Present End and the Future Begin?," *Journal of Experimental Psychology: General* 149, no. 4 (2020): 701–718; and S. J. Maglio and H. E. Hershfield, "Pleas for Patience from the Cumulative Future Self," *Behavioral and Brain Sciences* 44 (2021): 38–39.

95: Figure created by Neil Bage based on data from Hershfield and Maglio, "When Does the Present End and the Future Begin?" Percentages add up to more than 100 percent due to rounding.

Chapter 5: *Poor Trip Planning*

99: *biographers have described him* . . . J. M'Diarmid, ed., *The Scrap Book: A Collection of Amusing and Striking Pieces, in Prose and Verse: With an Introduction, and Occasional Remarks and Contributions* (London: Oliver & Boyd, Tweeddale-Court, and G. & W. B. Whittaker, 1825).

100: *The ink, in fact, was still wet* . . . This anecdote has never been officially verified. As one historian put it, of all the legends about *Don Giovanni*, this is the most enduring "perhaps because it may even be true." J. Rushton, *W. A. Mozart: Don Giovanni* (Cambridge: Cambridge University Press, 1981), 3. See also M. Solomon, *Mozart: A Life* (New York: HarperCollins, 1995). Thank you to Jane Bernstein for pointing me to this work.

101: *about 20 percent of people are chronic procrastinators* . . . J. R. Ferrari, J. O'Callaghan, and I. Newbegin, "Prevalence of Procrastination in the United States, United Kingdom, and Australia: Arousal and Avoidance Delays Among Adults," *North American Journal of Psychology* 7, no. 1 (2005): 1–6.

101: *85 percent do so in a way that bothers them* . . . This statistic comes from an informal poll that researcher Tim Pychyl conducted on his website.

101: *chronic procrastination is associated with a litany of* . . . F. Sirois and T. Pychyl, "Procrastination and the Priority of Short-Term Mood Regulation: Consequences for Future Self," *Social and Personality Psychology Compass* 7, no. 2 (2013): 115–127.

101: *this type of procrastination becomes a vicious cycle* . . . Procrastination is associated with putting off a host of appointments, including those in contexts such as medicine (F. M. Sirois, M. L. Melia-Gordon, and T. A. Pychyl, "'I'll Look After My Health,

Later': An Investigation of Procrastination and Health," *Personality and Individual Differences* 35, no. 5 [2003]: 1167–1184), dental care (F. M. Sirois, "'I'll Look After My Health, Later': A Replication and Extension of the Procrastination–Health Model with Community-Dwelling Adults," *Personality and Individual Differences* 43, no. 1 [2007]: 15–26), and mental health (R. Stead, M. J. Shanahan, and R. W. Neufeld, "'I'll Go to Therapy, Eventually': Procrastination, Stress and Mental Health," *Personality and Individual Differences* 49, no. 3 [2010]: 175–180).

102: *procrastination is also conceptually related to* ... C. Lieberman, "Why You Procrastinate (It Has Nothing to Do with Self-Control)," *New York Times*, March 25, 2019, https://www.nytimes.com/2019/03/25/smarter-living/why-you-procrastinate -it-has-nothing-to-do-with-self-control.html.

103: *The scientists asked the students about their procrastination habits* ... Blouin-Hudon and Pychyl were additionally focused on positive and negative emotional states in their research. Their work was correlational. Because more research is still being conducted in this arena, I've decided to focus on the core takeaways: simply put, those who can vividly imagine the future procrastinate less, and those who feel a sense of connection with their future selves also procrastinate less. E. M. C. Blouin-Hudon and T. A. Pychyl, "Experiencing the Temporally Extended Self: Initial Support for the Role of Affective States, Vivid Mental Imagery, and Future Self-Continuity in the Prediction of Academic Procrastination," *Personality and Individual Differences* 86 (November 2015): 50–56.

107: *And that, in turn, translated into less procrastination* ... It's important to note that it wasn't simply the case that the students who got better grades on the first exam were the ones who had an easier time forgiving themselves for procrastinating. M. J. Wohl, T. A. Pychyl, and S. H. Bennett, "I Forgive Myself, Now I Can Study: How Self-Forgiveness for Procrastinating Can Reduce Future Procrastination," *Personality and Individual Differences* 48, no. 7 (2010): 803–808. Other research has also looked at the link between self-forgiveness and procrastination (e.g., L. Martinčeková and R. D. Enright, "The Effects of Self-Forgiveness and Shame-Proneness on Procrastination: Exploring the Mediating Role of Affect," *Current Psychology* 39, no. 2 [2020]: 428–437). Although it seems like it should be straightforward to teach someone about self-forgiveness—something that's been successfully demonstrated with other problematic behaviors like gambling—no well-controlled research studies have looked specifically at the impacts of *teaching* people how to self-forgive and subsequent procrastination behavior.

108: *This is what psychologists Michael Wohl and Kendra McLaughlin have called* ... M. J. Wohl and K. J. McLaughlin, "Self-Forgiveness: The Good, the Bad, and the Ugly," *Social and Personality Psychology Compass* 8, no. 8 (2014): 422–435.

109: *People said they'd feel a higher level of happiness today* ... K. S. Kassam, D. T. Gilbert, A. Boston, and T. D. Wilson, "Future Anhedonia and Time Discounting," *Journal of Experimental Social Psychology* 44, no. 6 (2008): 1533–1537. One of the reasons we put things off till tomorrow—or "poorly plan our trips"—is that we underestimate the strength of our future emotions. But note: We don't *always* underestimate our future emotions. There are times, in fact, when we might think of our future emotional reactions as being *more* intense than they end up being (for instance, a potential break up might seem worse than it actually turns out to be; P. W. Eastwick, E. J. Finkel, T. Krishnamurti, and G. Loewenstein, "Mispredicting Distress Following Romantic Breakup: Revealing the Time Course of the Affective Forecasting Error," *Journal of Experimental Social Psychology* 44, no. 23 [2008]: 800–807).

111: *some women made a forecast based on a simulation*...After making their forecast about how much they'd enjoy the date, all the women received the piece of information that they hadn't yet gotten (that is, the women who just got the man's dating profile then received the surrogate report, and the women who just got the surrogate report then received the man's dating profile). In this way, all the women went into their date armed with the same information.

111: *When it came to how much women enjoyed the date*...D. T. Gilbert, M. A. Killingsworth, R. N. Eyre, and T. D. Wilson, "The Surprising Power of Neighborly Advice," *Science* 323, no. 5921 (2009): 1617–1619.

111: *"Before we set our hearts too much upon anything"*...F. de La Rochefoucauld, *Collected Maxims and Other Reflections* (Oxford: Oxford University Press, 2007).

112: *The computer surrogate...made superior predictions*...P. Khambatta, S. Mariadassou, and S. C. Wheeler, "Computers Can Predict What Makes People Better Off Even More Accurately Than They Can Themselves" (UCLA working paper, 2021).

115: *Wallace's memoir about his experiences,* Yes Man...D. Wallace, *Yes Man* (New York: Simon & Schuster, 2005).

117: *in one of Gal's studies*...G. Zauberman and J. G. Lynch Jr., "Resource Slack and Propensity to Discount Delayed Investments of Time Versus Money," *Journal of Experimental Psychology: General* 134, no. 1 (2005): 23–37. In the original paper, Zauberman and Lynch show that this tendency to perceive more "slack" — that is, more of a surplus of a given resource — in the future is stronger for time than it is for money. People still exhibit the "slack" effect for money, in that they think they will have more available money in the future than they do now, but it's just not as big an effect as it is for time. Why? It may be the case that we are relatively better at assessing our financial needs. From now until some later point in time, our financial commitments may be relatively similar (we know we'll still have the same bills to pay next month as we do now).

Chapter 6: *Packing the Wrong Clothes*

125: *he ordered a deluxe carne asada burrito*...J. Bote, "In 1998, These Men Got a Tattoo to Snag Free Tacos for Life. Here's What Happened After," *SF Gate*, September 20, 2021, https://www.sfgate.com/food/article/casa-sanchez-tattoos-free-meal-promo-san-francisco-16465800.php.

126: *as many as a quarter regret getting at least*...L. Shannon-Missal, "Tattoo Takeover: Three in Ten Americans Have Tattoos, and Most Don't Stop at Just One," Harris Poll, February 2016, https://www.prnewswire.com/news-releases/tattoo-takeover-three-in-ten-americans-have-tattoos-and-most-dont-stop-at-just-one-300217862.html. This survey was conducted on 2,225 US adults, and to assess regret, respondents were asked whether they ever regretted getting one of their tattoos. Almost a quarter (23 percent) said they regretted one. Another survey found a lower percentage (8 percent) but asked about regret for all tattoos rather than just one specific tattoo (Ipsos, "More Americans Have Tattoos Today Than Seven Years Ago," press release, 2019, https://www.ipsos.com/sites/default/files/ct/news/documents/2019-08/tattoo-topline-2019-08-29-v2_0.pdf).

126: *estimated to be worth about $4.7 billion* . . . WantStats Research and Media, "Tattoo Removal Market," Market Research Future, 2021, https://www.marketresearch future.com/reports/tattoo-removal-market-1701.

126: *Data from surveys support his observations* . . . R. Morlock, "Tattoo Prevalence, Perception and Regret in U.S. Adults: A 2017 Cross-Sectional Study," *Value in Health* 22 (2019): S778.

128: *considered to be one of the leading economists* . . . R. Partington, "Nobel Prize in Economics Due to Be Announced," *Guardian,* October 9, 2017, https://www.the guardian.com/world/2017/oct/09/nobel-economics-prize-due-to-be-announced.

129: *But when you are in the grip of powerful emotions* . . . Loewenstein first laid these ideas out in a paper on "visceral factors," which I briefly mentioned in Chapter 4. G. Loewenstein, "Out of Control: Visceral Influences on Behavior," *Organizational Behavior and Human Decision Processes* 65, no. 3 (1996): 272–292.

130: *the addicts were making a decision* . . . G. J. Badger, W. K. Bickel, L. A. Giordano, E. A. Jacobs, G. Loewenstein, and L. Marsch, "Altered States: The Impact of Immediate Craving on the Valuation of Current and Future Opioids," *Journal of Health Economics* 26, no. 5 (2007): 865–876.

130: *They coined the term "projection bias"* . . . G. Loewenstein, T. O'Donoghue, and M. Rabin, "Projection Bias in Predicting Future Utility," *Quarterly Journal of Economics* 118, no. 4 (2003): 1209–1248.

132: *they were more likely to opt for the apple* . . . D. Read and B. Van Leeuwen, "Predicting Hunger: The Effects of Appetite and Delay on Choice," *Organizational Behavior and Human Decision Processes* 76, no. 2 (1998): 189–205. I also spotlighted this study in Chapter 4 because, in addition to showing the impact of hunger on food choices, it demonstrates how preferences can reverse over time.

132: *convertible purchases increase* . . . M. R. Busse, D. G. Pope, J. C. Pope, and J. Silva-Risso, "The Psychological Effect of Weather on Car Purchases," *Quarterly Journal of Economics* 130, no. 1 (2015): 371–414. An earlier version of this paper also found that the effects uncovered extend to the housing market as well: houses with swimming pools sell for about 0.4 percent more in the summertime than when the same house goes up for sale in the winter.

132: *divorce rates significantly decreased after* . . . J. Lee, "The Impact of a Mandatory Cooling-Off Period on Divorce," *Journal of Law and Economics* 56, no. 1 (2013): 227–243.

133: *you might incorrectly attribute your fatigue to* . . . K. Haggag, R. W. Patterson, N. G. Pope, and A. Feudo, "Attribution Bias in Major Decisions: Evidence from the United States Military Academy," *Journal of Public Economics* 200 (August 2021): 104445. This paper adds a wrinkle to the other work on projection biases. When students decide on a major, they must try to call to mind their feelings about the earlier courses they've taken in that subject. Here, the students were recalling past feelings of fatigue, misattributing them to the subject matter, and then projecting ahead to their expected feelings moving forward. In this way, Haggag and colleagues demonstrate an interesting form of projection bias, where remembrance of our earlier self's feelings are weighted too heavily in projections about the future.

133: *"Even in a high-stakes context"*...Research backs up his assertions: For the impact of college major on well-being, see M. Wiswall and B. Zafar, "Determinants of College Major Choice: Identification Using an Information Experiment," *Review of Economic Studies* 82, no. 2 (2015): 791–824. As an example of the impact of college major on future earnings, see L. J. Kirkeboen, E. Leuven, and M. Mogstad, "Field of Study, Earnings, and Self-Selection," *Quarterly Journal of Economics* 131, no. 3 (2016): 1057–1111.

134: *we can end up expending too much effort on*...M. Kaufmann, "Projection Bias in Effort Choices," *arXiv preprint arXiv:2104.04327,* 2021, https://arxiv.org/abs/2104 .04327.

135: *reformed smokers who felt that they could better control*...L. F. Nordgren, F. V. Harreveld, and J. V. D. Pligt, "The Restraint Bias: How the Illusion of Self-Restraint Promotes Impulsive Behavior," *Psychological Science* 20, no. 12 (2009): 1523–1528.

138: *nearly twenty thousand people demonstrated a clear pattern*...J. Quoidbach, D. T. Gilbert, and T. D. Wilson, "The End of History Illusion," *Science* 339, no. 6115 (2013): 96–98.

139: *thousands of Americans consistently underestimated*...J. Quoidbach, D. T. Gilbert, and T. D. Wilson, "Your Life Satisfaction Will Change More Than You Think: A Comment on Harris and Busseri (2019)," *Journal of Research in Personality* 86 (June 2020): 103937. Additional research backs up this conclusion: in one study of nearly forty thousand Brazilians, researchers found that values changed in substantial ways over the life span from ages twelve to sixty-five (V. V. Gouveia, K. C. Vione, T. L. Milfont, and R. Fischer, "Patterns of Value Change During the Life Span: Some Evidence from a Functional Approach to Values," *Personality and Social Psychology Bulletin* 41, no. 9 [2015]: 1276–1290).

140: *"History, it seems, is always ending today"*...Quoidbach, Gilbert, and Wilson, "The End of History Illusion," 98.

140: *they implicitly call to mind the ways they've improved*...E. O'Brien and M. Kardas, "The Implicit Meaning of (My) Change," *Journal of Personality and Social Psychology* 111, no. 6 (2016): 882–894.

140: *we view our present selves in a positive light*...See R. F. Baumeister, D. M. Tice, and D. G. Hutton, "Self-Presentational Motivations and Personality Differences in Self-Esteem," *Journal of Personality* 57, no. 3 (1989): 547–579; and R. F. Baumeister, J. D. Campbell, J. I. Krueger, and K. D. Vohs, "Does High Self-Esteem Cause Better Performance, Interpersonal Success, Happiness, or Healthier Lifestyles?," *Psychological Science in the Public Interest* 4, no. 1 (2003): 1–44.

140: *we like to think that we know ourselves well*...S. Vazire and E. N. Carlson, "Self-Knowledge of Personality: Do People Know Themselves?," *Social and Personality Psychology Compass* 4, no. 8 (2010): 605–620.

140: *how well do we actually know who we are today*...In a conversation with me, Quoidbach suggested another reason, and one that he's recently uncovered in an ongoing project: it's possible that when we think about ourselves unfolding over time, we can change in two different ways. You could become, for instance, more conscientious or less. Not knowing the direction of change, when thinking ahead, you might cancel out the two probabilities, and report that you anticipate no or only minimal change.

141: *the "predictors"...anticipated far less change in their work motivations*...G. G. Van Ryzin, "Evidence of an 'End of History Illusion' in the Work Motivations of Public Service Professionals," *Public Administration* 94, no. 1 (2016): 263–275.

142: *the title of a 2017* New York Times *profile of B. J. Miller*...J. Mooallem, "One Man's Quest to Change the Way We Die," *New York Times,* January 3, 2017, https://www.nytimes.com/2017/01/03/magazine/one-mans-quest-to-change-the-way-we-die.html.

143: *"feel her lungs filled while she still has them"*...See, for example, B. J. Miller, "What Really Matters at the End of Life," filmed March 2015 in Vancouver, BC, TED video, 18:59, https://www.ted.com/talks/bj_miller_what_really_matters_at_the_end_of_life.

144: *are typically not viewed in positive ways*...M. S. North and S. T. Fiske, "Modern Attitudes Toward Older Adults in the Aging World: A Cross-Cultural Meta-Analysis," *Psychological Bulletin* 141, no. 5 (2015): 993–1021.

144: *only about one in three Americans have completed*...K. N. Yadav, N. B. Gabler, E. Cooney, et al., "Approximately One in Three US Adults Completes Any Type of Advance Directive for End-of-Life Care," *Health Affairs* 36, no. 7 (2017): 1244–1251.

144: *Fully 42 percent said yes*...M. L. Slevin, H. Plant, D. A. Lynch, J. Drinkwater, and W. M. Gregory, "Who Should Measure Quality of Life, the Doctor or the Patient?," *British Journal of Cancer* 57, no. 1 (1988): 109–112.

146: *From a practical standpoint*...D. J. Lamas, "When Faced with Death, People Often Change Their Minds," *New York Times,* January 3, 2022, https://www.nytimes.com/2022/01/03/opinion/advance-directives-death.html.

Chapter 7: *Making the Future Closer*

156: *donations to a Swedish Red Cross fund*...P. Slovic, D. Västfjäll, A. Erlandsson, and R. Gregory, "Iconic Photographs and the Ebb and Flow of Empathic Response to Humanitarian Disasters," *Proceedings of the National Academy of Sciences* 114, no. 4 (2017): 640–644.

156: *the Syrian crisis had been raging*...S. Slovic and P. Slovic, "The Arithmetic of Compassion," *New York Times,* December 4, 2015, https://www.nytimes.com/2015/12/06/opinion/the-arithmetic-of-compassion.html.

157: *but stories about mass poverty rarely produce*...D. A. Small, "Sympathy Biases and Sympathy Appeals: Reducing Social Distance to Boost Charitable Contributions," in *Experimental Approaches to the Study of Charity,* ed. D. M. Oppenheimer and C. Y. Olivola (New York: Taylor & Francis, 2011), 149–160.

157: *such framing led to higher contributions* . . . D. A. Small and G. Loewenstein, "Helping a Victim or Helping the Victim: Altruism and Identifiability," *Journal of Risk and Uncertainty* 26, no. 1 (2003): 5–16. See also D. A. Small, "On the Psychology of the Identifiable Victim Effect," in *Identified Versus Statistical Lives: An Interdisciplinary Perspective,* ed. I. G. Cohen, N. Daniels, and N. Eyal (Oxford: Oxford University Press, 2015), 13–16.

157: *people preferred to lend to individuals* . . . J. Galak, D. Small, and A. T. Stephen, "Microfinance Decision Making: A Field Study of Prosocial Lending," *Journal of Marketing Research* 48, special issue (2011): S130–S137.

158: *That activity, in turn, predicts donation behavior* . . . A. Genevsky, D. Västfjäll, P. Slovic, and B. Knutson, "Neural Underpinnings of the Identifiable Victim Effect: Affect Shifts Preferences for Giving," *Journal of Neuroscience* 33, no. 43 (2013): 17188–17196.

158: *closeness matters when it comes to our desire* . . . B. Jones and H. Rachlin, "Social Discounting," *Psychological Science* 17, no. 4 (2006): 283–286; T. Strombach, B. Weber, Z. Hangebrauk, et al., "Social Discounting Involves Modulation of Neural Value Signals by Temporoparietal Junction," *Proceedings of the National Academy of Sciences of the United States of America* 112, no. 5 (2015): 1619–1624.

162: *those who interacted with their age-progressed images* . . . H. E. Hershfield, D. G. Goldstein, W. F. Sharpe, et al., "Increasing Saving Behavior Through Age-Progressed Renderings of the Future Self," *Journal of Marketing Research* 48, special issue (2011): S23–S37.

162: *One Twitter user comically demonstrated such confusion* . . . Hunter (@Hunter-Mitchel14), "I signed up for my company's 401k, but I'm nervous because I've never run that far before," Twitter, July 9, 2019, 7:19 p.m., https://twitter.com/huntermitchel14/status/1148733329245528065?lang=en.

163: *seeing those older selves increased not only* . . . J. D. Robalino, A. Fishbane, D. G. Goldstein, and H. E. Hershfield, "Saving for Retirement: A Real-World Test of Whether Seeing Photos of One's Future Self Encourages Contributions," *Behavioral Science and Policy* (2022). The increase in saving behavior was relatively small, with 1.7 percent of customers who saw their distant selves contributing compared to 1.5 percent who did not. (Precisely, we saw a 16 percent increase from an intervention run solely by email and text message, a space where it's often hard to convince customers to respond.) The increase in amount saved was considerably larger: interacting with future selves increased the total amount saved by 54 percent (1,675,974 pesos) compared to customers who did not interact with their older selves (1,087,422 pesos).

163: *Those who met their future selves displayed* . . . T. Sims, S. Raposo, J. N. Bailenson, and L. L. Carstensen, "The Future Is Now: Age-Progressed Images Motivate Community College Students to Prepare for Their Financial Futures," *Journal of Experimental Psychology: Applied* 26, no. 4 (2020): 593–603.

163–164: *a future-self visualization exercise increased preventive health behaviors...* A. John and K. Orkin, "Can Simple Psychological Interventions Increase Preventive Health Investment?" (NBER Working Paper 25731, 2021).

164: *they did a better job of recognizing what sort of items...* N. Chernyak, K. A. Leech, and M. L. Rowe, "Training Preschoolers' Prospective Abilities Through Conversation About the Extended Self," *Developmental Psychology* 53, no. 4 (2017): 652–661.

166: *adults who "met" their future selves via age-progressed images...* S. Raposo and L. L. Carstensen, "Can Envisioning Your Future Improve Your Health?," *Innovation in Aging* 2, supplement 1 (2018): 907.

166: *led people to take the more righteous path...* J. L. van Gelder, H. E. Hershfield, and L. F. Nordgren, "Vividness of the Future Self Predicts Delinquency," *Psychological Science* 24, no. 6 (2013): 974–980.

166: *when high school students befriended...* J. L. van Gelder, E. C. Luciano, M. Weulen Kranenbarg, and H. E. Hershfield, "Friends with My Future Self: Longitudinal Vividness Intervention Reduces Delinquency," *Criminology* 53, no. 2 (2015): 158–179.

166: *he's found that doing so has reduced the self-defeating behaviors...* J. L. van Gelder, L. J. Cornet, N. P. Zwalua, E. C. Mertens, and J. van der Schalk, "Interaction with the Future Self in Virtual Reality Reduces Self-Defeating Behavior in a Sample of Convicted Offenders," *Scientific Reports* 12, no. 1 (2022): 1–9.

167: *Gordon Ramsay observed that this was what he'd look like...* M. No, "18 FaceApp Tweets That Are as Funny as They Are Accurate," *BuzzFeed,* July 18, 2019, https://www.buzzfeed.com/michelleno/funny-faceapp-tweets?bftw&utm _term=4ldqpfp#4ldqpfp.

167: *the FaceApp images weren't partnered with...* This is a point I also made here: H. E. Hershfield, "A Lesson from FaceApp: Learning to Relate to the Person We Will One Day Become," *Los Angeles Times,* July 26, 2019, https://www.latimes.com /opinion/story/2019-07-26/hershfield-faceapp-relating-to-our-future-selves.

167: *we must know that our future selves exist...* D. M. Bartels and O. Urminsky, "To Know and to Care: How Awareness and Valuation of the Future Jointly Shape Consumer Spending," *Journal of Consumer Research* 41, no. 6 (2015): 1469–1485.

169: *In an op-ed, Napolitano detailed...* A. Napolitano, "'Dear Me': A Novelist Writes to Her Future Self," *New York Times,* January 24, 2020, https://www.nytimes .com/2020/01/24/books/review/emily-of-new-moon-montgomery-letters-ann -napolitano.html.

172: *we discovered that when hundreds of college students...* A. M. Rutchick, M. L. Slepian, M. O. Reyes, L. N. Pleskus, and H. E. Hershfield, "Future Self-Continuity Is Associated with Improved Health and Increases Exercise Behavior," *Journal of Experimental Psychology: Applied* 24, no. 1 (2018): 72–80.

173: *customers who wrote such letters were...* A. Shah, D. M. Munguia Gomez, A. Fishbane, and H. E. Hershfield, "Testing the Effectiveness of a Future Selves

Intervention for Increasing Retirement Saving: Evidence from a Field Experiment in Mexico" (University of Toronto working paper, 2022).

173: *the participants were able to shed the shackles of*...Y. Chishima, I. T. Huai-Ching Liu, and A. E. Wilson, "Temporal Distancing During the COVID-19 Pandemic: Letter Writing with Future Self Can Mitigate Negative Affect," *Applied Psychology: Health and Well-Being* 13, no. 2 (2021): 406–418.

174: *They subsequently reported that they were more likely to engage in*...Y. Chishima and A. E. Wilson, "Conversation with a Future Self: A Letter-Exchange Exercise Enhances Student Self-Continuity, Career Planning, and Academic Thinking," *Self and Identity* 20, no. 5 (2021): 646–671.

174: *We've even found that this sort of "reverse time travel"*...K. L. Christensen, H. E. Hershfield, and S. J. Maglio, "Back to the Present: How Direction of Mental Time Travel Affects Thoughts and Behavior" (UCLA working paper, 2022).

175: *we feel like we're home when we've reached the first landmark*...P. Raghubir, V. G. Morwitz, and A. Chakravarti, "Spatial Categorization and Time Perception: Why Does It Take Less Time to Get Home?," *Journal of Consumer Psychology* 21, no. 2 (2011): 192–198.

176: *mentally journeying through days instead of years*...N. A. Lewis Jr. and D. Oyserman, "When Does the Future Begin? Time Metrics Matter, Connecting Present and Future Selves," *Psychological Science* 26, no. 6 (2015): 816–825.

Chapter 8: *Staying the Course*

179–180: *"the capillaries in the whites were so engorged"*...J. Cannon, "My Experience with Antabuse," Alexander DeLuca, MD, addiction, pain, and public health website, September 2004, https://doctordeluca.com/Library/AbstinenceHR/MyExperience WithAntabuse04.htm. Site last accessed on June 25, 2021, but now appears defunct. I confirmed details of this story with Dr. DeLuca in my interview with him.

181: *"I did not want to deal with my life"*...J. Cannon, "My Experience with Antabuse."

184: *"you can't get rid of me by Tuesday"*...J. Cannon, "My Experience with Antabuse."

184: *a specific problem that affects about 6 percent of the American population*...Substance Abuse and Mental Health Services Administration, "2019 National Survey on Drug Use and Health," 2019, https://www.samhsa.gov/data/sites/default/files /reports/rpt29394/NSDUHDetailedTabs2019/NSDUHDetTabsSect5pe2019 .htm#tab5-4a.

185: *he suggested that nations could lessen the likelihood of*...T. C. Schelling, "An Essay on Bargaining," *American Economic Review* 46, no. 3 (1956): 281–306.

186: *the threat of a definite and already committed-to response*...V. Postrel, "A Nobel Winner Can Help You Keep Your Resolutions," *New York Times,* December 29, 2005, https://www.nytimes.com/2005/12/29/business/a-nobel-winner-can-help -you-keep-your-resolutions.html.

186: *explorer Hernán Cortés deliberately sunk*...W. A. Reynolds, "The Burning Ships of Hernán Cortés," *Hispania* 42, no. 3 (1959): 317–324.

186: *Chinese general Han Xin placed them with their backs*...R. A. Gabriel, *The Great Armies of Antiquity* (Westport, CT: Greenwood, 2002). I first came across this anecdote in S. J. Dubner and S. D. Levitt, "The Stomach-Surgery Conundrum," *New York Times*, November 18, 2007, http://www.nytimes.com/2007/11/18/magazine/18wwln-freakonomics-t.html?_r=1&ref=magazine&oref=slogin.

186: *In the 1980s, Schelling switched gears*...T. C. Schelling, "Self-Command in Practice, in Policy, and in a Theory of Rational Choice," *American Economic Review* 74, no. 2 (1984): 1–11.

187: *A similar strategy was used by the poet Maya Angelou*...J. Krasny, "The Creative Process of the Legendary Maya Angelou," *Inc.*, May 28, 2014, https://www.inc.com/jill-krasny/maya-angelou-creative-writing-process.html.

187: *you could drink plenty of water at night*...G. Bryan, D. Karlan, and S. Nelson, "Commitment Devices," *Annual Review of Economics* 2, no. 1 (2010): 671–698.

188: *Some economists call this a "soft commitment"*...Bryan, Karlan, and Nelson, "Commitment Devices."

189: *employees enrolled in the program quadrupled*...R. H. Thaler and S. Benartzi, "Save More Tomorrow™: Using Behavioral Economics to Increase Employee Saving," *Journal of Political Economy* 112, supplement 1 (2004): S164–S187.

189: *to increase other behaviors such as donating to charities*...A. Breman, "Give More Tomorrow: Two Field Experiments on Altruism and Intertemporal Choice," *Journal of Public Economics* 95, nos. 11–12 (2011): 1349–1357.

189: *attending and completing weight loss classes*...M. M. Savani, "Can Commitment Contracts Boost Participation in Public Health Programmes?," *Journal of Behavioral and Experimental Economics* 82 (2019): 101457.

190: *offered in a way that doesn't signal urgency*...J. Reiff, H. Dai, J. Beshears, and K. L. Milkman, "Save More Today or Tomorrow: The Role of Urgency and Present Bias in Nudging Pre-Commitment," *Journal of Marketing Research* (forthcoming), http://dx.doi.org/10.2139/ssrn.3625338.

190: *entrepreneurs saved about three and a half times as much*...F. Kast, S. Meier, and D. Pomeranz, "Under-Savers Anonymous: Evidence on Self-Help Groups and Peer Pressure as a Savings Commitment Device," National Bureau of Economic Research, no. w18417, 2012.

191: *a sense of faith in ourselves*...R. Bénabou and J. Tirole, "Willpower and Personal Rules," *Journal of Political Economy* 112, no. 4 (2004): 848–886.

193: *By putting the key to the padlock in the Kitchen Safe*...JhanicManifold, "Extreme Precommitment: Towards a Solution to Akrasia," Reddit, September 5, 2020, https://www.reddit.com/r/TheMotte/comments/in0j6g/extreme_precommitment_towards_a_solution_to/.

194: *But if its owner could demonstrate that the fridge door*...W. Leith, "How I Let Drinking Take Over My Life," *Guardian*, January 5, 2018, https://www.theguardian.com/news/2018/jan/05/william-leith-alcohol-how-did-i-let-drinking-take-over-my-life.

195: *"a sudden change where the things I've adored all my life"*...M. Konnikova, "The Struggles of a Psychologist Studying Self-Control," *The New Yorker*, October 9, 2014, https://www.newyorker.com/science/maria-konnikova/struggles-psychologist-studying-self-control.

195: *customers who had SEED accounts increased their savings balances* ... N. Ashraf, D. Karlan, and W. Yin, "Tying Odysseus to the Mast: Evidence from a Commitment Savings Product in the Philippines," *Quarterly Journal of Economics* 121, no. 2 (2006): 635–672.

195: *Slightly different products have met with* ... P. Dupas and J. Robinson, "Savings Constraints and Microenterprise Development: Evidence from a Field Experiment in Kenya," *American Economic Journal: Applied Economics* 5, no. 1 (2013): 163–192; L. Brune, X. Giné, J. Goldberg, and D. Yang, "Commitments to Save: A Field Experiment in Rural Malawi" (World Bank Policy Research Working Paper 5748, 2011). If you're curious, to study whether restrictive savings accounts are genuinely effective, you'd ideally want to test them using outcomes that matter. Yet, experimenting with several months' income is expensive in *developed* countries, so these particular experiments are usually conducted in *developing* economies. The amounts of money are smaller, but the outcomes are just as consequential as when using larger amounts of money in developed countries.

197: *when the "half the side" offer was given to diners* ... J. Schwartz, J. Riis, B. Elbel, and D. Ariely, "Inviting Consumers to Downsize Fast-Food Portions Significantly Reduces Calorie Consumption," *Health Affairs* 31, no. 2 (2012): 399–407.

199: *"I am going home now to bake a cake"* ... A. Lobel, *Frog and Toad Together* (New York: Harper & Row, 1972), 41.

199: *a letter would be sent to the state medical board* ... Schelling, "Self-Command in Practice."

200: *It's "loss aversion" in action* ... A. L. Brown, T. Imai, F. Vieider, and C. F. Camerer, "Meta-Analysis of Empirical Estimates of Loss-Aversion" (CESifo Working Paper 8848, 2021), https://ssrn.com/abstract=3772089.

201: *for those who enrolled, there was a 3.5 percent increase* ... J. Schwartz, D. Mochon, L. Wyper, J. Maroba, D. Patel, and D. Ariely, "Healthier by Precommitment," *Psychological Science* 25, no. 2 (2014): 538–546.

201: *They were also more likely to pass a surprise urine test* ... X. Giné, D. Karlan, and J. Zinman, "Put Your Money Where Your Butt Is: A Commitment Contract for Smoking Cessation," *American Economic Journal: Applied Economics* 2, no. 4 (2010): 213–235.

201: *investment accounts with early withdrawal penalties* ... J. Beshears, J. J. Choi, C. Harris, D. Laibson, B. C. Madrian, and J. Sakong, "Which Early Withdrawal Penalty Attracts the Most Deposits to a Commitment Savings Account?," *Journal of Public Economics* 183 (2020): 104144.

203: *A recent analysis of almost twenty thousand Stickk.com users* ... C. Brimhall, D. Tannenbaum, and E. M. Epps, "Choosing More Aggressive Commitment Contracts for Others Than for the Self" (University of Utah working paper, 2022).

203–204: *the most self-aware consumers* ... *were the ones who* ... Ashraf, Karlan, and Yin, "Tying Odysseus to the Mast."

204: *Other work, conducted in better-controlled laboratory settings* ... S. Toussaert, "Eliciting Temptation and Self-Control Through Menu Choices: A Lab Experiment," *Econometrica* 86, no. 3 (2018): 859–889. See also H. Sjåstad and M. Ekström,

"Ulyssean Self-Control: Pre-Commitment Is Effective, but Choosing It Freely Requires Good Self-Control" (Norwegian School of Economics working paper, 2022), https://psyarxiv.com/w24eb/download?format=pdf.

Chapter 9: *Making the Present Easier*

207: *Consider his take on shaving* ... M. Hedberg, *Strategic Grill Locations* (Comedy Central Records, 2002).

207: *"Like you could eat a carrot with an onion ring"* ... Hedberg, *Strategic Grill Locations.*

211: *the less anxious and depressed they became* ... C. Classen, L. D. Butler, C. Koopman, et al., "Supportive-Expressive Group Therapy and Distress in Patients with Metastatic Breast Cancer: A Randomized Clinical Intervention Trial," *Archives of General Psychiatry* 58, no. 5 (2001): 494–501.

211: *those who did lived approximately eighteen months longer* ... D. Spiegel, H. Kraemer, J. Bloom, and E. Gottheil, "Effect of Psychosocial Treatment on Survival of Patients with Metastatic Breast Cancer," *Lancet* 334, no. 8668 (1989): 888–891.

211: *that amount of life extension may be extreme* ... D. Spiegel, L. D. Butler, J. Giese-Davis, et al., "Effects of Supportive-Expressive Group Therapy on Survival of Patients with Metastatic Breast Cancer: A Randomized Prospective Trial," *Cancer* 110, no. 5 (2007): 1130–1138.

211: *not only live longer but also live better* ... See, for instance, Spiegel and his colleagues' meta-analysis on survival (and how such treatments have a more positive impact for married women, women over fifty, and when introduced early in the course of cancer): S. Mirosevic, B. Jo, H. C. Kraemer, M. Ershadi, E. Neri, and D. Spiegel, " 'Not Just Another Meta-Analysis': Sources of Heterogeneity in Psychosocial Treatment Effect on Cancer Survival," *Cancer Medicine* 8, no. 1 (2019): 363–373. For a meta-analysis of the psychosocial impacts of the therapy, see J. Lai, H. Song, Y. Ren, S. Li, and F. Xiao, "Effectiveness of Supportive-Expressive Group Therapy in Women with Breast Cancer: A Systematic Review and Meta-Analysis," *Oncology Research and Treatment* 44, no. 5 (2021): 252–260.

211: *"I brought my cancer with me"* ... D. Spiegel, "Getting There Is Half the Fun: Relating Happiness to Health," *Psychological Inquiry* 9, no. 1 (1998): 66–68.

212: *"happiness and sadness were not two poles"* ... Spiegel, "Getting There Is Half the Fun."

212: *The concept of these sorts of mixed emotions* ... J. T. Larsen, A. P. McGraw, and J. T. Cacioppo, "Can People Feel Happy and Sad at the Same Time?," *Journal of Personality and Social Psychology* 81, no. 4 (2001): 684–696; J. T. Larsen and A. P. McGraw, "The Case for Mixed Emotions," *Social and Personality Psychology Compass* 8, no. 6 (2014): 263–274; J. T. Larsen and A. P. McGraw, "Further Evidence for Mixed Emotions," *Journal of Personality and Social Psychology* 100, no. 6 (2011): 1095–1110.

214: *"This has been a difficult couple of weeks"* ... J. M. Adler and H. E. Hershfield, "Mixed Emotional Experience Is Associated with and Precedes Improvements in Psychological Well-Being," *PLOS One* 7, no. 4 (2012): e35633, 3.

215: *The true benefit from taking the good with the bad* ... Adler and Hershfield, "Mixed Emotional Experience."

215: *bereaved adults who express positive emotions*...G. A. Bonanno and D. Keltner, "Facial Expressions of Emotion and the Course of Conjugal Bereavement," *Journal of Abnormal Psychology* 106, no. 1 (1997): 126–137.

215: *reliving happy memories alongside feelings of sadness*...S. Folkman and J. T. Moskowitz, "Positive Affect and the Other Side of Coping," *American Psychologist* 55, no. 6 (2000): 647–654.

215: *experiencing mixed emotions in the face of*...R. Berrios, P. Totterdell, and S. Kellett, "Silver Linings in the Face of Temptations: How Mixed Emotions Promote Self-Control Efforts in Response to Goal Conflict," *Motivation and Emotion* 42, no. 6 (2018): 909–919.

215: *by pairing the act of saving with something potentially*...S. Cole, B. Iverson, and P. Tufano, "Can Gambling Increase Savings? Empirical Evidence on Prize-Linked Savings Accounts," *Management Science* 68, no. 5 (2022): 3282–3308.

216: *She loved spending her nights reading engrossing fiction*...K. Milkman, *How to Change: The Science of Getting from Where You Are to Where You Want to Be* (New York: Penguin Random House, 2021).

217: *the intermediate form of temptation bundling...led to*...K. L. Milkman, J. A. Minson, and K. G. Volpp, "Holding the Hunger Games Hostage at the Gym: An Evaluation of Temptation Bundling," *Management Science* 60, no. 2 (2014): 283–299.

217: *In a different field experiment conducted with 24 Hour Fitness*...E. L. Kirgios, G. H. Mandel, Y. Park, et al., "Teaching Temptation Bundling to Boost Exercise: A Field Experiment," *Organizational Behavior and Human Decision Processes* 161 (2020): 20–35.

218: *in one study Allie and her colleagues conducted*...A. Lieberman, A. C. Morales, and O. Amir, "Tangential Immersion: Increasing Persistence in Boring Consumer Behaviors," *Journal of Consumer Research* 49, no. 3 (2022): 450–472.

219: *if a company wants to encourage its employees to*...A. Lieberman, "How to Power Through Boring Tasks," *Harvard Business Review*, April 28, 2022, https://hbr .org/2022/04/research-how-to-power-through-boring-tasks.

219: *a McDonald's in ·China recently made headlines*...H. Tan, "McDonald's Has Installed Exercise Bikes in Some of Its Restaurants in China So Customers Can Work Out and Charge Their Phones While Eating," *Insider*, December 22, 2021, https://www.businessinsider.com/mcdonalds-china-installed-exercise-bikes -in-some-restaurants-2021-12.

221: *They claim that their price-per-issue ads were*...J. T. Gourville, "Pennies-a-Day: The Effect of Temporal Reframing on Transaction Evaluation," *Journal of Consumer Research* 24, no. 4 (1998): 395–408.

222: *make the act of saving automatic*...See, for example, B. C. Madrian and D. F. Shea, "The Power of Suggestion: Inertia in 401(k) Participation and Savings Behavior," *Quarterly Journal of Economics* 116, no. 4 (2001): 1149–1187.

223: *four times as many users signed up for the savings plan*...H. E. Hershfield, S. Shu, and S. Benartzi, "Temporal Reframing and Participation in a Savings Program:

A Field Experiment," *Marketing Science* 39, no. 6 (2020): 1039–1051. Note that there were some users who eventually recognized that five dollars per day added up to too much savings over time. We followed users for three months, and sure enough, after about four weeks, about 25 percent of the folks from the five-dollars-per-day group had dropped out compared to 15 percent in the weekly group and 14 percent in the monthly group. But because of the big difference in initial enrollment between groups, even with this higher dropout rate, more users from the five-dollars-per-day group were still enrolled. What's more is that two months and three months after the initial intervention, dropout rates remained small and roughly equal across the three groups.

223: *You don't have to look far to see this strategy* . . . S. A. Atlas and D. M. Bartels, "Periodic Pricing and Perceived Contract Benefits," *Journal of Consumer Research* 45, no. 2 (2018): 350–364.

223: *economists suggest that there may eventually be a* . . . J. Dickler, "Buy Now, Pay Later Is Not a Boom, It's a Bubble, Harvard Researcher Says," CNBC, May 13, 2022, https://www.cnbc.com/2022/05/13/buy-now-pay-later-is-not-a-boom-its-a -bubble-harvard-fellow-says-.html.

224: *where they start by paying off smaller accounts* . . . D. Gal and B. B. McShane, "Can Small Victories Help Win the War? Evidence from Consumer Debt Management," *Journal of Marketing Research* 49, no. 4 (2012): 487–501.

224: *asking people to donate four hours of their time per week* . . . A. Rai, M. A. Sharif, E. Chang, K. Milkman, and A. Duckworth, "A Field Experiment on Goal Framing to Boost Volunteering: The Tradeoff Between Goal Granularity and Flexibility," *Journal of Applied Psychology* (2022), https://psycnet.apa.org/record/2023 -01062-001.

224: *once you get close to the end of your goal* . . . S. C. Huang, L. Jin, and Y. Zhang, "Step by Step: Sub-Goals as a Source of Motivation," *Organizational Behavior and Human Decision Processes* 141 (July 2017): 1–15.

226: *They typically only visited three attractions their first year* . . . S. B. Shu and A. Gneezy, "Procrastination of Enjoyable Experiences," *Journal of Marketing Research* 47, no. 5 (2010): 933–944.

227: *As one Twitter user commented* . . . Danny Baldus-Strauss (@BackpackerFI), "Don't wait till you're this old to retire and travel the world," Twitter, September 20, 2021, 11:31 a.m., https://twitter.com/BackpackerFI/status/1439975578749345797 ?s=20.

228: *"But cutting these things out came at the price of"* . . . L. Harrison, "Why We Ditched the FIRE Movement and Couldn't Be Happier," *MarketWatch*, October 1, 2019, https://www.marketwatch.com/story/why-we-ditched-the-fire-movement -and-couldnt-be-happier-2019-09-30.

228: *Researchers have labeled this sort of behavior "hyperopic"* . . . R. Kivetz and A. Keinan, "Repenting Hyperopia: An Analysis of Self-Control Regrets," *Journal of Consumer Research* 33, no. 2 (2006): 273–282.

229: *Harrison has come a long way from her happiness free fall*...Harrison, "Why We Ditched the FIRE Movement."

229: *But as Richards put it*...C. Richards (@behaviorgap), "Spend the money...life experiences give you an incalculable return on investment," Twitter, May 15, 2020, 8:04 a.m., https://twitter.com/behaviorgap/status/1261266163931262976. The *Atlantic* writer Derek Thompson recently made a similar observation: "Those who spend a lifetime delaying gratification may one day find themselves rich in savings but poor in memories, having sacrificed too much joy at the altar of compounding interest" (D. Thompson, "All the Personal-Finance Books Are Wrong," *The Atlantic,* September 1, 2022, https://www.theatlantic.com/ideas/archive/2022/09/personal-finance-books-wrong/671298/). Note that some recent academic work lends some support to these assertions: in a correlational study, researchers found a "u-shaped" relationship between the tendency to delay gratification (on laboratory tasks) and happiness. Whereas a moderate amount of patience may be optimal for happiness, an extreme amount of patience is associated with a downturn in well-being. P. Giuliano and P. Sapienza, "The Cost of Being Too Patient," AEA Papers and Proceedings 110 (2020): 314–318.

Epilogue

233: *the World Health Organization announced that in 2020 alone*...World Health Organization, "Mental Health and COVID-19: Early Evidence of the Pandemic's Impact; Scientific Brief," March 2, 2022, https://www.who.int/publications/i/item/WHO-2019-nCoV-Sci_Brief-Mental_health-2022.1.

233: *almost half of adults between eighteen and thirty-five don't see a point in*...Fidelity Investments, "2022 State of Retirement Planning," 2022, https://www.fidelity.com/bin-public/060_www_fidelity_com/documents/about-fidelity/FID-SORP-DataSheet.pdf.

233: *Stand-up comedian Hannah Jones, twenty-seven, explained it this way*...A. P. Kambhampaty, "The World's a Mess. So They've Stopped Saving for Tomorrow," *New York Times,* May 13, 2022, https://www.nytimes.com/2022/05/13/style/saving-less-money.html.

234: *milestone birthdays often create little breaks in our lives*...See A. L. Alter and H. E. Hershfield, "People Search for Meaning When They Approach a New Decade in Chronological Age," *Proceedings of the National Academy of Sciences of the United States of America* 111, no. 48 (2014): 17066–17070; and T. Miron-Shatz, R. Bhargave, and G. M. Doniger, "Milestone Age Affects the Role of Health and Emotions in Life Satisfaction: A Preliminary Inquiry," *PLOS One* 10, no. 8 (2015): e0133254.

234: *the pandemic created a sort of "universal midlife crisis"*...A. Galinsky and L. Kray, "How COVID Created a Universal Midlife Crisis," *Los Angeles Times,* May 15, 2022, https://www.latimes.com/opinion/story/2022-05-15/covid-universal-midlife-crisis.

236: *Sensing deeper roots in one's community*...C. J. Corbett, H. E. Hershfield, H. Kim, T. F. Malloy, B. Nyblade, and A. Partie, "The Role of Place Attachment and

Environmental Attitudes in Adoption of Rooftop Solar," *Energy Policy* 162 (2022): 112764.

236: *focusing on the long and rich history of one's country*...H. E. Hershfield, H. M. Bang, and E. U. Weber, "National Differences in Environmental Concern and Performance Are Predicted by Country Age," *Psychological Science* 25, no. 1 (2014): 152–160.

INDEX

Index

Index

Index

ABOUT THE AUTHOR

Hal Hershfield is a professor of marketing, behavioral decision-making, and psychology and holds the UCLA Anderson Board of Advisors Term Chair in Management at UCLA's Anderson School of Management, where he has won numerous teaching awards. His research on future selves has received widespread attention in the *New York Times*, the *Wall Street Journal*, the *Boston Globe*, the *Washington Post*, and *The Atlantic* and has been featured on the hit Netflix show *Money, Explained* and on NPR, CBS, ABC, and PBS. Hershfield's research has been published in prestigious business, psychology, and general science academic journals, as well as in the *Harvard Business Review*, *Scientific American*, and *Psychology Today*.